AMERICAN GUERRILLAS

AMERICAN GUERRILLAS

From the French and Indian Wars to Iraq and
Afghanistan—How Americans Fight Unconventional Wars

THOMAS D. MAYS

Guilford, Connecticut

An imprint of Globe Pequot

Distributed by NATIONAL BOOK NETWORK

Copyright © 2017 by Thomas D. Mays

Maps: Cristina Bauss, Humboldt State University

British Library Cataloguing in Publication Information available

Library of Congress Cataloging-in-Publication Data available

ISBN 978-1-4930-2229-8 (hardcover)
ISBN 978-1-4930-2230-4 (e-book)

∞™ The paper used in this publication meets the minimum requirements of American National Standard for Information Sciences—Permanence of Paper for Printed Library Materials, ANSI/NISO Z39.48-1992.

Printed in the United States of America

To my fellow Beirut Veterans of America
"The First Duty is to Remember"

CONTENTS

ACKNOWLEDGMENTS

THIS WORK WOULD NEVER HAVE MADE IT INTO PRINT WITHOUT THE support of many people. First I need to thank literary agent Roger S. Williams at Roger Williams Agency, who brought the concept of this project to my attention. Thanks as well to Eugene Brissie of Lyons Press, who originated the idea, and to Lynn Zelem and Kim Giambattisto for their careful editorial suggestions. The historiography of military history has changed over the years from the traditional "bugles and drums" battle narratives to more nuanced studies of common soldiers and the effect of war on culture. This work owes much to historians who have laid the foundation for the study of unconventional warfare in American history, including Daniel E. Sutherland, Clay Mountcastle, Max Boot, John S. Pancake, Alfred H. Paddock Jr., and John Grenier. Special thanks as well to James Zobel of the MacArthur Memorial Library and Archives for his interest and contributions and to the faculty and staff of the Humboldt State University Department of Geography—especially Amy E. Rock, Mary Beth Cunha, and Aaron Taveras—for their assistance with cartography. Most importantly, the greatest contributor to this work has been my primary editor, researcher, fact-checker, general critic, cartographer, and love of my life, my wife Cristina Bauss.

PROLOGUE

AT DAYBREAK ON MAY 28, 1754, A MIXED FORCE OF INDIANS AND VIR-
ginians approached a French military encampment on the Pennsylvania
frontier. Situated near the junction of the Allegheny and Monongahela
Rivers, the camp had been established under the protection of a rock
cliff in a narrow ravine. Leading the Indians was Tanaghrisson, known to
the English as the "Half King." He was serving as guide to the Virginians and their commander, a twenty-two-year-old militia major by the
name of George Washington. The force surrounded the camp, whisper-
silent; the French had scarcely begun to stir. As Washington would later
recall, an alert Frenchman spotted the attackers and cried out a warning.
Taken by surprise, the French fired a few misguided shots, to which the
Virginians responded with two well-aimed volleys. Now panicked, the
French ran for the cover of the forest, where they were no match for
the Half King's warriors. They were driven out into the open. A French
officer asked for quarter and Washington ordered an end to the firing.[1]

Of Washington's men, one was dead and three were wounded. Of the
French, fourteen were dead or wounded and twenty-one had been taken
prisoner. With the help of a translator, one of the wounded identified
himself as the unit's commander. He was a peace emissary on a mission
to deliver a letter to the English, demanding that they leave French territory. After the letter was translated and read, the Half King approached
the officer and told him in French, "Thou art not yet dead, my father."
He then raised his tomahawk and gruesomely butchered the man. As
if on cue, the other Indians killed all the wounded Frenchmen but one.
Washington had granted quarter and had expected it to be given. He
quickly placed the Virginians between the Indians and the remaining

French prisoners, who were escorted to safety. On this blood-soaked spring morning, little did Washington know that the raid would spark what is known in Europe as the Seven Years' War and in America as the French and Indian War.[2]

American military historians have tended to focus almost exclusively on narratives placing the nation's conventional forces against similarly organized enemies. From the American Revolution through the invasion of Iraq, military analyses have concentrated on individual commanders, their decisions, and the actions of opposing nation-states. While these are essential to military history, another element may be as vitally important to the study of warfare, and in turn the study of American history: unconventional guerrilla warfare. From the founding of the colonies through the current wars of the twenty-first century, Americans have always been involved in non-state-supported conflicts. Long before the word *guerrilla* was coined, Native Americans were engaging in classic guerrilla campaigns against Europeans encroaching on their lands. Left to their own devices against the Natives, settlers at first responded by adapting to Native warfare, then escalated their counterattacks and began targeting crops, villages, and non-combatants. This brutal form of warfare would last for nearly three centuries, until the end of the Indian Wars in 1890.

Having learned the Native forms of raids and ambushes, Americans began forming ranger companies. They actively attempted to prevent raids, penetrating as far as Canada to bring the war home to their enemies. During the Revolution riflemen continued waging this form of unconventional war, often confounding and defeating British regulars. Meanwhile, Patriots who found themselves under British occupation took up arms as well. Following the Revolution, guerrilla fighting did not dissipate on the American frontier. When a band of former soldiers rose up in rebellion in western Massachusetts, the Founders took the threat of guerrilla war so seriously that they met in Philadelphia in 1787 to establish a central government with the power to counter it. In fact, the first serious test the new nation and President George Washington faced came in the form of a guerrilla force in western Pennsylvania, threatening the nascent government over its whiskey tax.

The American Civil War was primarily fought with conventional forces, and its outcome was clearly determined by the successes (and failures) of those forces. But far from the battlefields of Gettysburg, Antietam, and Shiloh—names known to virtually every American—a concurrent guerrilla war was waged, a war in which quarter was rarely given and a personal vendetta could follow a man from his homestead to his bed in an army hospital. However, until recently historians have paid scant attention to this war, despite the fact that guerrilla fighting in Kansas pre-dated the Civil War by several years—and the spark that lit the conflict, John Brown's 1859 raid on Harpers Ferry, was a large-scale act of domestic terrorism. Throughout the war countless bands of pro-Union and pro-Southern guerrillas battled each other for control of their communities. In Union-occupied areas of the South, the U.S. Army adopted tactics learned from breaking Indian resistance movements against the Rebels, destroying communities, farms, and crops. As the leaders of conventional forces found themselves continually challenged by guerrillas, the United States began establishing the world's first military code specifically addressing guerrilla warfare.

Guerrilla warfare was not limited to the Civil War or even the United States during the nineteenth century. Guerrilla tactics have been used in every American conflict from the War of 1812 to the Mexican-American War, and even employed abroad by filibusters, groups of armed Americans who attempted to overthrow governments in Latin America and Canada. Having learned brutal lessons during America's bloodiest conflict, Civil War veterans used the same scorched-earth policies against civilians during the Indian Wars. By the end of the nineteenth century, as the United States stepped onto the world stage, the American military was deploying brutal anti-insurgency tactics in the Philippines and beyond.

The scope of World War II challenged the capacity of American conventional forces to the point of adopting the British model of Special Forces trained to operate behind enemy lines. The American experience in this unconventional war eventually gave birth to both the Central

Intelligence Agency (CIA) and the Army's Special Operations. Former World War II operatives and guerrillas, including General Robert A. McClure and Colonel Russell W. Volckmann, established the Army's Special Operations Command and developed some of the first written doctrine on the subject. Their concept of placing American teams behind enemy lines to train and equip indigenous fighters was tested in Vietnam, with the arming of Montagnard villagers. The modern era has seen fundamental changes in American military thought, with General David Petraeus's complete overhaul of counterinsurgency doctrine in 2006. The United States no longer relies on slash-and-burn tactics to punish civilians who support insurgents. Instead the military attempts to work with local populations to address grievances, build infrastructure, and develop alliances to target guerrillas.

"One man's terrorist is another man's freedom fighter," British novelist Gerald Seymour famously wrote in *Harry's Game*. Differentiating between terrorists and guerrilla insurgents is a tricky proposition at best. In modern terms, terrorists are defined as combatants who target unarmed civilians or symbols of the state. This work focuses on insurgencies and guerrilla warfare, in which fighters organize and target occupying military forces, generally from behind the lines. As Max Boot explains in his seminal *Invisible Armies: An Epic History of Guerrilla Warfare from Ancient Times to the Present*, "*Guerrilla* literally means 'small war'; the name derives from the struggles of Spanish irregulars against Napoleon from 1808–1814, but the practice is as ancient as mankind." Insurgencies arise in occupied areas among forces that are too weak to fight in conventional combat. In order to be effective in conducting raids, ambushing the enemy, and setting traps against an occupying army, an insurgency must have reliable sources of weapons and supplies. Hence the widespread support of the civilian population where it is based is essential to a guerrilla movement's success. Even then—as will be seen from numerous examples in American history—to emerge victorious, most successful guerrilla insurgencies have ultimately depended on the support of conventional forces.[3]

CHAPTER ONE

"Now we have just cause to destroy them by all means possible"

Captain John Smith

FOLLOWING THE SETTLEMENT OF JAMESTOWN IN 1607, NATIVES WERE at first cautious and curious about the first English colonists. A few settlers, including the original Quakers of Philadelphia, even went so far as to develop strong cultural and economic relationships with the Natives. Some Native groups also saw the Europeans as potential allies in their conflicts with other tribes. Within a generation, however, the invaders' incompatible cultural systems and greed for land and resources led to widespread warfare. Native Americans fought in classic hit-and-run guerrilla fashion and refused to stand and fight as was traditional in European battle. At first Europeans were baffled by Native methods of warfare, but in time they understood and successfully adopted these guerrilla methods. In contrast, Natives would continue traditional ways of fighting, although they would successfully incorporate firearms as well as iron and steel weapons into Native warfare.[1]

Native American culture on the East Coast differed dramatically from European culture. Most tribes were part of the Eastern Woodlands groups who lived as hunter-gatherers and farmers. Women allocated resources, raised children, gathered wild edibles, and tended crops. Men had the responsibilities of hunting, fishing, dealing with other tribes, and, most importantly, fighting. Contrary to modern-day mythology, warfare was very common among the tribes prior to European occupation. But the goals, methods, and scale of fighting were dramatically different. The reasons for conflict varied—often clashes over hunting, farming, and fishing grounds—and fighting frequently broke out in order to settle debts of honor. Many Iroquois groups conducted what was called a "mourning war": when a tribe suffered the loss of too many of its members, it would send a war party to capture others to be adopted and take the places of the dead.[2]

The Native American style of warfare is a perfect example of what is known today as low-intensity guerrilla warfare. They did not raise large armies meant to be used in great battles or siege operations. Instead they used stealth, the raid, and the ambush to utilize the element of surprise to their advantage. If surprised, Indians often retreated. Many of their villages were surrounded with palisades in order to take away the element of surprise from potential attackers. Guerrilla-style raids and ambushes could potentially last for years, but to outside observers' surprise were rarely fought on a large scale with massive casualties. Many colonists agreed with Roger Williams's observation that Native warfare was far less brutal than European conflicts. Captain John Underhill was of like mind: After witnessing a battle between tribes, he wrote, "I dare boldly affirme, they might fight seven yeares and not kill seven men: they came not neere one another, but shot remote, and not point blanke, as wee often doe with our bullets, but at rovers, and then they gaze up in the skie to see where the Arrow falls, and not untill it is fallen doe they shoot againe, this fight is more for pastime, than to conquer and subdue enemies." This method of fighting did not often feature the ferocity of total war. While captured warriors often faced brutal consequences of ritual torture and sacrifice, such consequences were generally limited to that class. Non-combatants including women and children were not always killed (though they were often captured). Such rules were logical to Natives. Groups in conflict would raid, launch ambushes, and capture resources, prisoners, and slaves until all sides either reached a compromise or conceded over the issues that had sparked the conflict. This would all change with the arrival of the Europeans.[3]

North American Natives lacked the political and social organization of the modern nation-state. They had no massive empires with monarchical resources used to enforce conscription and issue mandatory orders. Native war parties were led by local war chiefs who attracted volunteers. Each fighter volunteered on his own accord, fully aware that his standing as a warrior in the community would be largely based on his personal bravery in battle, destroying the enemy and capturing resources and captives. Raised as hunters, they were experts in stalking, stealth, midnight raids, and surprise ambushes. Warriors often had detailed plans for a raid or ambush, but when the fighting began each man acted as his own commander, moving as he saw fit without taking orders. Unlike Europeans, who fought to hold the field, when pressed in battle Natives had no problem fading back into the woods to return another day. As Colonel Henry Bouquet—a Swiss-born officer in British service during both the Seven Years' War and Pontiac's War who had as much experience in fighting Natives as anyone else at that time—noted, Indian combat strategy differed markedly from Europeans'. First Natives fought without ranks in open order. Then they attempted to surround their targets. Finally, if pushed, their forces fell back, only to return when the opportunity arose again. The English were appalled when they found their new enemy refused to settle fights in open fields of battle. The concepts of taking and holding a position and taking or following orders were simply foreign to the original American guerrillas.[4]

While Natives both held on to and adapted their methods of warfare after the arrival of Europeans, they were also adept at adopting the material culture of Europe and using it to their advantage. However, they might not have had much use for the first muskets brought over: matchlocks (large, cumbersome, slow-loading and -firing weapons). They took several minutes to load, and the matchlock itself was fired by a slow-burning fuse, resembling a modern clothesline and called a "match," that the soldier had to keep lit. The musketeer carried the burning match with him. When he needed to discharge the weapon, he placed the barrel of the gun on a stand, inserted the burning match onto an arm of the weapon, and then discharged it by bringing the burning point onto a flash pan that would ignite the charge. The difficulties of this process can be easily imagined. The match had to remain lit at all times—including in the rain, at night, and on the march. Natives certainly could hear, see, and smell approaching armed colonists from quite some distance. This all changed with the flintlock.

Colonists began importing the vastly superior flintlock in the mid-fifteenth century. The firing mechanism no longer required a burning match, but worked instead by using a hammer called a "cock" that held a flint. The weapon discharged as the trigger released a spring, sending the flint forward to strike a piece of steel called a "frizzen," which in turn sent a cascade of sparks burning down into the flash pan. This musket revolutionized the world of firearms and became the weapon of choice for Natives and colonists alike. As with all useful European material goods, the Natives did not simply assimilate the goods; they adapted them to the needs of their own culture. Although gun trade with Indians was prohibited by many English colonies—some legislators even made it a capital offense—many ignored the law. Too much capital was to be gained in the fur trade, and the French, Dutch, and English competed in a lively business of exchanging furs for what were known as "trade guns" with the Indians. In a short time, Indians became the finest marksmen in the colonies. Unlike the majority of Europeans, who never enjoyed the privilege of hunting the king's game, for Natives, who were raised as hunters and outdoorsmen, aiming and firing were second nature. In some areas, including New England, Natives became extremely proficient in knapping flints, casting shot, and repairing stocks. But one issue may have been essential to the development of their keen marksmanship: They could never produce gunpowder and constantly faced shortages. Therefore it was crucial that every shot count in hunting as well as fighting. By 1730, most Native fighters east of the Alleghenies were armed with flintlock muskets.[5]

The English who settled the East Coast brought with them well-established military traditions that may seem odd to the modern reader. Above all, the history of England produced a people who distrusted the idea of government keeping a standing army. The English Civil Wars (1638–1651) led to the army of the Parliament defeating the army of

King Charles I, resulting in what Winston Churchill called the military dictatorship of Oliver Cromwell. After Cromwell's death in 1660, Parliament restored the monarchy by placing Charles's son Charles II on the throne. England did not raise and keep standing armies until the late 1600s, and when it did, the king was restricted in his ability to keep them on the island.[6]

Immigrants found large-scale European nation-state warfare to be unfit for the North American continent. Colonies lacked the funding, logistical support, and manpower to organize, train, equip, and support large numbers of troops. The continent lacked the reliable transportation infrastructure essential to moving and supporting large forces, and the terrain was nothing like the developed fields and villages of Europe. Large formations were useless in a land of uncharted mountains and streams. Besides, the Natives had no concept of this kind of fighting. No, in America war was fought on a small scale. As noted earlier, small-scale raiding and guerrilla fighting had always existed in warfare, and the English were forced to adapt to it.

In 1607, when the English established their first permanent colony at Jamestown, Virginia, they did so without military support from the Crown. The colony was an independent joint stock company, forced to rely on its own resources for defense. What colonists did bring with them, however, was the English system of local protection. When threatened with invasion at home, the Crown and Parliament issued "commissions" for local officers to raise short-term volunteers. These men agreed to serve for a period of time in exchange for adventure and potential treasure. The militia system was a more permanent military organization, with units known as "trainbands." Each community established a local unit based on the need for all healthy men to be able to band together in case of attack on their home communities. Their mobilization in England had been limited, however, due to the aristocracy's fear of arming large groups of commoners. But this system would become the dominant early form of military organization in the colonies.[7]

The colonial militia system became the primary mechanism for local defense in all English colonies. Densely settled New England colonies established companies based in each town, whereas the sparsely settled

South created trainbands in larger counties. Membership was almost universal, with many colonies requiring that all men from sixteen to sixty serve. The officers were either elected by the trainband or appointed by the governor. The structure of the militia reflected society at large. Those with status and wealth received commissions and likely held local office. Musters were mandatory and men were fined for non-attendance. The frequency of musters varied depending on the threat to any given area. Most colonies faced Native resistance during the early years of settlement, and musters, training, and short campaigns were frequent. As the frontier advanced, the musters became far less frequent, with peaceful communities drilling perhaps as rarely as once a year. Many of these musters became community social gatherings where men marched, drilled, and executed basic maneuvers. After meetings and elections the events usually turned into social events where participants imbibed heavily, often resulting in dueling or fighting.[8]

Each man was required to furnish his own weapon, and all colonies drafted laws that provided for furnishing even the most destitute men with guns. In the early days, militiamen were armed much like European infantry. Men wore breastplates and helmets and carried either an unwieldy matchlock or a pike and perhaps a sword. While these types of arms and equipment might have made sense in Europe, the kit proved to be next to useless for fighting Indians in America. The pike, for example, was a fine weapon to guard against horsemen and massed frontal assaults, fighting that was foreign to Natives. Helmets and body armor did ward off arrows and tomahawk blows, but were a severe hindrance to men attempting to move quickly through wooded country. As already noted, the unwieldy and slow-firing matchlock had the drawback of necessitating that its slow-burning match be kept lit. It was also a real hazard to the musketeer, who had to keep a bandoleer with pre-loaded cartridges slung over his shoulder while carrying the burning match—a situation that made accidents frequent. In fact, one of the first trained soldiers in Virginia, Captain John Smith, had to leave the colony after suffering severe gunpowder burns on his leg during a fight with the Indians. In time the matchlock was replaced by the much more reliable flintlock, and many men carried a hatchet for close fighting. The hatchet was extremely useful in the field for other functions as well.[9]

A trainband rarely deployed as a complete company outside its home territory. To do so would strip the area of manpower and leave it vulnerable and defenseless. Instead colonial governors would commission officers to raise regiments of volunteers for specific campaigns or terms of service. Trainbands provided volunteers with a basic knowledge of soldiering, but defending local communities and isolated farms against Native guerrilla raids was difficult at best. By the time an alarm was raised and men mustered, odds were that the raiders had struck and moved on. Pursuing them set the trainband up for ambush and left the settlement unprotected. Colonists instead relied on local fortifications or blockhouses for protection.[10]

Beginning with Jamestown in 1607, English settlers built stockades and fortifications in central areas that could be used as refuges in case of alarm. When threatened the entire outlying population retreated to the fort, where the muskets of the militia kept attackers at bay. Often, especially in New England, these strongholds were made of heavy logs with loopholes for firing. A second story that projected outward to provide an overhanging gallery was frequently constructed as well to protect the place from being stormed. However, as often as not these strongholds were not close enough to support each other or protect outlying settlers. When the Yamasee and their allies attacked South Carolina in 1715, many frontier settlers were unable to make it to refuge. The colony subsequently authorized the construction of ten new forts.

Successful garrisons had enough food, water, and ammunition to hold out against attack. Natives did not necessarily have the logistical support, organization, discipline, or means to carry out large-scale siege operations or successfully burn out a well-protected post. This left the defenders to man their walls while watching their exposed homes burn and crops and animals be destroyed. In addition to small blockhouses, colonies also built large-scale fortifications for frontier defense. By the French and Indian War (1754–1763), the English colonies had attempted to establish a chain of frontier forts from New York to southwest Virginia. According to historian John K. Mahon, this idea could be ranked as the "Maginot Line in its time," as it "tended to lull the apprehensions of settlers" without doing much to nullify threats. In reality, the forts proved to be far too distant from one another to provide support or stop war parties from advancing. To patrol the areas between fortifications, colonies often used specially raised militia units known collectively as "rangers." In the southern colonies the rangers' mission was to actively seek out and intercept invading parties, and they often patrolled territory on horseback. In New England ranger units even utilized snowshoes during the winter. Maintaining fortifications and roving ranger units was taxing on colonial governments, and some paid a high price. During the Pontiac War of 1763, the Quaker-dominated assembly of Pennsylvania resisted the idea of fully defending the frontier and ultimately paid dearly in life and property. In contrast, the colony of Virginia mobilized one thousand men and had much more success defending outlying communities.[11]

More often than not, local militias acted as local police forces. In addition to being called up to respond to outside threats to the community, they were also frequently used to quell civil unrest. If propertied interests felt threatened by the lower orders of society, the militia often responded. At times militias representing various interests actually sparred off against each other. The militia was also used to maintain domestic order; for instance, in the South it was often used to back up slave patrols that enforced the slave codes. They recaptured runaway slaves and ensured that Blacks were not traveling and meeting clandestinely at night to plan revolts. More often than not the militia was used to put down riots and challenges to the established social order. In New England the militia supported the night watch as a form of civil police. In 1771, in the Piedmont of North Carolina, the colonial militia came to blows with a local guerrilla militia known as the Regulators. The Regulators were upset with what they saw as unfair taxes and corrupt officials who had been appointed by the wealthy planter class from the Tidewater-dominated legislature. This Tidewater-versus-backcountry resentment had been building up for years, and the creation of the Regulator movement was a direct response by the people of the Carolina Piedmont following the failure of diplomatic efforts to address their complaints.

The May 1771 Battle of Alamance saw Royal Governor William Tyron's well-supplied and somewhat better-trained forces disperse the movement. However, this unlawful guerrilla militia would be a precursor to the popular uprising of the American Revolution.[12]

When action was needed, colonial authorities organized temporary volunteer units for any planned campaign. Each trainband was required to furnish men based on the population of its district. This left the majority of men at home to tend to farms and be available for local defense. The trainbands were required to furnish a quota of men, and their selection was left to local authorities. The majority were volunteers—often younger sons who could be spared by their families and who may have been in search of adventure and reward for themselves. Bounties were used to entice volunteers, but when that failed, local officials turned to the draft. If the draftee wished to avoid service he could press his case to a high-ranking officer who could offer a deferment. He could also pay a fine or hire a substitute to go in his place. When all else failed, he could desert and move to a different community.[13]

In order to counter Native guerrilla raids, colonists adapted guerrilla methods of warfare. These included the element of surprise, the raid, the dawn attack, and the ambush. Most often using Indian allies as guides, colonial forces surrounded Native villages under cover of darkness and attacked at first light. When facing overwhelming numbers, Natives rarely bothered to stand and fight in open field battles, but when forced to defend their villages—including their families, crops, and supplies—they had no choice. When forced to make a stand in this fashion, many Native societies met their defeat. Euro-Americans first developed this form of counter-guerrilla warfare during the early colonial period, and this became the dominant form of Indian fighting through the 1890s. However, in each generation it had to be relearned through trial and error—and the results were often genocidal.[14]

The settlers eventually turned to extirpative warfare. That is, in the modern definition, unlimited total warfare targeting civilians and their property as well as warriors. When threatened by Native tribes, many settlers believed that their only chance of survival was by counterattacking with extirpative expeditions. In the first forty years in Virginia, colonists primarily focused on Indian warriors; in the 1640s, however, they turned to the killing of non-combatants as their primary method of warfare.[15]

From the very beginning of the colonial period, the Natives of Virginia used guerrilla tactics to defend themselves against encroachment by the Jamestown colonists. After years of intrusion on their lands and on and off again raids, on Friday, March 22, 1622, Natives of the Powhatan Confederacy under Chief Opechancanough skillfully launched a surprise attack on the colony. Writing from England in his *History of Virginia*, Captain Smith related that friendly natives "came unarmed into our houses with deer, turkeys, fish, fruits, and other provisions to sell us." Then they took up any and all tools and arms they could find and commenced killing men, women, and children. The attack surprised many in the outlying farms and resulted in the deaths of 347 colonists (about one-fourth of the population). It had the potential of being more successful, had a friendly Indian not informed the residents of Jamestown itself. The survivors retreated, consolidated themselves, and organized retribution. In London, Captain Smith wrote, "now we have just cause to destroy them by all means possible." In retaliation, the London Company instructed the governor to hire allied Potomack Indians and muster a standing force and to take the field to "persue and follow them, surprising them in their habitations, interrupting them in the hunting, burning their towns, demolishing their temples, destroying their canoes, plucking up their [fishing] weirs, carrying away their corn and depriving them of whatsoever may yield them succor or relief." During the next ten years the colonists raged a relentless campaign against the Powhatan Confederacy. In 1632 the colony finally struck a truce with Opechancanough, only to face a new war in 1644. Now close to a hundred years old, Opechancanough was able to kill around five hundred colonists. However, in the years since the 1622 uprising, the English population of the colony had grown to eight thousand settlers, leaving plenty of militiamen able to organize and take the field. The fighting in the two years that followed destroyed any ability the Confederacy had of stopping English encroachment. The old chief himself would be captured and subsequently murdered by a prison guard, effectively ending the conflict.[16]

In 1676, in what became known as Bacon's Rebellion, a number of Virginia colonists adopted guerrilla tactics in order to take on their own governor and overthrow their government. By this time the white population had grown to 38,000 people; the colony also had 2,500 African slaves and perhaps 3,500 friendly Natives. Most of the whites had at one time or another served as indentured servants. To become an indentured servant, a young man or woman would sell his or her services for five to seven years to whoever paid for his or her transatlantic voyage. By 1676 wealthy landowners in the Tidewater region had all but monopolized the best arable land, forcing the newly freed settlers toward the frontier and inevitable conflict with the Indians. In addition, the frontier settlers paid a far higher share of taxes than the wealthy planters who controlled the colonial assembly. The situation left many settlers incensed. In response to back-and-forth raiding with the Indians on the frontier, Governor William Berkeley proposed a passive plan for defense by building a series of militia-manned forts along the frontier. Those living on the frontier knew this was no solution. Raiding parties could easily bypass the outposts and attack at will. This strategy was unacceptable to the settlers, who wanted to actively launch attacks on Native settlements and either permanently subdue the Indians or drive them from the colony. Leading this resistance was the governor's first cousin by marriage, Nathaniel Bacon.[17]

Bacon had recently arrived in Virginia, and with a well-to-do background could have fit in well with the growing colonial oligarchy. Instead he became the voice of the dispossessed former servants in the backcountry. After several requests to the governor to launch offensive campaigns were denied, in April 1676 Bacon raised an unauthorized guerrilla force and commenced his own private campaign against the Indians. He began with an attack on a group of friendly Natives, the Occaneechee. To Bacon and his supporters, the disposition of the Indians was irrelevant—they were the enemy. Berkeley branded Bacon a rebel and had him incarcerated, but later let him go. Once free, Bacon threatened the capital of Jamestown with five hundred of his militia and demanded the governor turn out the militia for an offensive campaign against the Indians. Again Berkeley declared the guerrilla a rebel—but this time fled Jamestown, leaving Bacon free to launch his campaign. The guerrillas then attacked the peaceful Pamunkey tribe. That September the rebels learned the governor had returned to the capital with troops, and they marched on Jamestown. Outnumbered, Bacon's forces constructed their own fortification outside of town, where they fended off an attack by the governor's supporters. They then used two cannon to attack Jamestown, taking the town when Berkeley's supporters deserted him. After driving off the governor a second time, on October 19 the guerrillas burned Jamestown. But within days—at the peak of his power and after taking the colony— Bacon contracted dysentery and died. Berkeley and his supporters rallied and captured or drove the leaderless guerrillas off. One thousand English troops soon arrived to take over the colony, and the uprising dissipated.[18]

However, Bacon's Rebellion resulted in major changes within the colony. The Tidewater oligarchy began listening to the complaints of the frontier settlers. They also became sensitive to the threat of a large body of poor, discontented citizens within the colony. Wealthy planters began relying more on well-off mounted militia units to patrol the frontier and less on local militias. They also slowly started turning to another source of labor: African slaves. According to historian Edmund Morgan, after 1676 white Virginians turned to using slave labor in the belief that an enslaved workforce would be far easier to control than the armed band of former indentured servants currently on the frontier.[19]

In 1620 settlers in the New England colonies enjoyed relatively friendly relations with the Natives, only to see them resort to guerrilla warfare as the English population multiplied and pressed inland. As in Virginia, the English militia set upon a program to make examples of any Native groups who were considered threatening. In the 1630s the Pequots of New England had become the most threatening tribe in the region. After trader John Oldham was killed by Natives, settlers demanded retaliation. With the assistance of allied tribes, including Mohegans and Narragansetts, New England militia under Captain John Mason from Connecticut and Captain John Underhill from the Massachusetts Bay Colony led an assault on the Pequot fort along the Mystic River. On May 26, 1637, the raiding party surrounded the Pequot compound. The tribe put up fierce resistance. With nowhere to turn and fighting to defend their women and children, the Pequots stood their ground. Many barricaded themselves inside their wigwams. Unable to win the fight in the open, Captain Underhill observed, "but seeing the Fort was to hotte for us, wee devised a way how wee might save our selves and prejudice them, Captaine Mason entering into a Wigwam, brought out a fire-brand, after hee had wounded many in the house, then hee set fire on the West-side." Underhill and Mason then set fire to the dwellings inside the fort. In the end, as many as five hundred Pequot men, women, and children were killed. The colonists and their Native allies spared none; as Underhill noted, "downe fell men, women, and children, those that scaped us, fell into the hands of the Indians, that were in the reere of us." Captain Mason added that he left his enemies "dunging the Ground with their flesh." Over the next three months members of the tribe who had not fallen in the massacre were rounded up and sold as slaves to local allied tribes or to the West Indies. Here the English introduced a new form of warfare to the Indians: extirpative warfare. The issue was no longer to be settled with a raid, skirmish, or ambush or two. Now the target included the entire settlement. This would color American guerrilla warfare throughout the era.[20]

In 1675 the Wampanoag under Chief Metacomet (known to the English as King Philip) rose up after three of their number had been executed by the Plymouth colonists for killing a Christian Indian. King Philip's War developed into one of the bloodiest wars of the colonial period. During the war the Natives avoided the well-fortified block-houses and went about destroying the undefended frontier settlements. The Wampanoag and the Narragansetts now adopted the English mode of extirpative warfare by attacking settlements and destroying means of survival. Having now taken up the European flintlock and other steel weapons, the scale of violence grew. In the beginning the Natives were so successful that, according to one account, they had destroyed in excess of 1,200 of New England's 12,000 homes and had caused casualties to perhaps a tenth of the male population.[21]

In response, Captain Benjamin Church of the Plymouth militia decided to adopt Native guerrilla tactics. In 1675, after having limited success in campaigns attempting to force the Natives to stand and fight,

Philip, alias Metacomet of Pokanoket. Engraving of the famed Wampanoag chief, as featured in Benson John Lossing's *The Pictorial Field-Book of the Revolution* (1853).

Captain Benjamin Church. Church (1639–1718) defeated King Philip by successfully adopting Native American methods of guerrilla warfare. MIRIAM AND IRA D. WALLACH DIVISION OF ART, NEW YORK PUBLIC LIBRARY

Church argued that they "must make a business of the war as the enemy did." Church befriended the Sakonnet tribe and enlisted a few hardy militiamen for a rigorous winter operation. In early 1676, the mixed guerrilla unit set out along the Connecticut River into central Massachusetts in search of the Narragansetts. Church's plan was to use Native allies and their methods of stealth, surprise, and ambush to take on Metacomet's forces. This first campaign started well. Church recorded that his company "had success of killing many of the enemy until at length, their provisions failing, they returned home." As historian John Grenier has noted, by adapting Native guerrilla tactics Church and his men "inaugurated the American ranger tradition" in what Grenier coined "the first American way of war."[22]

Later Church organized a new unit of "scouts" who would avoid garrison duty in the settlements to "lie in the woods as the enemy did." In July 1676, Plymouth governor Edward Winslow commissioned Church to form the first ranger force in America. With 140 allied Natives and 60 militiamen, he was ordered to "discover, pursue, fight, surprise, destroy or subdue" the colony's Native enemies. As the numbers clearly indicate, the militia was dependent on Native leadership, survival skills, and tactical expertise to fight on the frontier. Without it, they knew the odds of being able to successfully seek out and engage Indians in their home territory would be very long. According to Grenier, "Americans in fact never could have become rangers without the tutelage of Indian allies." Deep in enemy territory, Church and his men learned the frontier skills essential for victory, including how to work with "Indian scouts, maneuvering, setting and avoiding ambushes, and close-quarter fighting." Although the formation of an alliance between the colony of New York and the nations of the Iroquois League was the primary reason for English success in King Philip's War, Church and his men gained valuable tactical experience and triumphed in the field, capturing the chief's wife and nine-year-old son. Then, guided by a Wampanoag turncoat, on August 12, 1676, they killed the chief himself. Because he had been a close ally of the settlers in the past, his body was subsequently drawn, quartered, and displayed publicly, per the English custom of dealing with traitors.[23]

In time the ranger companies gained enough competence and experience to act independently without what they considered their "fickle Indian allies." Several generations of New England militiamen would form successive ranger companies. By the 1740s most of the ranger companies were commanded by men who had a direct connection with Captain Church. The institutional knowledge of guerrilla tactics, ranging, and extirpative warfare is an important and often overlooked element of the military history of New England. During King William's, Queen Anne's, and King George's Wars many New England militia units served with the regular English or British forces, but by far the majority who saw combat fought as guerrilla rangers on the frontier.[24]

Mounted militiamen in Virginia developed roving ranger units to patrol the frontier during the same time period that Church and his New England rangers became active. The major difference between them was the heavy dependence the New England militia had on adapting Native forms of guerrilla warfare. Whereas Church and his rangers were reinventing themselves by adapting to Native guerrilla tactics, the Virginia horsemen were taking the concept of European cavalry and modifying it to American frontier conditions. As they learned, southern horsemen would also evolve into capable guerrilla fighters.[25]

One of the ugliest elements of frontier warfare was the addition of colonial bounties placed on Native scalps. Scalp buying, or the practice of paying privateers to kill native men, women, and children, enticed untold numbers of men to join guerrilla units and clear the frontier. During Queen Anne's War in 1702, Massachusetts hired scalp hunters. The colony offered £10 for "every Scalp of an Indian Enemy killed in a fight, that is, ten Years of age." They eventually raised the bounty to £100 "for the scalp of each adult Indian male capable of bearing arms." Children were to be taken as slaves, and the scalps of women were worth £10. The economic incentive for scalp hunting must have been tempting; for example, the bounty of £10 (the equivalent of two hundred shillings) was being offered when the daily wage of laborers was usually less than two shillings. In 1711 North Carolina established scalp bounties on the Tuscaroras, and even the Virginia House of Burgesses kicked in with a £20 bounty. The Virginia and Carolina militias and their Indian allies burned their way through Tuscarora villages, killing an unknown number of men, women, and children and enslaving several thousand more. Many of the survivors fled to New York to seek the protection of their Iroquois relatives.[26]

In South Carolina in 1715, the Yamasees, one time allies of the English, found themselves increasingly in debt to local traders as their traditional means of sustenance, the hunting of deer, was severely impacted by the destruction of their habitat. Another means of support, their heavy trade with the English of Indian slaves, also waned. Beset with heavy debts to English traders, many tribes rose up in rebellion. With the support of allied Catawbas and Creeks, they were successful in driving most settlers in the colony to the capital of Charles Town. In June the colonists struck back, sending a company of rangers to surprise and kill upward of sixty Yamasee fighters. The fighting would continue until 1728. In a war of extermination, the South Carolina militia, their Native allies, and scalp and slave hunters of all races all but destroyed the Yamasees in the colony. The majority of the survivors fled to Spanish Florida.[27]

Father Rale's War (also known as Lovewell's War or Dummer's War, 1722–1725) provides a perfect example of the nature of guerrilla warfare in colonial New England. The Native Wabanaki Confederacy, allied to New France, was in conflict with the British over the border between Nova Scotia, New France, and New England. The 1713 Treaty of Utrecht that ended Queen Anne's War, as it was known in America, failed to acknowledge Wabanaki sovereignty over the land. With the British in control of what became Nova Scotia, in 1710 New France still held claim to much of what is now present-day Maine, holding the Kennebec River as the boundary and sending Catholic missionaries and supplies to maintain the support of allied tribes.[28]

When New England settlers continued to cross the Kennebec River into French and Wabanaki land, raiding ensued. Combatants on all sides engaged in classic guerrilla raids and ambushes. The Colony of Massachusetts became convinced that the French Canadians were prompting the Natives to attack; however, it is doubtful the Natives needed any outside incentives to defend their sovereignty. In 1720, Massachusetts placed a bounty of £100 on the head of a Catholic missionary, French

Jesuit priest Sebastian Rale, who they were sure was instigating and supplying Natives for war. The colony expanded its efforts by enticing rangers to enlist with bounties for Wabanaki scalps. After several attempts to kill Father Rale failed over the winter of 1721–1722, the Wabanaki responded with attacks of their own, raiding the frontier and driving in settlers from Nova Scotia through New England. Toward the end of the summer of 1724, around two hundred rangers led by Native guides managed to overwhelm Father Rale's mission in Norridgewock, Maine. The priest was killed, and his supporting warriors and their families were either killed or scattered. The rangers returned to Falmouth to claim bounty on twenty-seven scalps, including "the Fyars."[29]

One of the most well-known rangers of the pre–Revolutionary War period was John Lovewell. Although relatively unheard of in the present era, he was a New England household name for generations. Henry David Thoreau, Nathaniel Hawthorne, and Henry Wadsworth Longfellow all wrote tributes to his exploits during the nineteenth century. While living in what is present-day Nashua, New Hampshire, Lovewell responded to a call by the Massachusetts Colony to hire scalp hunter rangers to drive back the French and Wabanaki from the Maine frontier. Captain Lovewell led three raids into Maine. In November 1724, Lovewell asked the Massachusetts Assembly for a commission to raise a company of forty or fifty frontiersmen to "range and keep out in the woods for several months together, in order to kill and destroy their enemy Indians, provided they can meet with Encouragement suitable." The assembly granted them a per diem and offered them a bounty of £100 for the scalp of each male brought to Boston. Using well-established ranger guerrilla methods, Lovewell raised a company of rugged frontiersmen and on December 10, 1724, surprised a Native adult male and a young boy in a wigwam while they slept. They were awarded £200 plus per diem for their efforts. In February 1725 a second raid of eighty-eight rangers set out in another late winter snowshoe expedition to the Maine frontier. This time they tracked a band of Natives for eleven days, from near Lake Winnipesaukee to where they caught up with their camp at dusk on February 20. Lovewell had his men lay low until well after sunset, and then sprang a surprise attack around midnight.

The Natives were overwhelmed and butchered. Whether they were all warriors or a mixture of combatants and non-combatants is unclear. However, the rangers returned with many French-produced muskets and extra blankets and moccasins that would be needed to bring in captives. At the time many may have agreed with an eighteenth-century biographer of Lovewell who wrote that this prevented a major attack on the frontier—"for these Indians were marching from Canada, well furnished with guns and plenty of ammunition."[30] The raiders gained fame throughout New England and were awarded £1,000 for ten scalps.[31]

Lovewell's final and most famous raid occurred in April and May of 1725. This expedition was with a new company of forty-seven townsmen, largely from Boston, with little backwoods experience. They planned to surprise the Abenaki town of Pequawket, now Fryeburg, Maine. Nearing the village, Lovewell constructed a small fort, leaving nine men behind. Later the raiders spotted a lone Native who retreated at their approach, and the men dropped their packs and equipment to run after the retreating Indian. This time it was the Natives who used surprise and ambush to wipe out the raiding party. The men fell into a pre-laid ambush of perhaps one hundred warriors, which resulted in the death of Lovewell on the first volley and the scattering of his command. The survivors managed to make it back to the fortification after the Abenaki broke off the chase. Only twelve of the original attackers survived the ambush. This battle brought about an even larger invasion by the New Englanders, eventually driving the Natives to Québec. Perhaps this disaster was attributable to the predominance of townsmen in the company, men with little backwoods skills and only the promise of bounties to motivate them. However, the fight became famous in New England history as the Battle of Pequawket or Lovewell's Fight. In retrospect, it is rather odd that such a poorly led and executed—and ultimately failed—raid would be hailed by such nineteenth-century literary giants as Thoreau, Hawthorne, and Longfellow.[32]

The colonial wars became increasingly brutal and at odds with European movements of the time. In the "Age of Limited Warfare," Natives and colonists were delving into total racial warfare. The combatants were not European-hired mercenaries fighting for some distant monarch, but rather local Native and colonial forces fighting for survival. In the European sense, simply winning and holding a battlefield settled nothing. One side or the other had to prevail. Both sides targeted unarmed civilians and property, and the militia would settle for nothing less than the complete conquest of the Natives.[33]

Guerrilla warfare was not unknown to the established nation-states of Europe. Irregular warfare, or what the French referred to as *petite guerre* ("small war"), was a well-known concept. The use of small and irregular forces in ambushes, attacks against isolated outposts, and surprise raids against supply lines was accepted. However, most European officers frowned upon the use of guerrillas who lacked discipline and professionalism. They believed irregular warfare quickly degenerated into total warfare targeting civilians. Raids led to rape, murder, displacement, and plunder of civilian property. This kind of warfare was to be confined to "barbarous Nations."[34] This did not mean Europeans entirely avoided using *petite guerre*; in fact, total warfare against civilian populations became a primary tactic for the English when they forced the people of Ireland and Scotland to submit to colonial control.[35]

Historically, Europeans understood the concept of total war perfectly. After a three-year siege at the end of the Third Punic War in 146 BCE, Romans under Scipio Aemilianus breached the walls of Carthage and systematically destroyed it. The Romans enslaved fifty thousand Carthaginians, burned the city, and razed its walls—essentially erasing it from the map. Roman forces under Germanicus waged a total war on German tribes, which according to Tacitus "ravaged and burnt the country for fifty miles around. No pity was shown to age or sex."[36] Medieval Crusaders saw Muslims as subhuman and had no issue with the killing of civilians including women and children. In Europe, the Reformation and subsequent Wars of Religion led to the widespread displacement and death of untold thousands.[37]

In the eighteenth century professional soldiers continued to study and write about guerrilla warfare. In 1752 Frenchman Armand de La Croix wrote a memoir of his service as a guerrilla fighter in *petite guerre*. Many French officers were interested in institutionalizing guerrilla units within the army. In 1756 Thomas-Auguste le Roy de Grandmaison, the leading advocate of guerrilla warfare in France, published *La Petite Guerre*. This work called for the French army to establish a permanent irregular force that would support the regular army by acting as guides and scouts and working in the rear of enemy-occupied positions. There they would conduct raids and ambushes on communications and supplies. In 1759 Louis Michel de Jeney published *Le Partisan*, a tactical manual for guerrilla operations. Rather than rely on poorly trained and undisciplined guerrillas, de Jeney called for highly trained forces to infiltrate the enemy's rear and cause havoc. This manual became the forerunner of what we know today as "Special Forces" doctrine. The manual called for highly trained and well-disciplined men to conduct raids, ambushes, and "secret marches." For example, in setting up an ambush, de Jeney pointed out that the force should have a pre-planned escape route in case it is outmatched. He even noted that men should be recruited with the language skills needed for their area of operations and that officers should have field medical training because regular medical care would not be available.[38]

Yet as modern nation-states developed in Europe, commissioned officers began to see themselves as a professional class whose obligation was to exercise the will of their monarchs. It was rarely in the best interest of the nation to wage war on non-combatants. The mission of the military was to impose the will of the monarch against a rival monarch, not necessarily the general population. These gentlemen considered it their mission to maintain strict control over the peasants who comprised the rank and file of the army. Rape, murder, looting, and pillaging could no longer be tolerated by eighteenth-century western forces. For the most part, career officers rejected the idea of irregular operations. After seeing the results of depredations committed by the Cossacks following the 1812 Battle of Borodino, the legendary strategist Carl von Clausewitz condemned all undisciplined bands that preyed on civilians. According to historian John Grenier, "In time, the relatively benign treatment of noncombatants became the norm for Western European armies."[39]

CHAPTER TWO

"No army can subsist in this country without rangers"

John Campbell Loudoun

AS THE NORTH AMERICAN FRENCH, ENGLISH, AND SPANISH COLONIES developed in the eighteenth century, it was inevitable that conflicts among the competing European powers would spill over to the provinces. Unlike the conflicts in Europe, however, the contests in America would be fought on the frontier, with surrogate Native allies using raids, ambushes, and the element of surprise. In the northeast, the English and French vied with each other for alliances with the two dominant Native groups of the region, the Iroquois and Algonquian Confederacies. The French supported their Algonquian allies, including the Abenakis, Ottawas, and Montagnais, in an extensive fur trading network across southern Canada. The Six Nations of the Iroquois Confederacy, which occupied northern New York, consisted of the Onondaga, Cayuga, Oneida, Mohawk, Seneca, and later the Tuscarora. This placed them in a unique geographical position between British and French colonies, which they used to pit the European trading competitors against each other. The French and Indian War (1754–1763)—or Seven Years' War, as it is known in Europe—was the bloodiest of these contests; unlike the other wars, it originated in America and grew to what many historians call the first great world war. In this conflict the British deployed large bodies of regular forces that, in the face of French and Native guerrilla fighters, were forced to adapt to the American way of guerrilla warfare.[1]

The French and Native forces of New France accepted non-conventional warfare from the start. Bloody raids had gone on since the sixteenth century along the northern American frontier, as the Natives teamed with French *coureurs de bois* (runners of the woods) who lived among the Indians and adapted to their native customs and guerrilla tactics. One observer called them "Half Indianized French, and Half Frenchified Indians." French officials learned to use independent mixed companies of Canadian militia, French regular forces known as *Troupes de la Marine*, and Native allies as raiding parties. Unlike British officers who purchased their commissions, the French promoted local men by merit. As historian William Eccles noted, "Great mobility, deadly marksmanship, skillful use of surprise and forest cover, high morale and, like the Royal Navy, a tradition of victory, gave the colonial regulars their superiority." These parties devastated northeastern British settlements, targeting men, women, and children, and they were successful time and again in driving colonists off the frontier to the protection of more densely settled areas. American militia were for the most part no match for these masters of the forest. The Americans and the British had to adapt to their form of warfare and develop their own ranger traditions in response.[2]

For much of the colonial period the British colonies had developed in close proximity to the Atlantic Ocean, but as they expanded through the gaps in the Appalachian highlands, they came to covet the fertile bottomlands of the Ohio River and its tributaries. Virginia and several other colonies laid claim to the area. The French—with their extensive alliances with Natives and knowledge of the transportation networks on the rivers and lakes of what is known today as the Midwest—were in a position to challenge American colonists as they moved west.

The French and Indian War was instigated by a guerrilla ambush on the Ohio River by militia and allied Natives under twenty-two-year-old George Washington. After failing to convince the French to leave the area, in April 1754 Virginia governor Robert Dinwiddie dispatched a small force under Washington to build a fort where the Monongahela and Allegheny Rivers join to form the Forks of the Ohio. Along the way Washington learned the French had driven a construction crew off the site and had built their own fortification, Fort Duquesne. Shortly thereafter,

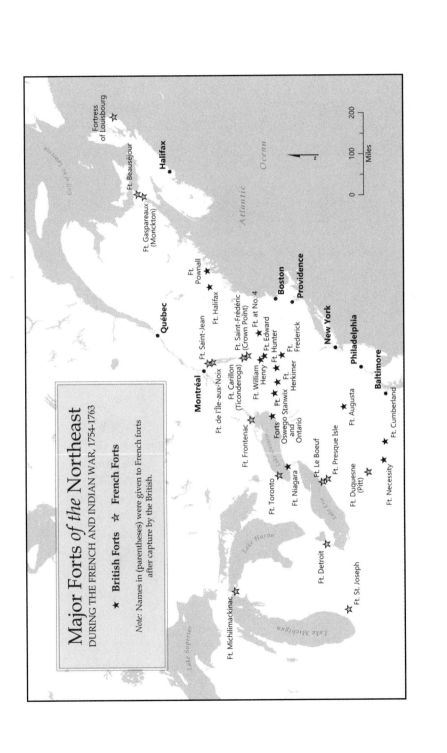

Major Forts *of the* Northeast
DURING THE FRENCH AND INDIAN WAR, 1754-1763

★ British Forts   ☆ French Forts

Note: Names in (parentheses) were given to French forts after capture by the British.

Fortress of Louisbourg

Ft. Beauséjour

Halifax

Ft. Gaspareaux (Monckton)

Atlantic Ocean

N

0   100   200
Miles

Gulf of St. Lawrence

Ft. Pownall

Québec

Ft. Saint-Jean

Ft. Halifax

Ft. Saint-Frédéric (Crown Point)

Ft. at No. 4

Boston

Providence

Ft. Edward

Ft. Hunter

Ft. Frederick

New York

Montréal

Ft. de l'Île-aux-Noix

Ft. Carillon (Ticonderoga)

Ft. William Henry

Ft. Herkimer

Philadelphia

Ft. Stanwix

Baltimore

Ft. Frontenac

Oswego Forts and Ft. Ontario

Ft. Augusta

Ft. Cumberland

Lake Ontario

Ft. Toronto

Ft. Niagara

Ft. Le Boeuf

Ft. Presque Isle

Ft. Duquesne (Pitt)

Ft. Necessity

Lake Erie

Lake Huron

Ft. Detroit

Lake Michigan

Ft. Michilimackinac

Ft. St. Joseph

Lake Superior

Washington's Native guides led the Virginians on a surprise attack against a Canadian force that had been sent out to warn the Virginians away from the area. Some of the French militia were killed and, according to one source, a Native ally of Washington used his hatchet to kill the French commander after he had surrendered—turning the incident into a guerrilla fight that would have international repercussions.

G. Washington. Stipple engraving of a young George Washington by J.B. Forrest, after a portrait by Charles Willson Peale.
MIRIAM AND IRA D. WALLACH DIVISION OF ART, NEW YORK PUBLIC LIBRARY

After hearing of a French force marching out to pursue him, Washington returned to a place called the Great Meadows, where his men had begun construction on a fort called Fort Necessity. It was located in an open valley where the walls and fortifications provided little protection from the French and their allies, who took to the hills around it. Disappointed with Washington's defensive efforts, his Native allies abandoned him. Washington and his men were forced to come to terms with the French. In signing a French parole document, one he could not read because he did not understand French, Washington admitted in writing to being responsible for the death of the French diplomat—thus kicking off the American phase of what would continue in Europe, two years later, as the Seven Years' War.[3]

The differences between the tactics of regular European forces and those of American guerrilla fighters are most clearly seen in British Major General Edward Braddock's 1755 campaign against Fort Duquesne. Upon learning of Washington's defeat, London sent Braddock with two regiments of Irish regulars and authority to raise American forces, with orders to eliminate the French at the Forks of the Ohio. Braddock embarked with 2,400 provincial and British forces in a long European caravan, including camp followers, wagons, and equipment, into the rugged Alleghenies. In order to move the wagon train, Braddock was forced to cut a road through the mountains. As the forces slowed to a crawl, he went ahead with half the men as a "flying column" in search of the enemy. Had he properly utilized Native guides and Virginia rangers, the ultimate result may have been different. Instead Braddock ignored the small number of rangers who had joined him and drove away around a hundred Native allies. Benjamin Franklin, who worked closely with him, wrote that Braddock stubbornly refused to adapt to American guerrilla tactics. He argued that had Braddock utilized the rangers and Natives who had volunteered as "Guides, Scouts, &c." and if "he had treated them kindly," he might have enjoyed more success. "But he slighted & neglected them, and they gradually left him."[4] The general had no respect for the fighting abilities of American Natives. Speaking with him prior to the campaign, Franklin warned Braddock that if he were to separate his troops and overextend his line of march, the French and Indians would cut his forces and ambush them from the dense woods along the line of march. "He smil'd at my Ignorance, & reply'd," remembered Franklin, "These Savages may indeed be a formidable Enemy to your raw American Militia; but, upon the King's regular & diciplin'd Troops, Sir, it is impossible they should make any Impression."[5]

By July 9, 1755, the flying column under Braddock had crossed the Monongahela and had advanced within nine miles of Fort Duquesne when they unexpectedly ran into a French and Indian force that had been sent to intercept them. The fight began as a complete surprise for both forces; however, the French and their experienced allies recovered first. The French militia and the Indians took to the concealment of the woods on both sides of the trail, pinning the redcoats in a deadly crossfire that provided no cover. Surrounded on three sides, the leading troops fell back and broke up the ranks of the rest of the column attempting to march forward. Braddock's officers found it impossible to deploy in a European line of battle, and the forces fell back on themselves in confusion. Braddock himself was mortally wounded, and the column flew back in retreat to the rest of the force's body along the trail. Volunteer aide George Washington made a stand here, and with the help of the Virginia militia may have provided the cover needed for the survivors to retreat. Crossing the Monongahela, the army destroyed its full baggage train and retreated back to its starting point at Fort Cumberland, Maryland. A force of around nine hundred French and Indian fighters had routed 1,400 mostly British regulars from the flying column, only losing about forty men, while around two-thirds of the British force was killed or wounded. Braddock succumbed to his injuries en route and was buried on the road so that his body would remain hidden and not recovered and mutilated. Franklin remembered, "This General was I think a brave Man, and might probably have made a Figure as a good Officer in some European War. But he had too much self-confidence, too high an Opinion of the Validity of Regular Troops, and too mean a One of both Americans and Indians."[6]

In 1755, as overall commander in America, Braddock had started off with several British advances against the French, most of which ended in disaster. The campaign seasons from 1755 through 1757 all went poorly for the colonists and the British. The French form of guerrilla warfare on the frontier was far superior to the major campaigns of regular forces that the British were attempting. As British general John Forbes neatly summarized, "the French have these several years by past, outwitted us with our Indian Neighbors, have Baffled all our projects of Compelling them to do us justice, nay have almost everywhere had the advantage over us, both in political and military Genius, to our great loss, and I may say reproach."[7] In 1757 the Crown charged William Pitt with the conduct of the war, and he began focusing on using the superior Royal Navy—combined with regular and provisional forces—in an attempt to drive the French from North America once and for all. The plan called for a naval blockade to cut off essential supplies and trade goods from Canada and increasing the resources needed to campaign on the ground. In addition to regular troops, the Crown took over the financing of provincial units, including the invaluable rangers.[8]

Braddock's defeat opened the floodgates for French and Indian frontier raids. From the end of 1755 until early 1756, attackers swarmed in from the Pennsylvania frontier south to Georgia. By the fall of 1756 the Ohio Valley Shawnees and Delawares had killed or captured upward of three thousand colonists in the Appalachian range. The frontier receded as survivors flocked east to more densely settled areas. In Pennsylvania, for example, the raiders pushed as close as seventy-five miles from Philadelphia. The French reported that "all these provinces are laid waste for forty leagues from the foot of the mountains, in the direction of the sea."[9]

After Braddock's defeat, colonial assemblies began commissioning ranger units and offering bounties for Native scalps. For example, the Virginia House of Burgesses raised three fifty-man ranger companies and offered a bounty of £10 (approximately $2,000 in today's currency) for each scalp of an Indian male over twelve years of age. Lieutenant Governor Dinwiddie noted that over the fall of 1755 and early winter of 1756, the rangers devastated many Native villages. In New Hampshire, Robert Rogers received permission to enlist experienced frontiersmen from Colonel Joseph Blanchard's militia to become "Rogers' Rangers."[10]

The problem of French and Indian raids was particularly acute in Pennsylvania, where the pacifist Quaker-dominated assembly had always avoided any kind of support for a militia system. The raiders made no distinction between pacifists and combatants, and even after the pacifist Moravian settlement of Gnadenhütten ("huts of grace" in German) was annihilated in November 1756, the Quaker assembly was slow to act. The main obstacle was an impasse over taxes between the assembly and the proprietors, the Penn family. The stalemate finally broke after Germans from the frontier began parading the dead and mangled bodies of their loved ones on carts down High Street in Philadelphia and the Scots-Irish on the frontier threatened to take up arms and march on the statehouse. In order to avoid breaking with their pacifist theology, the assembly passed a bill to provide £55,000 for "the King's use."[11]

On the Pennsylvania frontier, Lieutenant Colonel John Armstrong also formed a ranger unit of mountaineers to face the danger. Armstrong had attempted to protect the area with a string of traditional forts and militia garrisons, but found these were useless in ending the raids. He went on the offense, and in 1756, with three hundred men, led a strike against the village of Kittanning, a Delaware settlement on the Allegheny River north of Fort Duquesne. Just before dawn on the morning of September 8, 1756, the rangers overran the village, capturing and killing the inhabitants and then destroying the settlement. The idea was to eliminate the village as a forward operating base to attack the Pennsylvania frontier. But the rangers did not leave it at that. In retribution for prior attacks, the rangers took no prisoners, chasing surviving men, women, and children into the forest in search of scalps. Although the attack on Kittanning was a success, it was costly and in the long term prolonged the conflict: it came at the same time that Quaker representatives from the colony were in talks with the Delaware and Shawnee, hoping to convince them to return to the status of neutrality.[12]

Major General Braddock's defeat led the British to rethink their strategy on the continent and their reliance on the "fickleness" of the Indians as guides and scouts.[13] Major General Jeffery Amherst, now commander-in-chief of the British army in North America, chose instead to lean on the American settlers who knew guerrilla warfare the best, the rangers.[14] Well acquainted with the American tradition of using ranger units to counter the French and their Native allies, Amherst turned to Robert Rogers and his rangers. The most famous leader of

American rangers, Rogers had extensive experience in the field. He was a true backwoodsman, ideally suited to frontier warfare. He noted in his *Journals* that he became familiar with "some knowledge of the manners, customs, and language of the Indians," adding that he was knowledgeable of the "British and French settlements in North America, and especially with the uncultivated desert, the mountains, valleys, rivers, lakes and several passes that lay between and contiguous to the said settlements."[15]

In the summer of 1754, during King George's War, Rogers was a fourteen-year-old living with his parents, James and Mary Rogers, in the Great Meadow frontier of New Hampshire when Abenakis from Canada laid waste to their farm and the surrounding area. Rogers then joined Captain Daniel Ladd's company of rangers and began his storied career.[16] During this war Massachusetts governor William Shirley had enlisted colonists whom he called "snowshoe men," or rangers, to defend the frontier. They were to "hold themselves ready at the shortest Warning to go in pursuit of any Party of Indians, who frequently in time of War make sudden Incursions, whilst there is a deep Snow upon the Ground, and retreat as suddenly into the Woods after having done what Mischief they can."[17]

Robert Rogers's service began when he raised a unit of New Hampshire volunteers for service in the 1755 Lake George campaign. The backwoodsmen Rogers recruited were experienced hunters like he was. At times, British regulars were simultaneously shocked by the lack of discipline among provincial rangers and in awe of their skills in scouting and raiding. Rangers cared little for the redcoats and regulations of the regulars. One British officer observed that the rangers "have no particular uniform, only they wear their cloaths short." Each man carried his musket, hatchet, possibles bag containing sixty bullets, buckshot, and a long knife. They also carried a "bullocks horn full of powder" that "hangs under their right arm by a belt from their shoulder."[18]

Rogers spent 1755 and 1756 leading his men on scouting expeditions from Fort William Henry up to Lake George and Lake Champlain. In March 1756 he managed to approach the walls of France's greatest citadel, Fort Carillon (later renamed Fort Ticonderoga by the British), on Lake Champlain. By the time he was recalled to meet Governor Shirley

Robert Rogers—Commandeur der Americaner. Etching originally published in *Geschichte der kriege in und ausser Europa* (Nürnberg, G.N. Raspe, 1776–84). No known portraits of Robert Rogers were drawn or painted from life; this etching appears to have been based on a color mezzotint dating to 1776, currently located in the Anne S.K. Brown Military Collection at Brown University. RARE BOOK AND SPECIAL COLLECTIONS DIVISION, LIBRARY OF CONGRESS in Boston, now the overall British commander in North America, the papers had made him a celebrity. The Boston *Evening Post* hailed him as the man "who has made himself famous in these Parts of America, by his Courage and Activity with his Scouting-Parties near Crown-Point."[19] Rogers was pleased with the meeting, during which the governor "soon intimated his design of giving me the command of an independent company of Rangers."[20] Shirley authorized Rogers to raise a company of sixty-six men "used to traveling and hunting, and in whose courage and fidelity I could confide" in order to "distress the French and their allies by sacking, burning, and destroying their houses, barns, barracks, canoes, battoes, etc., and killing their cattle of every kind; and at all times to endeavor to way-lay, attack, and destroy their convoys of provisions by land and water, in any part of the country."[21]

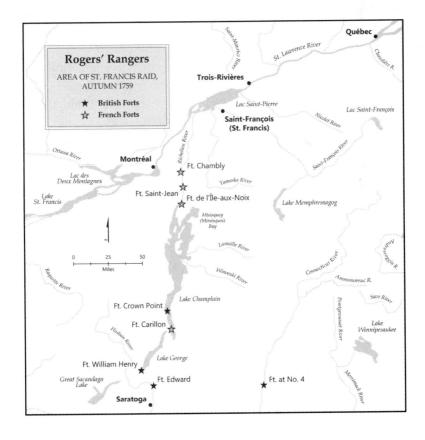

Throughout 1756 Rogers's Rangers scouted from Fort William Henry and Fort Edward to report on the French and their Native allies on Lake Champlain. Rogers looked for targets of opportunity and used the surprise of an ambush to capture and bring back prisoners for interrogation. The risks were extremely high; unlike regular forces fighting in Europe, the war on the American frontier did not always include the option of surrender. If captured by Natives, colonists could expect a level of torture that made death a blessed relief.[22]

When Major General James Abercrombie assumed command of British forces in America in the summer of 1756, he summoned Rogers to Albany. Pleased with Rogers's efforts, the major general added a new company of rangers to be commanded by his brother, Richard Rogers.[23] When General John Campbell, Fourth Earl of Loudoun, assumed command, Rogers reported that he had also taken command of a group of about thirty Stockbridge Indians, whom Rogers had sent scouting; Rogers reported they had returned with two "French scalps, agreeable to their barbarous custom."[24] Rogers used his knowledge of the French language to his advantage. On a scouting party within a mile of Fort Carillon, he spied a French sentry. Taking five men, he boldly approached the soldier and answered the sentry's challenge "in French, signifying that were friends; the centinel was thereby deceived, till I came close to him, when perceiving his mistake, in great surprize he called, *Qui etes vous?* I answered 'Rogers,' and led him from his post in great haste, cutting his breeches and coat from him, that he might march with the greater ease and expedition."[25] This prisoner, like others taken before, provided a boon of information for the British over the French and Indian strengths and plans.[26]

That winter Rogers's force was increased by two more ranger companies and split between Forts Edward and Henry. In mid-January 1757, Rogers set out from Fort Henry with a snowshoe-clad heavy scouting party down from Lake George in the direction of Fort Carillon. Due to injuries on the first day, by the second day the party was reduced to seventy-four officers and men. On January 21, 1757, midway between Crown Point and Carillon, the party spotted a sled traveling between the two posts. Sending Lieutenant John Stark with part of the force to intercept the sled, Rogers and another force attempted to block the sled's line of retreat back to Carillon. At that point Rogers spotted about ten more sleds that had spotted them, and all beat a path to safety back at the fort. "We pursued them," wrote Rogers, "and took seven prisoners, three sleds and six horses; the remainder made their escape."[27] Rogers learned from the prisoners that the fort was well garrisoned with French and their Indian allies, and the men who had escaped the ambush would surely rouse the garrison. Here Rogers held a council of war in which his officers suggested they should "return by a different route from that by which the party came." The men were soaked and exhausted, and Rogers ordered them back to the fires of their last camp to clean their wet weapons and prepare to fight or retreat. The cocky twenty-four-year-old was defiant, stating "that they would not *dare* pursue him."[28]

After the halt, at around two in the afternoon, the rangers marched on in single file about a half-mile, with Rogers in the lead and Lieutenant Stark taking up the rear. Rogers should not have wasted time returning to his camp; in fact, by doing so he violated one of his own famous "Rules of Ranging." Rule V states that "in your return take a different route from that in which you went out, that you may better discover any party in your rear, and have an opportunity, if their strength be superior to yours, to alter your course, or disperse, as circumstances may require."[29] Instead Rogers led his men into a deadly ambush in which the first sign they had of the enemy "was the noise in cocking their guns." Entering a valley where the French and Indians had taken positions in the wood line, they met "the enemy, who had here drawn up in the form of a half-moon, with a design, as we supposed to surround us, saluted us with a volley of about 200 shot, at the distance of about five yards from the nearest, or front, and thirty from the rear of their party."[30] As men fell all around, Rogers was wounded, but still ordered his men to rally with the rear guard on the closest hill. Several more were killed or captured as they fell back. "My people," noted Rogers, "however, beat them back by a brisk fire from the hill." Here Rogers placed his officers and men in a high defensive position, all the while fearing being flanked. Outnumbered, almost surrounded, and in a desperate situation, the rangers did have one distinct advantage: they were wearing snowshoes and could skim across the surface while the French had to plow through waist-high snow.[31] The

French and Indians moved to flank them on their right, and Rogers sent his reserves over to hold them off. Rogers noted they performed well, "giving them the first fire very briskly," forcing them to take cover where "it stopped several from retreating to the main body." They then made a head-on assault, but using the cover and concealment of the trees, Rogers recorded that "we maintained a continual fire upon them, which killed several, and obliged the rest to retire to their main body." The standoff continued in this way for several hours, with the enemy taunting Rogers by name with threats. They claimed that they were about to be reinforced, and if Rogers refused to surrender they would "cut us to pieces without mercy." They then tried flattery, stating that it was "a pity so many brave men should be lost; that we should, upon our surrender, be treated with the greatest compassion and kindness." The rangers turned down the offers, replying that "we were determined to keep our ground as long as there were two left to stand by each other."[32]

The fighting finally began to taper off at sunset, as human targets began to blend in with the growing shadows. At this time Rogers "received a ball thro' my hand and wrist, which disabled me from loading my gun. I however found means to keep my people from being intimidated by this accident; they gallantly kept their advantageous situation, till the fire ceased on both sides."[33] Under darkness the rangers fell back, making it to Lake George by sunrise. With many wounded, Rogers dispatched Lieutenant Stark and two other men to Fort William Henry to bring up transportation for the wounded. The next day a relief force with a sled guided the party back to the fort, where fifty-four survivors including six wounded men arrived. Rogers guessed they had been attacked by 250 French and Indian fighters, and he had heard that the French reported 116 men killed or mortally wounded.[34]

By late 1757 Loudoun and his commanders came around to the use of American guerrilla rangers and decided to increase their numbers for the upcoming campaign season to a thousand men. Rogers was then given the order to raise five companies of New England rangers that he would command.[35]

However, Rogers and his command saw the war through different lenses. This war in America was not a contest between the "King's

Champions" who, under bright banners in colorful uniforms, would meet their enemy on the field of honor while advancing by fife and drum. No. For Robert Rogers and his neighbors, the Seven Years' War in America was a fight for survival on the frontier, dominated by the guerrilla tactics of small-unit ambushes and raids, using the elements of stealth and surprise to dominate the enemy. Quarter was neither freely given nor expected by either side, and civilian settlements were considered fair game. As early as 1756, Rogers had pressed Loudoun for permission to "plunder Canada"[36] with attacks and raids upon the settlements of the French and their allied Natives. Loudoun demurred. He thought this would simply turn into a scalping party by the New Englanders, something he considered a "Barbarous Custom."[37] Besides, rather than enemy scalps, he needed the intelligence that prisoners could provide. He ended the practice of awarding bounties for scalps.[38] Loudoun's successor, Major General Abercrombie, freely used the rangers on scalping parties and reported to London that he had sent them out to do "as Much Mischief as they" could.[39]

While the scouting and raiding by the rangers proved valuable, British authorities had little faith in using American provincial troops. General James Wolfe opined that "Americans are in general the dirtiest, the most contemptible cowardly dogs you can conceive."[40] In fact, he considered rangers in particular to be "Lazy cowardly People."[41] The rangers developed a reputation of being poorly disciplined and insubordinate. After going on a scout with Rogers's men to Fort Carillon in late 1757, Captain James Abercromby (no relation to the general) complained that "the Ranger officers have no Subordination amongst them."[42] He advised his commanders that if the ranger force was to be expanded, they should be led by regular British officers "to introduce a great deal of Subordination."[43]

At Fort Edward in December 1757, Rogers's Rangers mutinied after the regulars flogged two privates. The rangers knew Rogers's first rule: "All Rangers are to be subject to the rules and articles of war."[44] This also included brutal forms of corporal punishment that were rare among provincials. Two respected veteran rangers, Samuel Boyd and Henry Dawson, were convicted of stealing rum from the fort. They were taken by the regulars and brutally whipped with a cat-o'-nine-tails, a whip with nine separate lashes, each tipped with a sharp metal barb. The rangers had seen enough. Unlike regular British troops, they did not consider themselves professional career soldiers, but rather colonial citizen-soldiers who had temporarily taken up arms under contract to protect their neighbors on the frontier. Their concept of discipline and service could not have been more foreign than that of the regular officers, who used the brute force of corporal punishment to ensure the discipline of the regular forces—many of whom enlisted from the most impoverished classes of Britain.[45]

The event may not have spiraled out of control had Rogers been there. But he had been bedridden fighting scurvy, and his men took action. First they focused their anger on the greatest symbol of oppression: the whipping post. After they gathered around it and cut it down, they attempted to free the prisoners from the guardhouse. They surrounded the stockade and began to knock boards off of it until two ranger officers, Captain Charles Bulkeley and Captain John Shepherd, intervened at some risk to themselves. Shepherd grabbed a weapon from one of the mutineers and ordered some of the men who had accompanied him to fire on the next man who attempted to destroy the guardhouse. The regulars heard the commotion in the American camp and went to investigate. The commander of Fort Edward, Lieutenant Colonel William Haviland, had little use for the rangers and demanded that Rogers turn over the ringleaders of the mutiny. Rogers complied, but warned Haviland that if the men were treated too brutally, he could not ensure that a good portion of his command would not desert. This stand simply convinced the lieutenant colonel that the rangers were unfit for service at the fort and should be transferred away due to their bad influence on the regulars. General Abercrombie concurred and informed his commander Loudoun that he had always felt that the rangers were "unfit for service.[46]

The legacy of what became known as the "Whipping Post Mutiny," combined with the great expense of equipping the ranger companies, led Loudoun to conclude it would be better if he could train regular troops to perform the scouting and raiding duties for the army. Indeed, Prince William, the Duke of Cumberland, wrote Loudoun, "I hope that you will, in time, teach your Troops to go out on Scouting Parties, for, 'till *Regular* Officers with men that they can trust, learn to beat the woods, & to act as *Irregulars*, you never will gain any Intelligence of the Enemy, as I fear, by this time you are convinced that *Indian* Intelligence & that of the *Rangers* is not at all to be depended upon."[47] In a break from tradition, Loudoun had started placing regular officers under provincial command in order for Rogers to teach them the fundamentals of ranging. Rogers accepted fifty-five "Gentleman Volunteers" for training in "ranging discipline." In December 1757, Lieutenant Colonel Thomas Gage (later of Lexington and Concord fame) offered to raise and pay for a five-hundred-man regiment of "light-armed foot," provided the Crown compensated him and advanced him to the rank of colonel. Loudoun approved, believing that this would cut the expenses and improve discipline. In 1758 Gage began recruiting, and by May Gage's new 80th Regiment of Foot was established with the newly minted colonel at its head. However, Gage had ignored officers with ranging experience, used very few of the men who had training under Rogers and his men, and instead filled positions with regular line officers. Gage would prove to be a competent administrator, but lacked the aggressiveness needed for battle. In time Gage's force proved to be inept at ranging, and when they were used, they were placed under the command of Rogers.[48]

In 1757, as Rogers trained his rangers on Rogers Island (across the Hudson from Fort Edward), he codified his method of guerrilla warfare into what has come down to us as Rogers's "Rules of Ranging." In attempting to standardize his rules for guerrilla warfare, Rogers distilled his concepts into twenty-eight "Standing Orders" that outlined his principles. Here he was training his men for "ranging, or wood-service, under my command and inspection; with particular orders to me to instruct them to the utmost of my power in ranging-discipline, our methods of marching, retreating, ambushing, fighting &c."[49] Rogers noted the list of rules were based on his own experience "which upon various occasions, I had found by experience to be necessary and advantageous."[50] The rules have proven to be a timeless guide to small-unit fighting. In fact, a fictionalized folksy version of the rules, originally printed in Kenneth Roberts's 1937 novel about Rogers, *Northwest Passage*, follows the "Ranger's

Creed" in the U.S. Army Ranger Handbook. However, the original rules from Rogers's journals are still studied by Army Ranger students today.

The rules cover a wide variety of subjects, even including the daily inspections during which men would appear "at roll-call every evening, on their own parade, equipped, each with a Firelock, sixty rounds of powder and ball, and a hatchet, at which time an officer from each company is to inspect the same, to see they are in order, so as to be ready on any emergency to march at a minute's warning." The rules contain timeless pieces of advice as well. For example, Rogers cautions rangers moving on patrol, "if your number be small, march in a single file, keeping at such a distance from each other as to prevent one shot from killing two men, sending one man, or more." When crossing wetlands where tracks are easy to follow, Rogers suggests that men shift from walking in single file to abreast "to prevent the enemy from tracking you," then to resume their former order on dry land. Men should keep moving and camp after it is "quite dark" in an area that will permit sentries the ability to see and hear "the enemy some considerable distance." In order to quickly respond to any threat, Rogers orders that half of the men remain awake "alternately through the night." He calls for prisoners to be separated "till they are examined" in order to extract the most information from each. He also warns against returning from a patrol using the same route, writing, "in your return take a different route from that in which you went out, that you may the better discover any party in your rear, and have an opportunity, if their strength be superior to yours, to alter your course, or disperse, as circumstances may require." While traveling in large bodies, he required units to send out flanking parties on all sides to "prevent your being ambuscaded, and to notify the approach or retreat of the enemy." In a rejection of standard practices of eighteenth-century European warfare, he calls for men to take cover under fire, adding, "If you are obliged to receive the enemy's fire, fall, or squat down, till it is over; then rise and discharge at them." He advises men to cover each other as they "advance from tree to tree, with one half of the party before the other ten or twelve yards."[51]

Robert Rogers foresaw many circumstances that modern fighters know well. Modern military tactics call for leaders to point out rally points for troops on patrol. If caught by an ambush and command is scattered, men automatically fall back to the rally point and set up a perimeter of defense. Rogers foresaw this, noting, "If the enemy is so superior that you are in danger of being surrounded by them, let the whole body disperse, and every one take a different road to the place of rendezvous appointed for that evening, which must every morning be altered and fixed for the evening ensuing, in order to bring the whole party, or as many of them as possible, together, after any separation that may happen in the day." The modern soldier is well acquainted with the whisper just before dawn of the order to "stand to," which is short for stand-to-arms. The twilight hour of dawn has historically been the preferred time for a surprise attack, a crucial fact not lost on Rogers. He ordered his men at daybreak to "awake your whole detachment; that being the time when the savages choose to fall upon their enemies, you should by all means be in readiness to receive them." He gave practical advice for avoiding being ambushed by following main roads and using common fords. He showed them how to follow the enemy without being discovered. Rather than following directly behind them, Rogers advised his men to circle around them "to head and meet them in some narrow pass, or lay in ambush to receive them when and where they least expect it."[52]

In January 1758 Loudoun ordered Rogers to recruit five new companies of rangers, including a company of Natives. All were to be "able-bodies, well acquainted with the woods, used to hunting, and every way qualified for the Rangeing service."[53] Four of the new companies were sent to Louisburg, North Carolina, and Rogers took command of the fifth at Fort Edward.

On March 10, 1758, Rogers led a force of 183 men up from Lake George to Fort Carillon. However, the campaign started off on the wrong foot. The British commander of Fort Edward, Colonel Haviland, had previously sent out a raiding party under the future American Revolutionary War hero, Israel Putnam, and had made it public knowledge that Rogers's command would venture out as well upon Putnam's return. One of the men had been captured and another had deserted to the French, and it was clear to Rogers that by sending his party out at this point, the commander had lost his most valuable commodity—the element of surprise. In addition, Rogers had originally been promised four hundred men for the raid, but had only 183. Rogers had a premonition about the events that would unfold: "I acknowledge I entered upon this service . . . with no little concern and uneasiness of mind," he recalled, "for there was the greatest reason to suspect that the French were, by the prisoner and deserter above mentioned, fully informed of the design of sending me out." He also questioned Colonel Haviland's motives for the orders. The rangers had nothing but problems with the regulars at the fort, and Rogers noted, "I must confess it appeared to me (ignorant and unskilled as I was then in politicks and arts of war) incomprehensible; *but my commander doubtless has his reasons, and is able to vindicate his own conduct.*"[54]

The rangers utilized advance scouts, flanking parties, and even ice skates to cross the lake. On March 13, advancing on the fort, they took to the woods and used snowshoes to remain under cover of the forest. Next they split the command into two divisions and proceeded along parallel routes to within two miles of the garrison's advanced guards. After advancing along a narrow valley following a creek, the advance scouts informed Rogers that perhaps as many as ninety-six Natives were advancing in their direction. Rogers ordered his men to drop their packs and set an ambush. After placing the men, "we waited till their front was nearly opposite to our left wing, when I fired a gun, as a signal for a general discharge upon them." The volley killed as many as forty Natives, and the survivors retreated. Rogers ordered a charge. But they did not go far: unbeknownst to the rangers, the party they had ambushed was but an advanced guard of six hundred or more French and Indians.[55]

Rogers ordered his men to fall back to their previous position, "which we gained at the expence of fifty men killed." He rallied the survivors and managed to drive off the enemy. With their backs to the mountain, Rogers's men were attacked on three sides and the rangers drove them back a third time. With around two hundred men, the Natives then proceeded to climb the mountain to their rear. Here Rogers sent a lieutenant with eighteen men to hold the ridgeline and sent more to cover his left. Rogers recorded that "the fire continued almost constant for an hour and half from the beginning of the attack, in which time we lost eight officers, and more than 100 private men killed on the spot." Rogers and about twenty survivors retreated to the ridge and reunited with the men previously sent there. Here one of the detachments was cut off and surrounded. They were offered what they thought were good terms and surrendered; only then did they discover that their fate was to be "inhumanly tied up to trees and hewn to pieces, in a most barbarous and shocking manner."[56]

"I now thought it most prudent to retreat," Rogers noted. Closely followed by Natives, the force retreated back to Lake George and gathered some of the surviving wounded with their sleds. He sent word to Fort Edward for help bringing in the wounded and resumed the march the next morning. Rogers summarized that he had faced perhaps a hundred Canadians, supported by no less than six hundred Indians; he thought his forces might have killed as many as 150 of the enemy, at a cost of nearly his entire command. Despite his prescience, Rogers never accepted responsibility for the disaster he led his men into and never questioned his own judgment in setting an ambush for an enemy force without first determining its size and composition. Instead he blamed Colonel Haviland for advertising the raid and sending out an undersized force.[57]

Rogers and his men continued to scout and support the British in 1758, taking part in the Battle of Carillon on July 7 and 8. Now promoted to the rank of Major of Rangers, the new British commander in North America Major General Jeffrey Amherst ordered Rogers on a mission he had long sought, an attack on hostile Native settlements in Canada. By summer of 1759 the situation for the British in America had improved much. In July the British captured Carillon (or Fort Ticonderoga) and Fort Niagara. They had now taken the war directly to Canada, with the key city of Québec under siege. Amherst was also set on revenge. He had sent a delegation under a flag of truce to parley a treaty with the Abenakis at St. Francis in Québec. Amherst became incensed when he learned that his men had been taken as prisoners. Rogers noted, "this ungenerous, inhumane treatment determined the General to chastise these savages with some severity." Amherst ordered Rogers to take a force of two hundred men and "march and attack the enemy's settlements on the south side of the river St. Lawrence, in such a manner as you shall judge most effectual to disgrace the enemy, and for the success and honour of his Majesty's arms." However, he added, although the enemy had "murdered the women and children of all ages, it is my orders that no women or children are killed or hurt."[58]

Rogers saw this as a golden opportunity to settle an old score. These were the same people who had attacked the Great Meadow in 1745, when he was just fourteen, destroying his homestead and killing so many of his neighbors.[59] In September 1759, half a lifetime later, Rogers paddled north from Crown Point in the company of two hundred men, with vengeance on his mind. Most were rangers, but the force also included Stockbridge Indians, Mohegans who were part of the rangers, and a few regulars. Ten days later they hid their boats at Misisquey Bay (present-day Missisquoi Bay) and began an overland march to St. Francis. They left two Natives behind to watch their boats and supplies, only to learn the French and Indians had discovered them and had a force of four hundred in pursuit. "This unlucky circumstance," noted Rogers, "(it may well be supposed) put us into some consternation." With their line of retreat blocked and supplies and boats captured, Rogers elected to press ahead with the mission. He sent a messenger back to Crown Point asking for supplies to be diverted over the mountains to the Connecticut River, offering the force a second route. After ten days of pushing through wetlands to avoid being easily followed, they reached the St. Lawrence about fifteen miles north of the town. Fording the river, they marched south. Climbing a tree, Rogers finally spotted St. Francis about three miles away. At around 8:00 p.m., as the light faded, he gathered two officers and left to observe the town. He found the Indians in "a high frolic or dance," guaranteeing the element of surprise. Returning to his force at 2:00 a.m., he set out with them an hour later. Reduced by the rigors of the journey to 142 men, they quietly approached to within five hundred yards of the village, stowed their packs, and prepared to attack. Rogers waited until half an hour before sunrise; then his men swarmed through.[60]

The surprise was complete. Rogers noted that the "enemy had not time to recover themselves or take arms for their own defence, till they were chiefly destroyed." A few broke for their canoes along the water, only to be chased down and shot by the rangers. The rangers had no sympathy for their victims and no reason, in their own minds, to follow

Amherst's "orders that no women or children are killed or hurt": Rogers explained that this tribe "had for near a century past harrassed the frontiers of New England, killing people of all ages and sexes in a most barbarous manner." In a six-year period, Rogers continued, this tribe had captured or killed "400 persons." As they looted and destroyed the village, Rogers noted, "we found in the town hanging on poles over their doors, c., about 600 scalps, mostly English."[61]

Rogers found two storehouses with corn that he planned on using for the return trip. Just after sunrise, he ordered that the town be burnt. Some Natives were incinerated alive, as "the fire consumed many of the Indians who had concealed themselves in the cellars and lofts of their houses." The Catholic church was looted and its bell was taken. By 7:00 a.m. Rogers concluded that the event was over. He bragged of killing "at least two hundred Indians, and taken twenty of their women and children prisoners." He released most, but brought away two boys and three Native girls; he also liberated five "English captives" with whom he would return. However, the French reported that Rogers and his men killed only forty people and carried away ten prisoners.[62]

Learning that a large force of French and Indians were actively searching for them and expecting them to return via Lake Champlain, Rogers met with his officers and they agreed that the Connecticut River was their only viable route back south. After marching south for eight days, provisions began to run short. Rogers divided the command into several independent companies who—split up with guides—would lead them along different paths to a predetermined rally point at the mouth of the Amonsook River. There supplies from Crown Point should have been waiting for them; however, when they arrived, Rogers and his men discovered that the officer who had been sent from Crown Point with supplies had given up and returned hours before their arrival. After building a raft, Rogers set out with a couple of men for the nearest settlement, a frontier fort known simply as the Fort at Number 4 (now Charlestown, New Hampshire). They arrived after several days and were able to send food and rescue to the rest of the party. Men continued to drift in, and by the time he reached Crown Point on December 1, 1759, Rogers tallied forty-nine men lost since leaving St. Francis.[63]

Rogers's St. Francis raid is significant for several reasons. It demonstrated that General Amherst and the British had accepted "the first way of war" in America, to use Grenier's phrase. This is war between partisan or guerrilla bands, targeting civilians and their farms and villages. It incorporates the raid and ambush and rarely includes quarter to men—and only occasionally to women and children. The British were now willing to use American rangers in place of their fickle Native allies to act as guides, scouts, and raiders. Rogers demonstrated that American forces could be just as well adapted to the same long-range raiding that the French and Indians had already practiced for a century along the frontier. Finally, it demonstrated to the French and Indians that their homelands were no longer immune from the terror they had long practiced themselves, with their own frontier raids into the northern British colonies.[64]

The fall of Québec in 1759 and Montréal the next year marked the end of much of the Native raiding along the frontier and foretold the demise of New France. Ultimately, however, the war was not won by the guerrilla tactics practiced by Rogers and others. The British under Gage had attempted to train forces for unconventional warfare, but met with little success. Instead it was William Pitt's use of naval and regular forces in conventional warfare that turned the tide. Cut off by blockades from trading with the French, many tribes declared neutrality, and some switched sides to the British.

Chapter Three

"An unfair way of carrying on a war"

British soldier William Carter

ONE OF THE MOST ENDURING MYTHS OF THE AMERICAN REVOLUTION is that the colonists defeated the British by adopting Native styles of warfare and developing a guerrilla militia system that overwhelmed the redcoats. According to the myth, the British found that Old World military formations, bright uniforms, and fife-and-drum parade-ground maneuvers were no match for the plainly dressed frontiersman who—under cover and concealment of the wood line—took careful aim at the enemy with his trusty Kentucky rifle. As with all myths, this one has an element of truth. Ultimately, however, the war was won by using conventionally trained and equipped American and French forces supported by an allied navy. American militia did make a significant contribution in many campaigns and battles, including Lexington, Concord, and Bunker Hill. Riflemen were a deciding factor in several battles, including Saratoga and Cowpens. The short-term militia comprised no small part of the American forces in all battles of the war. However, at best the militia were unreliable, untrained, and unable to use a bayonet or withstand a charge by well-disciplined troops. For every Bunker Hill, where the militia made a determined stand, there was a corresponding Battle of Camden, where hundreds of militiamen threw down their loaded weapons—before firing a single shot—and fled from the field.

But the militia and riflemen played an important role in the conflict, especially in the beginning, when the Americans—lacking any standing continental forces—were forced to rely on their militia traditions. When General George Washington took command of the army before Boston in 1775, he immediately began training the short-term militia and pleading to the Continental Congress for help building a "respectable army." Washington expressed his disregard for the militia, noting, "To place any dependence upon Militia, is assuredly, resting upon a broken reed; . . . unaccustomed to the din of Arms; totally unacquainted with every kind of Military skills, when opposed by Troops regularly train'd, disciplined and appointed, makes them timid and ready to fly at their own shadows."[1] Although much of his experience in the Seven Years' War had been at the head of a militia that fought guerrilla-style, at the beginning of the Revolutionary War Washington called for a professional, disciplined army, well-trained and equipped with musket and bayonet, led by educated upper-class officers. In order to defeat the British on the field— and perhaps win the support of France and other "civilized" western nations—the Americans had to stand toe-to-toe with British regulars. This meant possessing the ability to maneuver in linear tactics of the line; stand in ranks, shoulder to shoulder, and fire volleys on command; and most important, be disciplined enough to hold their ground when faced with a bayonet charge and be able to return one in kind.[2]

But militia were the only forces Washington had in the spring of 1775, and some were far more irregular than others. In August of that year ten companies of riflemen from Virginia, Maryland, and Pennsylvania arrived in Washington's camp. One of these companies was led by a man destined to become one of the greatest guerrilla fighters in American history, a stout Virginian named Daniel Morgan. After a falling out with his father at around age seventeen, Morgan had set out from his family's New Jersey home and moved to Virginia's lower Shenandoah Valley. As a young man he developed a reputation for enjoying cards, taverns, and a good fistfight. In time Morgan found employment as a wagoner, hauling supplies to frontier settlers. During the French and Indian War, he had an altercation with a British lieutenant while en route to Fort Chiswell, Virginia. The lieutenant hit Morgan with the flat side of his sword; true to form, Morgan responded by knocking the gentleman out cold with a single blow to the head. A court-martial sentenced Morgan to five

Danl. Morgan. Engraving of "The Old Wagoner," Daniel Morgan, as featured in *The Pictorial Field-Book of the Revolution* (1853), sporting attire
clearly adapted from Native American dress. MIRIAM AND IRA D. WALLACH
DIVISION OF ART, NEW YORK PUBLIC LIBRARY

hundred lashes. Unsurprisingly, he subsequently developed a deep loathing for the British regulars and enjoyed telling a story of how, during his punishment, the drummer charged with keeping time and count of the lashes miscounted—and he received only 499. "The Old Wagoner," as Morgan became known, always contended that the redcoats owed him one more lash. Later, Morgan was shot in an Indian ambush during the war. The bullet entered the back of his neck, took out his teeth, and exited his left jaw, leaving him scarred for life.[3]

Riflemen in Morgan's mold would have a lasting impact on military history. Although a few rifles were used by rangers during the Seven Years' War, their increased use (and on a larger scale) during the Revolutionary War would have long-ranging effects on American military strategy. Short rifles were first used in Germany, but on the Virginia and Pennsylvania frontier gunsmiths lengthened the barrel considerably, creating what is erroneously called by many the Kentucky long rifle. The weapon differs from the smoothbore musket in that the rifle barrel has a set of spiral grooves turning its full length. After the powder is measured and poured down the barrel, the rifleman rams a ball that is set in a greased patch down the barrel. The seal must be tight and loading is time-consuming. When the weapon is fired, the ball spins down the barrel, adding distance and accuracy. Onlookers were amazed by the sharp marksmanship of the frontiersmen. As the Maryland company of Captain Michael Cresap passed through Lancaster, Pennsylvania, on the way to rendezvous with Washington's army, one witness remembered:

> *Captain Cresap's company . . . have been in the late expedition against the Indians . . . and show scars and wounds which would do honor to Homer's Iliad. . . . Two brothers in the company took a piece of board five inches broad and seven inches long, with a bit of white paper, about the size of a dollar, nailed in the center, and while one of them supported this board perpendicularly between his knees, the other, at a distance of upwards of sixty yards . . . shot eight bullets through it successively. . . . The spectators appearing to be amazed at these feats, were told that there were upwards of fifty in the company who could do the same thing.[4]*

After Lexington and Concord, Morgan answered Virginia's call for riflemen, and in only ten days he raised a company of ninety-six men who then raced six hundred miles from Winchester, Virginia, to Washington's camp outside of Cambridge, Massachusetts, in three weeks. They were quickly followed by a second company from nearby Shepherdstown, Virginia. The stodgy New England farmers and fishermen in the army were amazed by the "shirtmen," as they called the riflemen. In lieu of a uniform jacket they wore a hunting shirt or frock, either pulled over the head or wrapped around the body, with shirts fringed like buckskin and capped to keep out the elements. Once in camp, they constantly violated Washington's rules by drinking, fighting, and discharging weapons. Much of this excitement seemed to drain from them, however, after thirty-three men were fined for riotous conduct.[5]

The riflemen quickly caught the attention of the British as well. Whereas a New England musket was a threat to a British guard or sentry at about 150 yards, a rifle could hit a man at upward of 400 yards. British soldier William Carter complained that sniping was "an unfair way of carrying on a war"; another soldier grumbled that the riflemen were "the most fatal widow-and-orphan makers in the world."[6]

After hemming in the British in Boston and driving them from power in the thirteen colonies, Congress and Washington looked to Canada as a possible fourteenth colonial ally. John Adams, for example, saw the northern colony as a threat: from the north, he opined, the enemy had the capacity to supply and support Natives, "inflame all the Indians upon the continent . . . as well as to pour down Regulars, Canadians, and Indians upon the borders of the Northern [provinces]." In addition, taking and holding Montréal and Québec would cut off support for far-flung British posts along the Great Lakes in the interior. In short, taking Canada would result in major advantages for the Americans.[7]

In June 1775, Congress authorized an expedition led by General Philip Schuyler to move north along Lake Champlain against Montréal, while Washington independently planned a second invasion force to move north along the Kennebec River in Maine. The campaign got off to a very slow start, with General Richard Montgomery eventually replacing the sickly and slow Schuyler. Now with winter approaching, the Americans hoped to capture approximately seven hundred British regulars to whom the Royal Navy could not send reinforcements due to ice clogging the St. Lawrence. Foremost on the Americans' minds was whether local French militia would support them, support the British, or remain neutral.

Benedict Arnold. MIRIAM AND IRA D. WALLACH DIVISION OF ART, NEW YORK PUBLIC LIBRARY

To lead the Maine invasion, Washington organized a force of ten companies totaling 1,050 men under the capable Colonel Benedict Arnold from Connecticut. To act as scouts and guides, he attached three rifle companies under Daniel Morgan. The commanders grossly underestimated the challenges they would face. The force needed to move upriver and then cross a pathless northern wilderness to the St. Lawrence, a distance of more than 350 miles. A journey they estimated would take three weeks instead took six; they consumed all their supplies and were ultimately forced to cook their dogs and turn their soap into gruel. By the time they made it to the St. Lawrence in November, they were reduced to a force of six hundred men. A full third had turned back before completing the trek.[8]

On December 2, 1775, forces under General Montgomery and Colonel Arnold united to take the city of Québec, waiting for a snowstorm to make a surprise nighttime attack. Montgomery's force was set to storm the town from the lightly defended river side, called Lower Town. Many enlistments were about to expire at the end of the year, and fortuitously, a snowstorm arrived on New Year's Eve. Alas, unbeknownst to the attackers, they had lost the element of surprise: a deserter had informed the garrison of the impending attack, and they were awaiting the ambush. Things went poorly in Lower Town for the Americans, with Montgomery receiving a mortal wound and Arnold being injured as well. Meanwhile, Morgan took the lead in attempting to breach several of the walls with which the British had blockaded the streets. Supported by his riflemen, Morgan pressed through hesitant New England militia and breached one of the walls; then, almost single-handedly, he captured a house full of redcoats and Canadian militia. Confusion reigned on the British side as Morgan pressed to take a second barrier. However, the New England officers called a halt to the attack, preferring to await news from Montgomery's forces. They never arrived, and the British were able to encircle Morgan's force. At the first light of dawn, Morgan pressed his men forward for a final assault, but it was too late. As one of his riflemen noted, however, the Old Wagoner was "brave to temerity": upon surrendering he shocked those present by refusing to give up his sword to a British officer, handing it instead to a visibly stunned priest and declaring, "not a scoundrel of these cowards shall take it from my hand."[9]

In the long run, the assault and subsequent failed siege of Québec proved to be a disastrous waste of resources for the strapped Americans. Their hopes for a Canadian alliance never materialized, and at that point in the war it became painfully clear that Washington and the newly assembled army had encountered a challenge they could not surmount.[10]

Morgan was captured with almost four hundred of Arnold's men, and in January 1777 was exchanged. Upon returning to the army, he found he had been promoted to colonel. In June 1777 he was placed in command of the five-hundred-man Provisional Rifle Corps, comprised of riflemen from Pennsylvania, Maryland, and many of his own Virginia compatriots. Noting Morgan's talent for unconventional warfare, at the end of August 1777 Washington dispatched him, with part of his corps, to help General Horatio Gates stem British General John Burgoyne's offensive down Lake Champlain from Canada.

General Burgoyne's 1777 plan was to head south from Canada, using Lake Champlain and the Hudson River in New York to cut off communication between the troublesome New England colonies and their American allies. Burgoyne hoped to move eight thousand regulars, Canadian militia, and Native allies far down the Hudson River, supported by a secondary force moving east along the Mohawk River. After taking Albany, he assumed that George Germain, First Viscount Sackville, would direct the British commander in America, General Sir William Howe, to cooperate with him somewhere north of New York City. However, General Howe had his own plan of action that summer—to capture the American capital at Philadelphia and force Washington's Continental army to make a stand to defend it. In short, the plodding "Gentleman Johnny" (as Burgoyne was known to his men) would be left to his own resources in upstate New York.[11]

General Burgoyne's procession down Lake Champlain was a truly remarkable sight. His force got underway in mid-June, sailing down the lake with the Green Mountains to the east and the Adirondacks to the west. Leading the procession were the birch canoes of five hundred Natives, all in war paint. After these were the "advanced corps" of 650 Loyalists and Canadian militia, followed by the British naval flotilla under sail. The force also consisted of three thousand Brunswick

Hessians, German mercenaries hired by the Crown to augment the British forces. At the south end of the lake the force took to land and attempted to cut a road through the wilderness to the Hudson River. They were woefully unprepared for uncharted territory, traveling with a heavy baggage train that would have been far more useful along the well-developed roads of Europe than in the wilderness of New York. It included a 138-piece artillery train, a number of two-wheeled carts constructed out of green unseasoned wood, more than thirty carts holding Burgoyne's magnificent wardrobe, and chests of champagne. The force was followed by the usual entourage of wives, children, camp followers, and civilian merchants known as sutlers. American forces blocked Burgoyne's progress by felling trees and flooding creeks; as a result, his forces took twenty-four days to advance a mere twenty-three miles to Fort Edward on the Hudson. Nevertheless, Burgoyne seemed to enjoy the great adventure, spending his evenings "singing and drinking and amusing himself in the company of the wife of a commissary, who was his mistress, and like him, loved champagne."[12]

Yet while Burgoyne enjoyed the music and champagne (it was rumored he also developed a taste for rattlesnake), dark clouds shrouded the horizon. The general had warned the Natives not to take the scalps of innocent women and children, but they paid this order no heed. Nine members of the Allen family were executed in their house as they sat down for dinner. Other families were also killed as they attempted to flee invading forces. Most notoriously, Jane McCrea, a young woman who had been engaged to one of Burgoyne's Loyalist officers, was shot and scalped by Natives. When Burgoyne refused to turn over or punish the accused murderers, the settlers of upstate New York, Vermont, and New Hampshire mobilized into deadly guerrilla bands. Men who had generally been content to let the war pass them by now picked up rifles and muskets in a fight for frontier survival. This became alarmingly evident when Burgoyne sent a Hessian, Lieutenant Colonel Frederick Baum (who did not speak English), to Bennington, Vermont, in search of pack horses and supplies. On August 16, 1777, mistaking the armed men he saw shadowing his forces on all sides as Loyalist militia, the eight-hundred-man force under Baum was attacked from all directions.

Baum was killed and the survivors captured. The Yankee militia was almost overrun as well by a force sent by Burgoyne to relieve them. They rallied, however, and sent the defeated to tell Burgoyne that he had just lost nine hundred men. He subsequently complained that "wherever the King's forces point, militia to the amount of three or four thousand assemble in twenty-four hours."[13]

The arrival of reinforcements, including Morgan's riflemen, may have inspired General Horatio Gates, the new commander of the Northern Department. Washington suggested that news of the riflemen should be spread to the enemy and his Native allies "with proper Embellishments ... It would not be amiss, among other Things, to magnify numbers." Gates fortified a raised blocking position on the west side of the river at Bemis Heights, south of Saratoga. Here he hoped Burgoyne would take the bait and attack his position. In the meantime, Morgan's riflemen and the militia swarmed Burgoyne's force and so frightened the Natives that "not a man of them was to be brought within the sound of a rifle shot." As Indians who were allied with the Americans caught stragglers, most of Burgoyne's allied Natives and Loyalists melted away. With exaggerated "hooting and hollowing," the American-allied Natives staged fake torture and executions by pretending to bury or burn their captives alive.[14]

Not knowing where Gates had posted his men, on the morning of September 19 Burgoyne pushed forward. Morgan's riflemen were waiting in the woods with orders to slow their advance. Benedict Arnold, who had now joined forces with Gates after dispatching the British force that had attempted to advance east down the Mohawk River, wanted a far more aggressive movement. But Gates was willing to wait for Burgoyne to advance. As Burgoyne organized his forces in a clearing at a settlement known as Freeman's Farm, Morgan's riflemen, supported by Arnold's forces, attacked from the cover of the wood line. At more than a hundred yards and protected by the cover and concealment of the forest, the riflemen fired for deadly effect. However, when the enraged redcoats charged the wood line with bayonets, the riflemen were forced to retreat. The battle went back and forth like this for some time, with Morgan's men taking deadly aim at the officers. They especially seemed interested in targeting the Tories in their ranks. "This misfortune," protested British

Sergeant Roger Lamb, "accelerated their estrangement from our cause and army." One of the Hessians remarked, "In the open field the rebels do not count for much, but in the woods they are formidable." The combination of riflemen firing at long ranges supported by standard forces marked Freeman's Farm as a victory.[15]

From September 19 until October 7, Gates remained in his fieldworks as Burgoyne vacillated over his next move. On October 7 he attempted to turn the left flank of the American line with a 1,500-man force deploying in an open wheat field. Gates responded by deploying part of his force including Morgan's riflemen and Enoch Poor's brigade. The Americans used the wood line for cover and flanked the British on three sides of the field. The riflemen played havoc with the British officers. Many were cut down with their fire, including General Simon Fraser. Burgoyne himself had his horse and clothing hit. The British retreated back to their lines, where they had built up fieldworks of their own, closely followed by the Patriots. Traditional accounts written years after the war—and after Arnold earned infamy as a traitor to the American cause—describe a battle scene in which Gates had relieved Arnold for insubordination. According to this narrative, as Gates directed the battle from the comfort of his tent, Arnold, in direct disobedience of Gates's orders, boldly rode forward, rallied the troops, and captured a redoubt on Frazier's Farm. A letter that surfaced in mid-January 2016 disputes this story, however. Written two days after the fight by a New Hampshire militia adjutant, Nathaniel Bacheller, to his wife Suzanna, it describes close coordination among the officers, not conflict. "General Gates Soon arived to our Lines & Inquired for General Arnol," Bacheller wrote, "& was Told he was out of the lines to View the Enemy." Gates then ordered that some regiments be sent forward, sending word to Arnold to be careful not to fire on the advancing friendly units. According to Bacheller, Arnold reported back to inform Gates that the "Enemy Design was To Take Possession of a hill about a Quarter of a mile To the west of our lines." Bacheller added, "General Arnol says to General Gates it is Late in the Day but Let me have men & we will have some fun with them before Sun Set." This account rings true. Had Arnold actually taken command without orders, Gates would have had him charged and court-martialed for it.[16]

Arnold led the pursuit of the fleeing redcoats as they attempted to rally at two field fortifications, or redoubts that guarded their camp. With Morgan's riflemen flanking one side, Arnold drove his men between the redoubts, recklessly riding between the lines. The Americans eventually captured one of the positions, ultimately surrounding Burgoyne's army in Saratoga and forcing its surrender. Arnold's luck did run out during the battle, though, when he and his horse were hit and he suffered a broken leg. While partially recovering Arnold may have felt unrecognized for his role in the battle, a slight many historians believe led to his joining with the British. The role Daniel Morgan and his riflemen played was also pivotal to the campaign, which proved to be a major turning point in the war. After word reached Europe of Burgoyne's surrender, France and (later) other allies joined the war in support of the Americans.[17]

The war on the frontier fell into a familiar pattern. Many Native tribes attempted to remain neutral, while others noted that the real threat to their sovereignty and homelands lay not with the British but with the Americans. The Crown had sought to protect Native rights with the Proclamation Line of 1763, which barred American colonial settlement west of the Alleghenies. The British had filled the void left by the French in the American interior after the Seven Years' War, occupying Fort Detroit, Fort Niagara, and trading forts in the north at Michilimackinac. In addition, they occupied Kaskaskia in the Illinois territory, and even Pensacola and Mobile on the Gulf of Mexico. The British employed full-time Indian agents who bestowed gifts to tribes and armed them with muskets, powder, and shot—commodities they were unable to produce on their own. But as the war was ignited, a fresh wave of American settlers began moving through gaps in the mountains, including the Cumberland Gap, to establish settlements in Kentucky and what would become Tennessee. New settlements were established along the Watauga and Holston Rivers in Tennessee, and settlers began to squat around Pittsburgh as well.[18]

Alexander Cameron, Britain's deputy commissioner for Indian affairs in the southern colonies, showered the Cherokee with cash and supplies (including arms and ammunition) and encouraged them to make war on the frontier. In the summer of 1776 the Cherokee raised a force of around six hundred warriors and attacked highland settlements in Georgia, the Carolinas, and Virginia, striking as far as Fort Chiswell (near present-day Wytheville). In response, frontier militia forces and the governors of the newly formed states took defensive measures. South Carolina revived the bounty system and offered £75 for Cherokee scalps. Leading two hundred militia, Colonel Samuel Jack successfully drove off Cherokee raiders before destroying their villages between the Tugaloo and Chattahoochee Rivers. North and South Carolina militia united, forming a force of 3,400 to destroy thirty-six Cherokee villages in the Piedmont region. The Virginians advanced on the Cherokee as well; a force of 1,800 men cleared Cherokee settlements to the French-held Broad River, finding mounted scalps and other evidence of atrocities along the way. The Cherokee War ended in May 1777, with Native representatives signing treaties with the states that eventually ceded all claims to South Carolina and all lands east of the Blue Ridge.[19]

One group of Cherokee refused to capitulate, however. Led by Chief Dragging Canoe, they gathered at Chickamauga Creek, near the Tennessee River, and continued to raid the frontier. Counter-raids in 1779 destroyed several Chickamauga villages, but these served only to antagonize the warriors. Raids and counter-raids continued until Dragging Canoe's men laid siege to Bluff Fort (present-day Nashville) and were defeated there by the fort's defenders, who unleashed dogs on the attackers. Although the violence subsequently stopped for a short while, this frontier would continue to be the scene of atrocities for the next decade.[20]

In Kentucky, Natives and Americans had been fighting since before the Revolution began. In 1774 the Shawnee grew tired of the encroachment of the "Long Knives," as they called Virginians, into their traditional hunting grounds. They began frontier raids in the Ohio River Valley, targeting settlers and surveyors. The royal governor of Virginia, John Murray (Fourth Earl of Dunmore, or Lord Dunmore), raised 150 rangers and ordered them to destroy Shawnee towns. He also sent men to the confluence of the Kanawha and Ohio Rivers under the leadership of Colonel Andrew Lewis to engage the Shawnee in pitched battle at Point Pleasant. Although the Virginians were defeated, Lewis continued his campaign against Shawnee towns and ultimately defeated them. In the end, the Shawnee were forced to give up any claim to their Kentucky hunting grounds. In 1775 Henry Hamilton, Fort Detroit's lieutenant governor and superintendent of Indian affairs, referred to the Virginia Long Knives as being "hauty Violent and bloody," but added that "the savages had a high opinion of them as Warriors."[21]

The "bloody year of the three sevens," as 1777 came to be known in Kentucky County, Virginia, was one of frontier brutality on an unprecedented scale. Settlers including Daniel Boone were driven away from farmsteads to the protection of fortified towns, including Harrodsburg

George Rogers Clark. MIRIAM AND IRA D. WALLACH DIVISION OF ART, NEW YORK PUBLIC LIBRARY

and Boonesborough. Many gave up farming completely and trekked back east through the Cumberland Gap to the safety of more developed areas. George Rogers Clark, a frontier surveyor and the ranking militia officer in the county, believed that the loss of Kentucky would simply open up the frontier in western Virginia to further attacks. The six-foot-tall, twenty-five-year-old redhead collected a band of followers and traveled east to Williamsburg to propose launching a counterattack into Ohio country. Governor Patrick Henry and the Virginia Council agreed and issued public orders authorizing Clark to recruit his own force on the frontier, supported by the state, to protect Kentucky settlers. On January 2, 1778, Clark also received private orders from Governor Henry: He and his force were to attack British outposts in what was known as the Illinois country. The governor wrote that he was authorized to "raise seven companies of soldiers to consist of fifty men each, officered in the usual manner & armed most properly for the Enterprise, & with this Force attack the British post at Kaskasky [Kaskaskia, a French town in Illinois with around one thousand inhabitants]." The only way to protect settlers on the frontier was to remove the British from their outposts and control the area north of the Ohio River. Thousands of Natives were economically tied to these posts for trade goods, and many French still occupied settlements as far west as the Mississippi River. Clark also wanted to cut the head off the snake, so to speak, by capturing Fort Detroit.[22]

Clark and his officers recruited men from western Virginia, and in May 1778 traveled from Pittsburgh down the Monongahela to the Falls of the Ohio, where he established camp on an island across from what would become Louisville, Kentucky. He had hoped to attract Kentucky volunteers, but most of them were living under constant threat of attack; even the vaunted Daniel Boone had been captured by Natives in February 1778. When Clark announced the plan to march on Illinois, some of the men who thought they were enlisting to defend Kentucky became disheartened and deserted. On June 24, 1778, Clark and 175 riflemen pushed off in their boats down the Ohio. Knowing the British were watching the Mississippi and river junctions carefully, on June 29 Clark landed in western Illinois, a few miles down from the mouth of the Tennessee River, and began a 120-mile march to Kaskaskia. Enlisting the help of local hunters as guides, on

July 4 the band made it to within a mile of the town. The next day they secured replacement boats, crossed the Kaskaskia River, and rushed the town in two columns. They took the settlement completely by surprise, with one group taking the fort and the others securing all roads leading in and out. The town consisted of around five hundred French and an equal number of blacks. French-speaking riflemen called out to the villagers, announcing that the fort had been captured and all should remain in their homes; anyone venturing out or attempting to leave the town would be shot. Clark had learned that the French knew of the war and had "a most horrid idea of the barbarity of the rebels, especially of the Virginians." He used this to his advantage, taking their militia leaders in chains and keeping the village in lockdown. In time, town leaders and the priest approached Clark and asked permission to hold services in the church. Clark assented. Later they approached Clark again to ask if their property would be taken and their families broken up and taken away as prisoners. Clark responded, "Did they suppose that we meant to strip women and children and take the bread out of their mouths? Or that we would condescend to make work on the women and children, or the church?" On the contrary, he replied, they were simply there to protect settlers from Indian attacks. Then he informed them that Louis XIV of France had signed a treaty of friendship and military alliance with the United States and that the war might soon be over. With this revelation, the mood in the village changed from dread to outright celebration. Residents subsequently crowded the streets to meet and greet their new friends, the Long Knives of Virginia.[23]

Using the influence of the French settlers of Kaskaskia, Clark soon won the allegiance of the other French settlements along the Mississippi as far north as Cahokia. Located across the river from Spanish-held St. Louis, this granted Clark the opportunity to meet with Fernando de Leyba, Spain's lieutenant governor of upper Louisiana. Clark and his men then traveled east across what is now the state of Illinois to capture Vincennes, a key British-held village along the Wabash River. Lieutenant Governor Hamilton did not stand passively by: A retired soldier himself, he led a force of 35 regulars, 130 French militia, and 70 Indians to successfully retake Vincennes. Hamilton planned on waiting until the spring for reinforcements in order to drive the Long Knives from the territory altogether.[24]

This development placed Clark in a difficult position. Some of his men had returned home, and Hamilton was in position to block Clark's retreat to Kentucky and Virginia. Hamilton elected to wait until spring, when the floodwaters that covered much of lower Illinois receded and he could be reinforced and resupplied from Fort Detroit. In one of the boldest moves of the war, Clark decided to attack Vincennes. He set out during the first week of February 1779 with 172 men, about half of them French recruits, on a 180-mile journey. The conditions were dreadful: The men splashed through driving rains, crossed four flooded rivers, slept in mud without tents, and ran out of provisions in the last two days. Arriving at the flooded Wabash on February 22, Clark found no alternative but to ford the neck-deep river. After scouting it himself he returned to his men, who watched in awe as he "immediately put some water in my hand, poured on powder, blackened my face, gave the warwhoop and marched into the water. . . . The party gazed and fell in, one after another, without saying a word . . . and the whole went on cheerfully."[25]

The next day Clark and his forces reached their objective, the town of Vincennes and its fort. Hamilton—or "the Hair Buyer," as he was known to the Americans for allegedly paying Natives for the scalps of murdered settlers—faced many problems. His force of six hundred or so dwindled during the winter to less than one hundred men. Most of the Natives had moved on, and Hamilton was forced to let his Detroit militiamen return home to feed their families. Upon arrival in Vincennes, Clark had his French allies tell the villagers they themselves were supporting the Long Knives. He also sent word to the villagers that if they remained in their homes, they would not be harmed. Hamilton learned that most of his militia refused to fight their neighbors and relatives and deserted in droves; he was subsequently left with a squad of redcoats and militia totaling perhaps seventy-nine men. Clark's force entered the town, where the locals retrieved powder and shot they had buried and gave it to Clark's French American force, who then surrounded the fort. The stockade was poorly constructed, and the riflemen played havoc with the defenders by sniping at anyone whose head appeared out of a building.[26]

Hamilton wavered over whether or not to surrender, asking for a three-day truce that Clark flatly rejected. Clark did temporarily halt the firing so Hamilton could confer with his men. During this lull a French and Native war party, returning from the Kentucky frontier with scalps and oblivious to the siege, walked blindly into the attackers' hands. Clark later wrote to George Mason, "I had now a fair oppertunity of making an impression on the Indians . . . that of convincing them that Governour Hamilton could not give them that protection that he had made them to believe he could." Clark then "ordered the Prisoners to be Tomahawked in the face of the Garrisson: It had the effect that I expected." The garrison watched in horror as four Natives were tomahawked and their lifeless bodies were thrown into the river. Hamilton recalled that "about two in the afternoon the party of Indians which had gone towards the falls of Ohio returnd . . . they were placed in the street opposite the Fort Gate. . . . One . . . was tomahawked either by Clarke or one of his Officers, the other three . . . were butchered in succession. . . . The Blood of the victims was still visible for days afterwards, a testimony of the courage and Humanity of Colonel Clarke."[27]

A shaken Hamilton met again with Clark to discuss terms. Hamilton wrote, "In consequence I met him on the parade outside the Fort. He had just come from his Indian tryumph all bloody and sweating." Hamilton was appalled as Clark "seated himself on the edge of one of the batteaus, that had some rainwater in it, & while he washed his hands and face still reeking from the human sacrifice in which he had acted as chief priest, he told me with great exultation how he had been employed." Hamilton's force formally surrendered the next day, February 24, and he and twenty-six other prisoners were taken east through Kentucky to Williamsburg, Virginia. Once there, Governor Thomas Jefferson refused to treat the Hair Buyer as a captured enemy officer, placed in chains in the town jail. He was exchanged in New York in October 1780.[28]

In the past, many writers have vastly exaggerated the importance of Clark's expedition. He cannot be credited with securing what became known as the Old Northwest Territory, which is the territory to the north of the Ohio River that lies between the mountains to the east and the Mississippi River to the west. Shortly after the successful Vincennes expedition, Clark fell back to the Louisville area and worked in vain throughout most of the war to recruit a force to march on Detroit. In fact, even after ceding the territory to the United States at war's end, the British continued to occupy Detroit until 1796. Some of the Natives along the Wabash did declare neutrality at the time, but many others were more than willing to fight for their land and sovereignty in a war that would continue on the frontier until 1795.[29]

The British at Fort Niagara supported the Mohawks, Cayugas, Senecas, and Onondagas of the Six Nations of the Iroquois in the north (the Oneidas and Tuscaroras did not participate). The British Indian agent Sir William Johnson had developed a close relationship with the Six Nations during the previous colonial wars, and after his death in 1774 his son, Sir John Johnson, his nephew and new Indian superintendent Guy Johnson, and his son-in-law Daniel Claus carried on the relationship. Key to it was the Mohawk chief Joseph Brant (Thayendanegea), a practicing Anglican who had been educated in Lebanon, Connecticut. During the Revolution the Iroquois, many of whom had longstanding friendly relationships with settlers in upstate New York, actively aided the British, supporting them during the failed American invasion of Canada and Burgoyne's disastrous Saratoga campaign. Using Fort Niagara as a supply base, the British fueled a continuous guerrilla war waged by Natives, Loyalists, and Canadians on the northern frontier.[30]

On July 3, 1778, Loyalist Colonel John Butler led a mixed force of 1,100 Tories, regulars, and militia and five hundred mostly Seneca allies from Niagara into the Wyoming Valley of Pennsylvania. Stretching for thirty miles along the north branch of the Susquehanna River, the valley was defended by a Continental officer named Colonel Zebulon Butler, who was there on furlough with sixty Continental soldiers backed by three hundred militia. Most of the force was crowded in with civilian refugees at Forty Fort, the area's main garrison. Alas, Colonel Butler committed the classic error of frontier warfare—venturing out from the protection of his palisade. Upon marching out, the American force was surrounded by Natives in the woods and destroyed without quarter, an event that came to be known as the "Wyoming Massacre." Twenty-eight officers and 268 enlisted men were killed, while on the attackers' side only one Native was killed and a handful of Tories and Indians were wounded. Tory commander John Butler attempted to restrain his force from looting and harming prisoners, but after he left the Senecas disobeyed his orders. Non-combatants were spared, but the soldiers were not as lucky: around sixty of them escaped, but the Senecas killed seventy others. The raiders moved on to destroy hundreds of farmhouses, barns, and fields, and the Natives later returned to Niagara carrying 227 scalps. Refugees flooded from the area as raids continued into the fall in the German Flats and the Cherry Valley of New York.[31]

Responding to petitions by New York and Pennsylvania refugees, in February 1779 Congress ordered Washington into action for "the chastisement of the savages." An old Indian fighter himself, Washington agreed, believing that the only way to bring the Natives to terms was by totally destroying their farms and villages. In May 1779 he gave orders to Major General John Sullivan to take three brigades of Continentals, supported by light infantry and riflemen, into Iroquois territory. Washington barred Sullivan from coming to any terms with the Natives "before the total ruin of their settlements is effected." In short, he wanted nothing less than "the total destruction and devastation of their settlements and the capture of as many of every age and sex as possible" to be held as hostages against further raids.[32]

In May 1779 Sullivan's force blazed a roadway northwest from Eaton, Pennsylvania, to the Wyoming Valley, then on to Tioga, where they united with a second wing of the army under Brigadier General James Clinton. Now an army of 4,445, the force set out to the homeland of the Mohawks and Senecas. As the army moved, Sullivan wisely sent his light infantry and riflemen far and wide to warn of ambush and to act as scouts. Meanwhile, between six hundred and eight hundred Delaware and Seneca warriors disregarded the advice of Joseph Brant and Tory leaders and attempted—alongside Tory militia—to make a stand at Newtown. Hoping to set a classic ambush for the Americans, they built breastworks along the route of advance. However, sharp-eyed riflemen spotted the works in advance, and on August 30 Sullivan assaulted the position. After opening with artillery he advanced on the front while sending a flanking force on the right, scattering the defenders with few casualties on either side. With the Native and Tory forces retreating to Niagara, Sullivan's force was free to carry out its plans of destruction. The soldiers marched on the Onondaga, Cayuga, and Seneca, destroying forty villages and countless homes in addition to chopping down orchards and destroying 160,000 bushels of corn. American major Jeremiah Fogg described the expedition as "hunting wild turkeys, with light horse." Their "nests are destroyed but the birds are still on the wing." If Washington thought that by destroying their villages he could bring the Iroquois to terms, he was wrong. No longer tied down with the need to protect their villages, the Indians sought vengeance along the frontier. Raids and counter-raids continued even after Yorktown.[33]

While some militia performed well during the war, they also were responsible for some of the ugliest episodes in American history. The war on the frontier provided an excuse to continue patterns of warfare against Native tribes that had been perfected over a hundred years of frontier strife. The pattern was the same: in response to any real or perceived threat, frontier militia units organized raids of retaliation on Indian villages. No one would be spared, not even non-combatant women and children. Raiders burned buildings, killed farm animals, and destroyed crops and orchards. Perhaps the most horrible example of this kind of warfare was the March 8, 1782, Gnadenhütten Massacre. In search of hostile Delaware, Pennsylvania frontier militia under the command of Colonel David Williamson set out into the Ohio country. Failing to find their quarry, they came instead across the Moravian mission town of Gnadenhütten, where the Natives had adopted the faith of the pacifist German sect. The raiders gathered up around a hundred men, women, and children, held a drumhead court-martial, and sentenced the villagers to die. The condemned spent their last night alive holding hands and singing Christian hymns. The next day, still singing and praying, they were executed with tomahawks, one after another. The raiders then piled the bodies in the dwellings and set fire to the settlement. In a later act of retaliation, the Delaware captured Colonel William Crawford, a veteran frontier leader and friend of George Washington. Although Crawford had no connection to the massacre, the Delaware tortured him in the most brutal fashion and roasted him alive.[34]

CHAPTER FOUR

"Tarleton's Quarter"

THE BRITISH DISASTER AT SARATOGA CHANGED THE DIRECTION OF THE Revolutionary War. By early 1778, with the French (and later the Dutch and Spanish) entering the conflict, the British found their resources for fighting in North America limited. The Crown now focused on holding on to its Caribbean islands and Gibraltar. It also had a legitimate fear of a combined French and Spanish invasion of England. Thus the aftermath of General Burgoyne's disaster brought new leadership to America. General Henry Clinton, with his second-in-command Charles Cornwallis, First Marquess Cornwallis, directed the last campaigns of the war. Overseeing the war effort for the king, Lord George Germain felt that as long as Clinton could not bring Washington's wary army to a decisive battle in New York, perhaps the Crown would make better use of its resources by focusing on the southern colonies. Unlike New England and the North, the South was sparsely populated, with no city larger than Charleston, South Carolina, which had an approximate population of twelve thousand. With uncontested control of the sea by the Royal Navy, the British could move at will and occupy important ports. The South produced staple crops including rice, indigo, and tobacco, as well as naval stores such as timber and tar from the Carolinas. The British believed Southerners were far too worried about Indian uprisings and losing control of their slaves to offer much organized resistance. As one official noted, Southerners would not be nearly as much of a problem as some New Englanders because "their numerous slaves in the bowels of their country, and the Indians at their backs will always keep them quiet." In

The Southern Colonies

MAJOR GUERRILLA ACTIONS DURING THE REVOLUTION, 1775-1783

addition, the displaced governors and royal officials convinced the Crown that thousands of southern Loyalists would flock to the colors when they arrived, and they could be recruited and organized into an American Loyalist military force that could free the redcoats for work elsewhere.[1]

In November 1778 Clinton dispatched 3,500 men, commanded by Lieutenant Colonel Archibald Campbell, to take Savannah, Georgia. The British succeeded in their mission and began a campaign to win over the population. Campbell offered amnesty to Georgians who would renounce the rebels and support the king. He also threatened to punish those who did not. On February 14, 1779, newly raised Loyalist militia under Colonel James Boyd were nearly destroyed at the Battle of Kettle

Creek, Georgia, by a force led by South Carolina guerrilla leader Andrew Pickens. From this point on, the Loyalist forces never ventured forth without the support of British regulars. The British and Americans spent the next year sparring between Savannah and Charleston. In September 1779 a French fleet with an embarked army arrived. The French commander, Admiral Charles Hector, comte d'Estaing, landed 3,500 men eight miles from Savannah and was joined by 1,500 Americans. The American commander, the portly General Benjamin Lincoln, wanted to lay siege to the town, but d'Estaing—light on supplies and with sickness taking its toll in his ranks—called for a general assault on the fieldworks guarding the town. The October 9 attack ended in disaster for the allied force, with perhaps a third of the attacking men suffering casualties. A dejected d'Estaing sailed with his fleet on October 19, an action the British interpreted as an invitation to take Charleston.[2]

By the spring of 1780 General Henry Clinton himself had brought part of his army from New York and assembled a force of 12,500 men for a siege of Charleston. They were successful, and—in what became the largest defeat of the war for the Americans—on May 12 the British captured more than five thousand Continentals and militia. Before departing for New York and leaving the South under the command of Cornwallis, Clinton ordered all residents of South Carolina to proclaim loyalty to the king. Even though they had already accepted a parole, they were now forced to swear an oath of allegiance to His Majesty and actively support the royal government. Left with no choice but to choose sides, many who had previously accepted parole once again took up arms. After the city fell, a 350-man regiment of Virginia Continentals traveled south in hopes of supporting the defenders under Colonel Abraham Buford with a small contingent of Lieutenant Colonel William Washington's (second cousin to George Washington) cavalry. Learning of the city's fall, the force retreated north—followed by Cornwallis, who sent Lieutenant Colonel Banastre Tarleton and three hundred of his mounted Tory Legion dragoons in pursuit. On May 29 they caught up to the Virginians near the North Carolina line at Waxhaws. Tarleton's men charged the Virginians with bayonets, and Buford ordered his men to hold their fire until the enemy closed on them, but they paused too long and were overrun. At some point Buford displayed a white flag to surrender, but the killing continued. Dr. Robert Brownsfield, who witnessed the event, wrote, "Not a man was spared . . . for fifteen minutes after every man was prostrate they went over the ground, plunging their bayonets into everyone that exhibited any signs of life." The Virginians suffered 113 killed, 150 terribly wounded, and 53 taken prisoner. The story of "Bloody Tarleton" and his "Tarleton's Quarter" would become as legendary in the South as Sherman's March to the Sea would be during the Civil War.[3]

Many southern whites became resigned to the reality that the British were back in power and willingly accepted parole and took oaths of allegiance to the Crown. Even the venerable Colonel Andrew Pickens—who had served in the Indian wars and wiped out a band of Tories at Kettle Creek in 1779 before retiring to his home near Ninety Six, South Carolina—took the oath. But here the British plan to pacify the South went wrong. As word of "Tarleton's Quarter" spread and Cornwallis lost control of the Tory militia, the war turned into a civil war between Loyalist and Patriot factions. Pickens is the perfect example of a leader who felt driven to rejoin the fight. The quiet Presbyterian elder rarely spoke, and when he did paced his words "between his fingers and examined them" before he spoke. He likely would never have taken up arms again as a guerrilla had the Tories left him in peace. But after they plundered his farm, he formed a militia band that would wreak havoc on them.[4]

One of the first guerrillas to take a stand against the British in South Carolina was Captain John McClure. The twenty-five-year-old Patriot served in the local militia, but after the fall of Charleston the unit had disbanded and the men had returned to their homes. After learning of Tarleton's alleged massacre of Buford's men at Waxhaws, McClure and his followers "arose upon their feet and made this united and solemn declaration: 'that they would never surrender to the enemies of their country; that "Liberty or Death" from that time forth should be their motto!'" Rather than taking the oath, McClure collected his own men and attacked and scattered local Tories—some of whom took the opportunity to switch sides and join the Whigs, "believing that they were now the strongest party." News of their success drew new recruits from the Fairfield and Chester districts of South Carolina. However, the same

Lt. Col. Tarleton. Banastre Tarleton's actions on May 29, 1780, at the Waxhaws in North Carolina—where he allegedly granted no quarter to men who had raised a white flag of surrender—would haunt the Tories for the remainder of the Revolutionary War. MIRIAM AND IRA D. WALLACH DIVISION OF ART, NEW YORK PUBLIC LIBRARY news drew the attention of the British. The force then retreated to North Carolina, where they joined fellow Carolinians uniting under guerrilla chief Thomas Sumter.[5]

The British and their Tory allies in South Carolina intended to use a show of force to bring the Carolinians into line. They confiscated food and property with little regard to whether the owners were loyal to the Crown or to the Patriots. When they suspected a farm owner of being a Patriot, they confiscated all they could carry away and burned the property. Farmer Thomas Sumter had served in the Continental army and following the British occupation of Charleston would likely have been content to sit out the rest of the war at his plantation along the Santee River. That is, until Tarleton's Legion came in search of him. They missed "the Gamecock" (as he would later be known), but took and destroyed everything he owned—leaving him in a state of "all sweat and fury." General Cornwallis turned a blind eye to the actions of his subordinates, who repeatedly ravaged the countryside.[6]

After losing his home, Sumter traveled to the American head-quarters in Salisbury, North Carolina, to reactivate his commission and receive permission to establish a partisan guerrilla band to raid behind enemy lines in South Carolina. Establishing camp at Tuckasegee Ford along the Catawba River in North Carolina, he sent messengers to his South Carolina neighbors to invite them to join his force. The guerrillas had little to no civil support, as no Patriot civil government existed in South Carolina. Even Governor John Rutledge had to flee Tarleton's raiders to the safety of North Carolina. As the band grew, its members realized they would have to be completely independent of organized civil support, supplying their own arms, ammunition, horses, and food. The men vowed to "oppose the British and Tories by force of arms," Patriot Richard Winn recalled, "which was never to be laid down until the British troops was drove from the State of South Carolina and the independence of the United States acknowledged." Without authorization from Congress or much more than a nod from their exiled governor, the band elected its own colonels and named Sumter brigadier general. From the beginning, however, Sumter and his men would cooperate with civil and military authorities when deemed convenient. Their clear objective was to drive the British and their Tory allies from the state; as James Williams, a veteran of the Cherokee fighting of 1776 from the Ninety Six District, wrote to his son in 1779, he was "obliged to take the field in defence of my rights and liberties, and that of my children." This was not a voluntary fight, but rather a war "of necessity, and from the consideration that I had rather suffer anything than lose my birthright, and that of my children."[7]

Unfortunately, the guerrilla wars in the Carolinas quickly degenerated into a bloody civil war marked by escalating acts of retaliation. Some historians bicker over which side was most at fault in committing atrocities or how accurate the accusations of Tarleton's men bayoneting wounded prisoners at Waxhaws was. Regardless of what actually happened during the battle, the massacre was accepted as fact at the time and motivated hundreds to take up arms to "remember Buford"—and to offer nothing but "Tarleton's Quarter" to the British and the Tories.[8]

After several Tories were captured in battle, Patriot militiaman Moses Hall witnessed firsthand the application of "Tarleton's Quarter" (that is, killing all prisoners). Approached a site where six captured Loyalists were being held, he recalled:

> Some discussion taking place, I heard some of our men cry out, "Remember Buford," and the prisoners were immediately hewed to pieces with broadswords. At first I bore the scene without any emotion, but upon a moment's reflection, I felt such horror as I never did before nor have since. [The following morning] I discovered lying upon the ground . . . [what] proved to be a youth about sixteen who, having come out to view the British troops through curiousity, for fear he might give information to our troops, they had run him through with a bayonet. . . . The sight of this unoffending boy, butchered . . . relieved me of my distressful feelings for the slaughter of the Tories, and I desired nothing so much as the opportunity of participating in their destruction.[9]

Henry Lee also recalled the effect of Waxhaws, comparing the massacre to the worst atrocities of the Natives on the frontier. "This tragic expedition sunk deep in the American breast," he wrote, "and produced the unanimous decision among the troops to revenge their murdered comrades whenever the blood-stained corps should give an opportunity."[10]

One of the most hated Tories in South Carolina was the German-born Philadelphia lawyer Christian Huck, who raised a unit of German horsemen when the British occupied Philadelphia. He was sent south to command a squad of horsemen attached to Tarleton's Legion and participated in the fight at Waxhaws. In June 1780, while commanding part of the British Legion, Captain Huck raided the Catawba River Valley to recruit Loyalists. Assembling the old men and boys who remained behind at New Acquisition, he earned the nickname "the Swearing Captain" after complaining loudly about his failure to capture a prominent local Presbyterian clergyman who had taken up arms with the Patriots. Huck told the community it seemed that "God almighty had become a Rebel, but if there were 20 gods on that side, they would all be conquered," adding, "if the Rebels were as thick as trees, and Jesus Christ himself were to command them, he would defeat them." If he thought this kind of profanity would subdue the community, he was mistaken: the last thing a German Loyalist should have done in a devout community of Scots-Irish Presbyterians was to take the Lord's name in vain.[11]

As the raid progressed along the Catawba River Valley and word spread of Huck's blasphemy and abuse against community members, many able-bodied men rushed to join the Patriot militia. Members of Tarleton's Legion stripped homes of all food, valuables, and clothing, going so far as to take away one housewife's rings, neckerchief, and shoe buckles. Word of the Legion targeting women during the raid raced through the Catawba backcountry. On July 11 the raiders fell on the home of Captain John McClure, who was away serving with Sumter. Although the raiders missed capturing the captain, they did find his son James and son-in-law Edward Martin, who were in the process of melting down pewter kitchenware to be recast into bullets. Huck declared the two to be traitors and "violent rebels" and sentenced them to hang at sunrise. When Captain McClure's wife Mary protested, one of the soldiers struck her with the flat side of his sword. According to family legend, however, the British failed to notice the McClures' daughter, also named Mary, who slipped out and rode to Sumter's camp to spread news of the raid.[12]

The raiders continued pillaging from house to house, capturing men and threatening women along the way. At last they chose the plantation of James Williamson, who was likely away with the militia, to settle in for the night. In addition to a handful of prisoners, Huck's force consisted of twenty New York Tories, sixty Carolina Tories, and thirty-five dragoons from the British Legion—115 men in all. They locked the prisoners in a corncrib to await their execution at daybreak. But a local slave made it to the Patriot militia at Fishing Creek and told them where Huck was camped. Another local who had been held by Huck's men escaped during the night and was able to give the Patriots an exact layout of the British camp. Not fearing any resistance, Huck's force set out only four sentries that night and did not send out any pickets. In addition, most of the men slept in open fields along the road. Tarleton later reported that Captain Huck "neglected his duty, in placing his party carelessly at a plantation."[13]

Captain John McClure and Colonel William Bratton led a force of around 150 men in hopes of surprising Huck's force. By the time they reached the plantation, the force had grown to as many as 250 men. They intended to attack from three directions at daybreak on July 12 in hopes of using the element of surprise and perhaps cutting off a route of retreat. They rode to the woods outside the plantation, dismounted, and advanced on foot, surprising the camp right after sunrise. A scene of chaos and panic ensued as some legionaries attempted to mount their horses and others grabbed muskets and cartridge boxes. The Patriots advanced to a split-rail fence surrounding the property and used it to rest their rifles, "with which they took unerring and deadly aim." British legionaries stepped into formation and attempted a bayonet charge, a move that almost always drove away militia bands. Three times they charged, only to be devastated by rifle fire and driven from the field themselves. Huck emerged from the house, mounted his horse, and attempted to rally his men for one more charge. A local militiaman, Thomas Carroll, placed a well-aimed shot that hit Huck behind the ear. Huck dropped his sword and fell lifeless to the ground. This was the final straw for his desperate men, who panicked and scattered into the woods. The entire battle was over in minutes.[14]

As the Patriots overran the camp, some of Huck's men dropped their weapons and begged to be taken alive. Others ran for the woods. Many of the attackers mounted horses and "pursued the flying Loyalists for thirteen or fourteen miles, wreaking vengeance and retaliating for their cruelties and atrocities." Tarleton reported that only twenty-four of the men escaped; another noted that the death toll was unclear, as "there were many carcasses found in the woods some days after." While the British and their Loyalist allies felt the full brunt of "Tarleton's Quarter," in the battle that became known as "Huck's Defeat," the Carolinians had only suffered one man killed and one wounded. In addition to capturing a great number of horses and supplies, they also freed the prisoners Huck's force had promised to kill. The destruction of Huck's Tory and provincial regular British force both electrified the Patriot movement and accelerated the war of retaliation.[15]

Huck's Defeat galvanized the Patriot movement throughout the South. It also sent a chilling message to the British and the Tories: The American militia could be more than a match for the king's forces. Loyalist recruiting efforts declined. Colonel Nesbit Balfour, the commander of the British garrison at Ninety Six, complained that the rebel victories had a strong effect in the countryside. "I find the enemy exerting themselves wonderfully and successfully in stirring up the people," he wrote. "Many that had protection have already joined them. . . . They have terrified our friends." Small bands of guerrillas appeared everywhere, and countless skirmishes occurred. During one three-month period alone, between Huck's Defeat on July 12 and the Battle of King's Mountain on October 7, there were twenty-two recorded fights between the militia and British forces, some large, others small.[16]

Despite the glory of Huck's Defeat, the war in the South continued to go poorly for the Patriots. After the loss of General Lincoln's entire army, Congress—over the objections of Washington—placed the hero of Saratoga Horatio Gates in charge of a new army being created to meet the threat. Gates's army and career came to an ignominious end at Camden, South Carolina, a supply outpost Gates thought he could take by surprise. The general had assembled a mixed force of Continentals, with perhaps two-thirds of his forces being Virginia and North Carolina militia. However, General Cornwallis learned of his movements and countered by bringing up his main force. While conducting a night march down the same road, the two armies literally bumped into each other about eight miles from Camden. The next morning, August 16, 1780, both sides lined up for action. Gates's force was in poor shape: Supply shortages had forced the men to subsist on green apples, green corn, partially cooked meat, and molasses during the march. Diarrhea and dysentery ran rampant through the ranks. Gates also did a poor job of placing his militia, investing too much faith in them and leaving them to hold the left side of his line without support. When the British charged with the bayonet, the militia panicked. Maryland Continental colonel Otho Williams observed that the bayonet charge "threw the whole body of militia into such a panic that they generally threw down their *loaded* arms and fled in the utmost consternation. The unworthy example of the Virginians was almost instantly followed by the North Carolinians. . . . A great majority of the militia . . . fled without firing a shot." The Continentals valiantly held their ground as long as they could, but when surrounded they too were forced to flee for their lives. Gates also made a narrow escape, galloping sixty miles to Charlotte. Later on, only seven hundred survivors of the 3,700-man army would rally at Gates's headquarters at Hillsborough.[17]

With Gates properly taken care of, Cornwallis turned his attention to the guerrillas under Sumter. Sumter had been successful in harassing Cornwallis's supply lines, capturing numerous wagons and prisoners. As Sumter's force slowly moved north—following the west side of the Catawba and loaded down with wagons and prisoners recently taken—Cornwallis dispatched Tarleton and his British Legion along the east bank in pursuit. On August 18 Tarleton's force surprised Sumter's men as they took shade from the midsummer's heat along the banks of Fishing Creek, a tributary of the Catawba. Even though Sumter had been warned of the enemy's presence in the area, he had taken few precautions: the men stacked their arms, rested in the shade, or headed to the stream. When the Legion attacked, the surprise was complete. Tarleton recorded that he needed no time to decide on whether or not to attack. "The cavalry and [mounted] infantry were formed into one line," he wrote, "and, giving a general shout, advanced to the charge." Sumter had been napping under the shade of a wagon when he awoke to the sight of legionaries swarming through the camp. Unable to reach his horse, he cut the traces from a draft horse, mounted it, and attempted to reform his force. Finding this impossible, he fled for his life. At Fishing Creek Tarleton killed or wounded 150 of Sumter's force, captured more than 300, released British prisoners, and took 800 horses and 1,000 weapons—the entire American supply train and all their artillery—at a loss of only sixteen men killed or wounded. Sumter retreated to Charlotte, North Carolina, where he arrived without his army.[18]

In late September Cornwallis led his command north from the Waxhaws to Charlotte. The heat and sickness of the summer had decimated the command. With some difficulty they took the town, only to discover that the Patriots were regrouping and swarming around them—leaving the command cut off from Charleston. Meanwhile, the Patriots left behind in South Carolina were far from passive. Francis Marion (the "Swamp Fox") organized a guerrilla force that ambushed supply trains and raided British outposts from the safety of his hideouts along the Pee Dee swamps. At the same time, Cornwallis complained to Clinton in New York that Sumter had "reinstated and increased his corps to upwards of 1,000 men."[19]

Cornwallis dispatched part of his army into the Carolina highlands under a young Scottish officer, Major Patrick Ferguson. A career soldier, prior to the war Ferguson had invented a breech-loading rifle that he hoped the army could adopt. However, the machine tools needed to create the intricate screw system that operated the breech-loading mechanism did not yet exist, and only a few prototypes of the rifle have survived. Ferguson began his duties in the Revolution as the leader of an experimental corps of British riflemen, but was wounded in the Battle of Brandywine on September 11, 1777. With his right arm permanently crippled, while recovering Ferguson assumed new duties in the Carolinas as inspector general of the militia. Although his job was to raise and train Loyalist militia, he was also ordered to keep the Loyalists "from offering violence to innocent and inoffensive people, and by all means in your power [to] protect the aged, infirm, the women, and the children of every denomination from insult and outrage."[20]

By late September, Ferguson drove into western North Carolina with a force of more than a thousand Loyalists. Reaching as far west into the Blue Ridge as Davidson's Old Fort, the Tories terrorized all communities in their path. Here Ferguson issued a proclamation that may have led to his downfall: he sent forth a message into the mountains of present-day Tennessee, asserting that if the Patriots "did not desist from their opposition to British Arms," his force would "hang their leaders and lay their country waste with fire and sword." Rather than scattering the rebel resistance, the threat had the opposite effect. Militia commanders called for their men to unite and rendezvous on September 25, 1780, at Sycamore Shoals (close to Elizabethton, Tennessee). Militiamen from the Holston River area, known as "Overmountain Men," gathered under Colonels Isaac Shelby and John Sevier. Bringing 240 men each, they were joined by 400 Virginia mountain men under Colonel William Campbell and 200 men under Charles McDowell. As they traveled into North Carolina, they were joined by 350 more men under Benjamin Cleveland. By the time they arrived at the Catawba at the end of September, they had amassed a force of nearly 1,300 men. The Overmountain Men were almost universally mounted and armed with their frontier rifles.[21]

Finding himself exposed and seventy miles away from Cornwallis's force in Charlotte, Ferguson prudently began to fall back. Within forty miles of Charlotte, he decided his thousand-man force was in a position to again take the offensive. However, he wrote Cornwallis that he was unsure he had the numbers to win and requested "three or four hundred good soldiers, part dragoons, would finish this business. Something must be done soon." As it turned out, his commander would never receive the message.[22]

On October 2 the leaders of the Overmountain Men held a war council at Gilbert Town, North Carolina. They requested that American authorities place a general in overall command of the force, elected Colonel Campbell as "Officer of the Day" to coordinate their forces, and decided to pursue Ferguson's force as quickly as possible in order to strike before he reached Charlotte. After selecting 910 men with the fleetest mounts to lead the pursuit, they departed early on October 3 with the rest of the force following closely behind. Through driving rain, they pushed on nonstop during the next day and night until learning from locals that Ferguson was camped nearby on a clearing at the top of a ridge called King's Mountain. Just twenty-five miles away from Charlotte and the main force—and perhaps confident in his odds against the enemy—Ferguson proclaimed that "God Almighty himself could not drive him from [the mountain]."[23]

On the morning of October 7 the Overmountain Men reached King's Mountain. The ridge itself is part of the Piedmont foothills of the Blue Ridge, rising sixty feet from its base to form a ridgeline that is clear at the top but surrounded by thick forest. Without seeing the need for any fortifications, Ferguson placed his camp in the clearing on the higher north end. Upon arrival, the Americans dismounted, secured their horses, broke into separate commands, and encircled the entire ridge. Using the cover and concealment of the wood line, they advanced from all directions. The attack began at around three in the afternoon, as Colonel Campbell urged his men on with the shout: "Here they are boys; *shout like Hell, and fight like devils.*" Upon spotting them, the Loyalists began firing downslope on the attackers, perhaps firing too high and over their heads. Militia under Shelby and Campbell drove the defenders from the exposed southern crest to fall back to the main camp in the north. Ferguson countered with bayonet charges, something that men armed with rifles struggled to defend. But with each charge the militia fell back to the cover of the wood line and continued their deadly hail of well-aimed shots. Eventually the attackers had the Tory force encircled on the northern crest, and the battle turned into a wild free-for-all. Charging down the mountain on a white horse and shouting "Huzza brave boys, the day is our own," Ferguson vigorously attempted to rally his men. Both rider and horse went down in a hail of bullets. As one American observer noted, "seven rifle balls had passed through his body, both his arms were broken and his hat and clothing literally shot to pieces."[24]

The death of Ferguson all but ended organized resistance, but the killing continued. Isaac Shelby recorded that the disorganized attackers continued to make their way up the mountain and fire into the Loyalist ranks before word could reach them that the battle was over. Others, who he admitted "had heard that at Buford's defeat the British had refused quarters . . . were willing to follow that bad example." After considerable effort, the officers brought the killing to a halt. One hundred fifty-seven

Death of Major Ferguson at King's Mountain. A typically romantic portrayal of an officer's death on the field, although by all accounts Ferguson did meet his fate bravely. MIRIAM AND IRA D. WALLACH DIVISION OF ART, NEW YORK PUBLIC LIBRARY

Tories lay dead, 163 were too badly wounded to be moved from the field, and the vast majority of the rest—around seven hundred men—were taken prisoner. The Patriots fared far better, with only twenty-eight killed and sixty-two wounded. According to Tarleton, "the mountaineers . . . used every insult and indignity . . . towards the dead body of Major Ferguson." Some sources maintain that the Overmountain Men stripped his body and urinated on his corpse, then placed him into a raw cowhide and buried him on the field. Perhaps fearing the approach of Cornwallis's main body, the rest of the dead were "thrown into convenient piles and covered with old logs, the bark of old trees and rocks, yet not so as to secure them from becoming prey to the beasts of the forests. . . . Also the hogs in the neighborhood gathered into the place to devour the flesh. . . . In the evening there was a distribution of plunder, and we were dismissed." The killing apparently resumed later at Gilbert Town, forcing Colonel William Campbell to step in and order an end to the "slaughtering and disturbing [of] the prisoners." But the Carolinians, believing that some of the prisoners had been guilty of frontier injustice, demanded a hearing. Before the business was ended, thirty-six men were found guilty and nine were executed.[25]

In the fall of 1780 Congress authorized General Washington to choose his own commander in the South to replace the hapless Gates. While Washington was at a loss to supply the South with much material support and manpower, he did send two of the most talented officers in the war: "The Old Wagoner," Daniel Morgan, had already been sent to the department, and Washington added his most trusted lieutenant, General Nathanael Green. A Rhode Island native, the thirty-eight-year-old former Quaker had never set foot south of the Potomac River, yet proved to be the ideal commander for the South. Although Green began the war as a private, he had risen through the ranks to quartermaster general, where he did a remarkable job of straightening out Washington's supply system. While many revolutionaries were provincial in their outlook, Green was a firm nationalist. "For my part," he remarked, "I feel the cause and not the place. I would as soon go to Virginia as stay here [in the North]." Green was also a skillful diplomat and proved apt in winning the support of local civil authorities, Continentals, and partisan commanders alike. He realized the guerrillas considered themselves semi-autonomous and shunned outside leadership. Nevertheless, he asked Sumter to coordinate his actions with him, advising, "You may strike a hundred strokes and reap little benefit from them, unless you have a good Army to take advantage of your success."[26]

Upon arriving in Charlotte on December 2, 1780, Green immediately began gathering intelligence about the topography of the area, available manpower and supplies, and possible courses of action. It was clear to him that he was in far too weak a position to challenge Cornwallis in standard battle—therefore (as he informed Congress) he would resort to guerrilla warfare, focusing on harassing Cornwallis on all flanks, intercepting his supply wagons, and disrupting communications. Green then performed the unconventional maneuver of splitting his force in the face of the enemy and taking half his men himself to Cheraw along the Pee Dee River. Here he hoped to train and equip the army. He placed his most able troops under the newly promoted General Daniel Morgan, with orders to move along the border of the Carolinas southwest of Charlotte. This decision, Green admitted, "makes the most of my inferior force for it compels to divide his, and holds him in doubt as to his own line of conduct."[27]

After King's Mountain, Cornwallis found his supply lines were jeopardized and fell back below Camden to establish winter quarters. The Swamp Fox was challenging his supply lines and communications from Charleston, and Sumter and other bands were cutting his lines in the backcountry. Following Green's new moves, Cornwallis wrote to Clinton that "events alone can decide the future Steps." He too split his forces, sending Tarleton's Legion after Morgan over the Enoree and Tiger Rivers while he led the rest of the army along the east bank of the Broad River in hopes of cutting Morgan off.[28]

Morgan fell back north to the nearby North Carolina border, avoiding an open battle with the Legion; with half of his force being undisciplined militia, he saw no choice but to do so. True to form, Tarleton drove on, catching Morgan where he decided to make a stand. Morgan chose a ridge and field on the west side of the swollen Broad River near Chesnee, South Carolina, known locally as the Cowpens, a popular area for farmers to gather their free-range animals. Morgan had been calling out for the local militia to join him. Men serving under Presbyterian guerrilla Colonel Andrew Pickens filed into camp, as well as many veteran Overmountain Men. In addition to the Carolina militia there were many Virginians as well, some former Continentals with a good deal of experience. The core of Morgan's command consisted of a three-hundred-man Continental infantry battalion under Lieutenant Colonel John Eager Howard, consisting of companies from Delaware, Virginia, and Maryland. These—along with some of the Virginia militia—were the only men trained and experienced with the key weapon of Tarleton's regulars, the bayonet. Mounted support came from several companies of state dragoons and parts of the First and Third Continental Light dragoons, commanded by Lieutenant Colonel William Washington. Morgan had eight hundred men. He worked throughout the night of January 16 and 17, 1781, drafting a plan of attack and sharing it with his officers while the men prepared their evening meals. He elected to make a stand on a hill in the center of the Cowpens pastureland, a position with open flanks and swollen rivers to the rear—which, as Morgan later wrote, he hoped would motivate the militia to make a stand, as they had during Gates's debacle at Camden. "I would have thanked Tarleton had he surrounded me with his cavalry," Morgan wrote, adding later, "it would have been better than placing my own men in the rear to shoot down those who broke from ranks. . . . When men are forced to fight, they will sell their lives dearly."[29]

Morgan's Cowpens plan was unconventional, to say the least. Rather than trying to coax his militia to stand shoulder to shoulder with the Continentals on the main line, he devised a new method of deploying them that played to their strengths as riflemen. Placing Andrew Pickens in charge of everything, he split the men into two lines that would be deployed not with the Continentals on the hill but in front of the battle line to act as skirmishers. In the front, as the Legion drove up the slope, the first line of riflemen had orders to sharpshoot, taking deliberate interest in the enemy officers (a tactic perfected at Saratoga). The first group would then fall back to the second and larger line of militia, where the combined force was to hold its fire until the enemy was within fifty yards. They were then to fire two rounds and, avoiding the inevitable bayonet charge, march to the left and rear of the Continentals while being protected by Washington's dragoons. The Continentals and reliable Georgia and Virginia militia on the hill would then make a final stand.[30]

After dismissing his officers, Morgan walked the campfires for the rest of the night, conversing with the men. Morgan's reputation as a fighter must have preceded him, and he surely told many tales of his dealings with the British in Boston, Canada, and Saratoga. As an adopted Southerner and Virginia frontiersman himself—and as a captain of a rifle company—the Old Wagoner spoke their language and had earned their respect. He knew that men equipped with their own personal muskets and rifles had no bayonets to face the regulars. He told them to just make two shots and fall back. He also told them not to worry about being overrun with dragoons; as they fell back "Billy" Washington's horsemen would cover them. When the battle was over, he told the men, they could go home to where "the old folks would cheer them and the girls would kiss them." The men reacted enthusiastically. Major Thomas Young watched as Morgan greeted new arrivals with the same exhortations all night. As he recalled, "I was more perfectly convinced of General Morgan's qualifications to command militia, than I had ever before been."[31]

Early on the morning of January 17, Tarleton took the bait. In fact, he was surprised to see the Americans making a stand in the open, with flooded rivers to the rear and their flanks hanging in the air. He later wrote that the battlefield was "certainly as proper a place for action as [I] could desire: America does not produce many more suitable." At seven in the morning, Tarleton advanced with the Legion infantry and light infantry on his right and the 7th Regiment on his left. Both flanks were supported by fifty mounted dragoons, with the rest of the mounted men in reserve. Major Thomas Young was amazed at the sight and discipline of the green- and red-clad regulars, opining that "it was the most beautiful line I ever saw." Eyeing the advance, Morgan rode among the men, encouragingly yelling "give them an Indian halloo, by G[od]!" True to their word, the first line of riflemen began their deadly work and fell back to Pickens's line, where he and his officers ordered the men to hold their fire. As they came up, Young watched: "first . . . pop, pop, pop, then a whole volley; but when the British fired, it seemed like one sheet of flame from right to left. Oh! It was beautiful." After performing their agreed-upon duty, the militia began to file to the rear when British dragoons began to charge them down. James Collins, a seventeen-year-old King's Mountain veteran who believed he would be skinned and hung as a wild animal if caught, "thought . . . 'my hid is in the loft.'" However, that would not come to pass: "Billy" Washington's dragoons galloped in "like a whirlwind" to the rescue and drove away the British.[32]

Eyeing the American militia as they scattered, the British gained confidence and pressed the attack of Howard's main line of Continentals and militia on the hill. Here they were stopped by the steady and disciplined fire of the American veterans. As Tarleton sent his 71st Regiment around the American right flank, some confusion over orders ensued in Morgan's ranks, and his men backed down the reverse slope of the hill. The mix-up was brief and the Delaware Continentals repulsed the attackers on the right. But seeing the Americans turn heel and march down the reverse slope, the Legion took it for a retreat and broke ranks to charge forward. Morgan rode forward and brought the retreat to a halt. As they crested the hill, the charging British found that Howard had "made a perfect line. . . . Our men commenced a very destructive fire, which they little expected, and a few rounds occasioned great disorder in their ranks." Howard then "ordered a charge with bayonet." On the British right, Washington and his horsemen jumped at the opportunity to charge. Thomas Young remembered, "at this moment the bugle sounded; we made a half circuit at full speed and came upon the rear of the British line, shouting and charging like madmen. . . . The British line broke." At the same time, Pickens's riflemen rallied behind the lines. "Morgan rode up in front and, waving his sword, cried out, 'Form my brave fellows. . . . Old Morgan was never beaten.' We then advanced and gained the [left] flank of the enemy." Almost completely surrounded, Tarleton's force disintegrated; many members of the Legion and the regulars "laid down their arms and surrendered, while the rest took to the wagon road and did their prettiest kind of running away." Tarleton had kept two hundred mounted dragoons from his legion in reserve and attempted to order them into battle; they refused and joined in the general retreat. Tarleton then made one final attempt with about sixty followers to drive off the attackers. He was met with a charge by Washington's horsemen, and in a textbook saber fight, the two commanders dueled personally before Tarleton broke it off and retreated. The loss was devastating to the British. In addition to the destruction of Tarleton's Legion, two of Cornwallis's finest regular units were crushed, the 7th and the first battalion from the 71st. The fight had lasted less than an hour, but Tarleton had lost 86 percent of his army—110 killed, more than two hundred wounded, and five hundred captured. In sharp contrast, Morgan suffered only twelve dead and sixty wounded.[33]

Knowing that Cornwallis and the main British force were close at hand, Morgan hastily buried the dead and, slowed by prisoners and the wounded, retreated north. The triumph of victory was bittersweet: Years of campaigning and rough weather had finally taken their toll on him and—suffering from rheumatism and perhaps malaria as well—the Old Wagoner retired from the army shortly thereafter to his home in the Shenandoah Valley. Meanwhile, Cornwallis, one of the most daring

British commanders in America, was not about to stand by idly after his crack unit had been destroyed. He drove north after the Americans at a blistering pace, at one point shedding the army of its baggage train while discarding tents, medical supplies, and food. To set an example for his forces and encourage them to keep up with the Americans, he personally put his own wagon to the torch. With Cornwallis in heated pursuit, Green retreated north of the Dan River into Virginia, where he took up the boats he could find along the river in order to hold off his pursuers. Drawing in Virginia and North Carolina militia, Green recrossed the Dan and made a stand at Guilford Court House (near present-day Greensboro, North Carolina). Inspired by Morgan's experience at Cowpens, Green set out two lines of militia in advance. But unlike Morgan, who placed his men at a distance of 150 yards from each other, Green separated his lines at nearly 400 yards, too far ahead of each other to provide mutual support. When Cornwallis attacked, his forces were hardly slowed by the two lines, and they drove directly up to the main line of Continentals. Although Green outnumbered the British with 4,200 men, most were untried militia, and Cornwallis was certain his 2,000 veteran fighters could meet the challenge. Near the courthouse the main line of Continentals held off the British for nearly three hours, and the 1st Maryland Regiment even replied with a bayonet charge of its own. Green was ultimately forced to withdraw, but not without inflicting devastating casualties on the enemy: Cornwallis lost a quarter of his force, with 93 dead, 413 injured, and 26 missing. Green also had 93 men killed, but with 183 wounded lost far fewer to injury.[34]

On March 15, the night following the fight, a cold rain fell on Cornwallis's exposed and battered command. His victory was Pyrrhic, his war almost lost. Retreating across North Carolina, the force was resupplied by the Royal Navy in Wilmington. Later General Clinton ordered them north to Virginia to establish a naval base of supply at Yorktown, effectively abandoning the Carolinas. Major fighting in the war came to an end on October 18, 1781, with Cornwallis's surrender to Washington, who was commanding a regular force of French and American forces backed by the French navy. But the British still occupied posts across the Carolinas, with a total of 8,000 men facing Green's meager force of 1,500. Green sparred with the British in a guerrilla war that would continue until they finally evacuated the area in 1782. He maintained close contact with his guerrillas, urging them to isolate the extended British garrisons. He also pressed Sumter to hit Camden from the west, encouraged Pickens to threaten Augusta, Georgia, and directed Francis Marion, supported by Henry Lee's Legion, to break up communications between the main British garrison at Charleston and the isolated outpost at Ninety Six. Green was not deterred by the occasional defeat: After one loss during an attack on a British outpost near Camden, he remarked that "this repulse, if repulse it may be called, will make no alteration in our general plan of operations." He famously added, "We fight, we get beat, rise, and fight again." By the spring and summer of 1781, Green had made life so difficult for the occupiers—despite having been defeated in most engagements—that, with the exception of a band of land between Charleston and Savannah, they had retreated from the South's interior. (The British occupied this area until withdrawal from the South in 1782.) By 1781 the British were fighting for national survival in a world war against the combined forces of the French, Spanish, and Dutch. Their resources for continuing the American fight were limited, and in the end—almost a year and a half after Cornwallis's surrender at Yorktown and the loss of Parliamentary support—the British came to terms with the Americans.[35]

Did American guerrilla riflemen and militia win the American Revolution? While some historians have championed this position, a careful look at all aspects of the war points to a different conclusion. In time Congress and Washington came to be of one mind and agreed to create a Continental army that could stand toe-to-toe in fighting a European-style war with the British. Their logic? If successful, this army—employing widely accepted ways of war—could win the support of France or Spain. Service in this army proved unpopular, and at times Washington would resort to irregular operations when his options were limited; he even did so with his own Continentals when he famously crossed the Delaware and surprised a thousand Hessians on the day after Christmas 1776. Washington accepted the presence and limited experience of militia because, for the most part, he knew these were the only men he could get. However, as an experienced frontier fighter himself, he appreciated rangers and riflemen such as Morgan and skillfully used them as a force multiplier around Boston, New York, Canada, and (to the best effect) the Saratoga campaign.

Rather than extolling frontier fighters like George Rogers Clark and the militia as heroes, historians today are more inclined to favor the Native American viewpoint. New and important questions are being asked about American advances into Canada, the Illinois territory, Kentucky, the southern highlands, and the Iroquois nations. Was this a defensive war focused on protecting the border settlements or an aggressive war justified by an early version of the doctrine of Manifest Destiny? In these frontier attacks, all sides eventually adopted a war of extermination. Both Native and settler villages were destroyed, with women, children, and prisoners all killed in what amounted to a total war difficult to celebrate for its widespread carnage and horror. Thanks to thoughtful historians including John Grenier, one can clearly see this was a continuation of longstanding Indian-settler conflicts, fighting for control and dominance of an ever-changing frontier.

But the role of the militia and riflemen in the South marked major turning points in the conflict as a whole. Much of the blame for the British defeat lies squarely with the high command of Lord Germain, General Henry Clinton, and his southern commander, Lord Cornwallis. In occupying Georgia and the Carolinas they failed to reestablish any kind of civil royal government that recognized the rights of either Patriot or Loyalist citizens. They permitted Loyalist bands to retaliate on their Patriot neighbors, driving many who had taken the oath, were riding the fence, and, in some cases, even Loyalists into the ranks of the guerrillas. The actions of "the Swearing Captain" Huck and countless bands of roving gangs, and the real or imagined atrocities committed by Tarleton at the Waxhaws, drove Southerners by the thousands to organize and recognize their own guerrilla bands. From Huck's Defeat through the arrival of Green and Morgan, the British occupation of the South turned into a failure that led directly to Cornwallis's surrender at Yorktown.

CHAPTER FIVE

"The Kentucky reinforcement, in whom so much reliance had been placed, ingloriously fled"

Andrew Jackson

THE AMERICAN REVOLUTION DID NOT BRING AN END TO PARTISAN uprisings. In fact, the exact opposite occurred. In 1786 and 1787 Shays' Rebellion, an anti-government guerrilla uprising in western Massachusetts, brought the Founders together in Philadelphia to draft the United States Constitution. Under the Articles of Confederation, following the Revolution the states, which for all intents and purposes were sovereign unto themselves, were left with the burden of war debts. Some, including Virginia, were able to pay off their debts, while others, such as Massachusetts, were forced to continue levying heavy taxes on citizens in order to relieve their own debts. In response, many partisan groups rose up throughout the country to challenge tax collectors and block courts from foreclosing on private property and placing men into debtors' prisons. The uprisings occurred nationwide and were extensively covered in the press. George Washington—who had resigned his commission and wished for nothing more than to retire to a quiet life running his estate at Mount Vernon, Virginia—recognized these developments as a threat to the nascent United States, warning that "there are combustibles in every State which a spark might set fire to." Some thought the rioters were nothing more than anarchists, opining that they were "rascals" and "the most despicable . . . that ever disgraced any country." According to their detractors, the insurgents' goal was, quite simply, "the total subversion of the Constitution and the equal distribution of all property."[1]

In August 1786, after the Massachusetts legislature refused to address the grievances of debtors, former Continental captain Daniel Shays, among many others, led a partisan band against the courts and government of the state. Shays and his self-styled "regulators" blocked courts and stopped debt collectors from performing their duties. Many observers thought this "rage of excess democracy," quickly dubbed "Shaysism," represented nothing more than the actions of a revolting mob using the pretext of overtaxation to avoid paying legitimate debts. Henry Lee wrote Washington that the rebels intended to overthrow state governments, cancel debts, and confiscate property: "In one word, my dear General, we are all in dire apprehension that a beginning of anarchy, with all its calamities, has approached." Washington responded that "commotions of this sort, like snow-balls, gather strength as they roll, if there is no opposition in the way to divide and crumble them." Many urged Washington to take the field himself, arguing that his presence alone would "bring them [the rebels] back to reconciliation." But ultimately the U.S. government was powerless to oppose the rebellion. The army had been all but disbanded and the treasury was busted. The United States was a country in name only, with neither the infrastructure nor the resources to enforce laws; even the state of Massachusetts could not raise enough money to pay its militia to put down the rebellion. Eventually, Revolutionary War general Benjamin Lincoln succeeded in collecting money from Boston's merchant class to pay the militia, who subsequently took the field to challenge the rebels. On January 26, 1787, 1,500 men of Lincoln's state militia were challenged by the Shayites in front of the U.S. military arsenal at Springfield. As the insurgents approached, Lincoln's forces first fired warning shots—to no effect—and then discharged artillery, killing four and wounding twenty. The force subsequently melted away and many, including Shays, were later charged. However, Washington (among others) called for leniency and most were granted pardons.[2]

Shays' Rebellion spurred Washington out of retirement to chair what is now known as the Constitutional Convention of 1787. To Washington and many other nationalists, the guerrilla uprising in western Massachusetts challenged the very fabric of freedom. Insurgents must be stopped, Washington argued, for "if there exists not a power to check them, what security has a man to life, liberty or property?" A strong federal government was essential, he continued, "whereas a liberal and energetic Constitution, well guarded & closely watched, to prevent encroachments, might restore us to that degree of respectability & consequence, to which we had fair claim, & the brightest prospect of attaining."[3]

The role of the military and state-controlled militias weighed heavily on the delegates meeting in Philadelphia in 1787. Americans had inherited the British distrust of maintaining a standing army. Although the Revolution was won by the disciplined regulars of Washington's Continental line, the myth of the Minute Men and the perceived superiority of the militia remained strong. The new Constitution they created centralized the power of the federal government, granting the new Congress the power to directly levy taxes and declare war. However, war-waging powers were divided between the new president, who would be commander-in-chief of all the armed forces, and the Congress, which had the authority to declare war and raise the capital needed to fund it. The states also maintained a great deal of military sovereignty. While they could not make treaties and keep standing armies, they were permitted to keep their independent militia, appointing officers "according to the discipline prescribed by Congress." In addition, the Second Amendment—which echoed many state constitutions—clearly maintained that the right of individuals to bear arms was an essential right states needed to maintain their militia. Many wanted strict federal control over state militias in order to prevent guerrilla uprisings like Shays' Rebellion from occurring. Once in office, President Washington and Secretary of War Henry Knox urged Congress to pass legislation placing the states' militia under federal control. In 1792 Congress passed the Calling Forth Act and Uniform Militia Act, effectively delegating the authority of nationalizing the militia to the commander-in-chief. While state governors could call out their militias, the president remained the overall commander of all armed forces. The Uniform Militia Act made all white males between eighteen and forty-five members of the militia. Ironically, it fell well short of establishing anything remotely "Uniform": States could promote officers at will, and there was no standardized form of organization and training.[4]

Washington spent much of his presidency trying to avoid European wars, defending the frontier against Natives, and dealing with the Whiskey Rebellion, a guerrilla uprising in western Pennsylvania that resulted from the taxation of distilled spirits. Congress had directly established the tax in 1791, under the urging of Secretary of the Treasury Alexander Hamilton. The tax was met with armed resistance on the frontier, as many farmers who had no market for their bulky corn had found that distilling it into whiskey was a profitable alternative. In scenes reminiscent of how the Patriots' resistance to royal taxation led to the Revolution, tax collectors in western Pennsylvania and other states were threatened and sometimes even tarred and feathered. But this situation, the new nation's leaders argued, was different: There was an elected government, and the farmers had representatives in Congress. Washington considered the Whiskey Rebellion a fundamental challenge to the new government and its Constitution. To allow a disgruntled minority to "dictate to the majority," he reasoned, "there is an end put at one stroke to republican government."

On August 1, 1791, a group of around six thousand rebels gathered at Braddock's Field near Pittsburgh, promising to forcefully block any government agent trying to collect the tax. The rebels even called for the guerrilla force to seize the U.S. garrison in Pittsburgh. Washington conferred with the political leaders of Pennsylvania, who hesitated to call out their militia. Nevertheless, Washington viewed the rebels' action as a threat to civil governance, and on August 7 issued a proclamation mobilizing the militia of several states and warning the guerrillas to "disperse and retire peaceably to their respective abodes." As he wrote Governor Henry Lee of Virginia, "I consider this insurrection as the first *formidable* fruit of the Democratic Societies." After Washington had no luck negotiating with the insurgents, Hamilton urged that "moderation enough has been shown; 'tis time to assume a different tone." Washington realized that a show of military force against the insurgency was necessary.[5]

Calling out thirteen thousand of the militia, the sixty-two-year-old president donned a military uniform and, accompanied by Hamilton, went to central Pennsylvania to organize and lead the force. Political opponents, including Thomas Jefferson and James Madison, viewed this as a bold move intended to justify the creation of a standing army, with Madison opining that the action was meant to "establish the principle that a standing army was necessary for enforcing the laws." Jefferson thought the whole thing was a political farce: An "insurrection was announced and proclaimed and armed against," he asserted, "but could never be found." Meanwhile, as his confidante Hamilton led the troops into western Pennsylvania, Washington returned to his presidential duties in Philadelphia. Upon Hamilton's arrival, the rebellion lifted like an early morning fog. Around 150 dissidents were rounded up, and Washington insisted they be tried in civil rather than military courts. After two of the ringleaders were found guilty and sentenced to death, Washington—for the first time—used his constitutional authority to pardon them.[6]

The rebellion tested the limits of the new government and its ability to respond to an insurgency. In this endeavor Washington was decidedly successful. However, while he was dealing with the Whiskey insurgents, the Ohio frontier was roiling with Native unrest. Although Great Britain had ceded the Northwest Territory—a vast swath of land from north of the Ohio River to the Mississippi—to the United States in 1783 as part of the Treaty of Paris, the Native inhabitants of the land had not been solicited to partake in negotiations. Many Natives wished to halt American settlement at the Ohio River and actively raided frontier settlements in what was essentially a continuation of the frontier warfare that had been endemic to North America since Jamestown. Congress sent peace emissaries to meet with the Natives, and Washington preferred the establishment of treaties and outright purchase of land from the Natives. But many Indians refused to abandon their ancestral territory.

In 1784 Colonel Josiah Harmar led the 1st American Regiment into the area, but the force proved to be too small to accomplish much. In October 1790 he led 300 of his regulars, supported by 1,200 Kentucky and Pennsylvania militia from Fort Washington (modern Cincinnati, Ohio), against the villages of the Miami and Shawnee. The Natives skillfully lured the militia away, then fell on the regulars. Harmar's men subsequently retreated back to Fort Washington. Secretary of War Knox blamed the debacle on the poorly trained and led militia, many of whom were old men and boys hired as substitutes. Washington tried again the next year, with Congress creating a new infantry regiment and the army recruiting two thousand "levies" for a six-month term. In time the government gave up attempting to depend on state militia units and instead turned to short-term volunteers raised specifically for the campaign. Arthur St. Clair, the governor of the Northwest Territory, led this force of mostly militia and volunteers. Just before dawn on November 4, 1791, as the men had begun stirring in their camp along the Wabash River, a thousand Shawnee and Delaware Native warriors overran the camp. Many of the militia simply turned and fled. What became known as the Battle of the Wabash (or St. Clair's Defeat) ended in one of the worst defeats in American history. More than half of St. Clair's force was lost and nine hundred out of the one-thousand-man force were casualties.[7]

Congress subsequently sent new envoys to negotiate with the Natives, while concurrently rebuilding the army. Pay and conditions were improved, and the army was expanded to five thousand men. Washington also placed Revolutionary War general Anthony Wayne in command and granted him the time needed to train his force for the task of driving the Natives away from the Northwest Territory should negotiations fail. The Legion of the United States, as Wayne's force was known, would perform much better than the two previous forces. Using rangers, he planned to destroy Native villages and crops. In the summer of 1794, screened by rangers and Native allies, he led an advance on Indian villages. On August 20, near the Maumee River (near present-day Toledo, Ohio), Wayne and his Legion fought the Battle of Fallen Timbers. (A storm had felled many trees in the area, giving the battlefield its name.) This time the Americans drove the Natives from the field. The Indians then retreated to a nearby British garrison, Fort Miami. Although the British had been supplying them and some Canadian militia had participated as well, they were surprised when they received neither shelter nor aid. This was a crushingly demoralizing defeat, and with the Americans destroying their crops and villages, in 1795 the Natives signed the Treaty of Greenville, effectively ceding much of Ohio and some of Indiana to the Americans.[8]

The peace would not be long-lived. The pressure of western settlement and American demands for land combined with tensions with Great Britain, eventually leading to the War of 1812. Two Shawnee brothers, Tecumseh and Tenskwatawa (known as "the Prophet" for his spiritual visions), exhorted all Native tribes to unite to stem settlements on the western frontier. They also called for the end of separate treaties ceding land to the Americans, arguing for all Native lands to be held in common with no more sold or ceded without universal consent. Other prominent Native leaders, including Pontiac, had made similar calls in the past, but the growing force at Prophet's Town (established in 1808 at the confluence of the Wabash and Tippecanoe Rivers) worried American authorities, including Indiana Territory governor William Henry Harrison. Harrison met several times with Tecumseh, who demonstrated that the northern Natives had formed a unified confederacy. When Tecumseh told Harrison he was traveling south to unite with the Chickasaws, Choctaws, and Creeks, Harrison knew he had to take military action.[9]

Harrison was a veteran of the Battle of Fallen Timbers, where he had served as Anthony Wayne's aide-de-camp. He understood the need for a partisan force of backwoods riflemen rather than regular troops to win the fight. Using regulars as a base, he moved in on Prophet's Town, sending Kentucky and Indiana rangers ahead to scout "every place which seemed calculated for an ambuscade." The governor stopped at what would become Terre Haute, Indiana, and constructed Fort Harrison. Before traveling south, Tecumseh had warned his brother not to get into a fight with the Americans before he returned, but with the force now advancing on Prophet's Town, Tenskwatawa was forced into action. Arriving on November 6, 1811, Natives approached Harrison's force and announced that the Prophet would meet with them in the morning. Sensing duplicity, Harrison ordered his force to sleep with loaded weapons. At approximately 4:00 a.m. on November 7, the Natives attacked. Harrison was not entirely surprised by the attack, but was stunned as "they manifested a ferocity, uncommon even with them." Both sides suffered tremendous losses, and after the Natives had suffered two hundred casualties, the Americans counterattacked and drove them through Prophet's Town. Harrison's men then continued the well-established pattern of destroying the village, granary, and supplies. The Native warriors retreated to the safety of Fort Malden in British-held Canada, where they were welcomed and supported by the garrison.[10]

During the War of 1812, the British effectively used their Native allies on the frontier. Many pro-war congressmen, known as War Hawks in the United States, viewed the conflict as an opportunity to take Canada—and with only a few thousand regulars in the territory, the British were forced to turn to the Indians for help. During the first months of the conflict, the redcoats and Natives enjoyed stunning victories along the Great Lakes frontier. Forts Michilimackinac, Dearborn, and Detroit were all taken with only token resistance. After Fort Dearborn was captured, the men and women of the garrison were promised safe passage. Instead fifty-two of them were massacred by a scalping party. By the end of the season Americans held only Forts Harrison and Wayne. In essence, settlers in the Northwest Territory faced the same challenges other frontier settlers had faced in previous periods of hostility. Thousands were now driven from their isolated Illinois and Indiana farmsteads to the safety of older, better-established communities. In September Harrison brought two thousand militia to relieve the besieged defenders of Fort Wayne. After relieving the post, Harrison retaliated in the usual manner on Indian villages and farms. Other militia bands led similar campaigns across the territories.[11]

During the war, America's senior major general Henry Dearborn had little use for ranger forces on the frontier. He focused instead on British regulars in Canada and neglected the threat from the Native alliance in the Northwest. In 1813, after the stunning American victory on Lake Erie, Lieutenant Colonel Richard Mentor Johnson's Kentucky rangers and 140 regulars drove British Major General Henry Proctor's army and Native allies across Canada. During the Battle of the Thames, William Henry Harrison and Johnson's Kentucky rangers were key to the victory, with perhaps Johnson himself killing Tecumseh. The lopsided American victory decisively eliminated the threat of Natives retaking their old Northwest homeland. While American volunteers and regular forces conducted the main campaigns along the Niagara and up the Chesapeake River, the Ohio, Indiana, Kentucky, and Illinois rangers cleared the threat to the frontier.[12]

The war sparked conflict in the old Southwest as well. Florida had been ceded back to Spain at the conclusion of the Revolution; with Spain allied with the British in the Napoleonic Wars, the War Hawks naturally turned their eyes to Florida. When the United States took Mobile in what was then West Florida, a faction of the Creek Nation, the Red Sticks, rose up. Many of them had warmed to the northern confederacy after Tecumseh's 1811 visit, and—with much of their land being threatened by the expansion of the Americans' booming slave and cotton economy—they elected to strike. Americans suspected that Spanish traders in Pensacola were arming the Red Sticks, and in the summer of 1813 an American force attacked a group of Natives who had been trading at the fort. The Creeks were divided, with some supporting the Americans and others (the Red Sticks) at war with the frontier militia. The war escalated on August 30, 1813, when the Red Sticks attacked and captured Fort Mims, about thirty-five miles north of Mobile. The attackers killed around 250 people, including slaves and Native women and children.[13]

The First Creek War, as this conflict became known, marked the rise of Andrew Jackson. Jackson was raised at war; although he never had any formal military training, his life story was one of unrelenting frontier violence. His Scots-Irish parents had joined the mass migration into the Carolina hill country in the 1760s, and after his father's death (before Jackson was born), his mother raised her three sons in the Waxhaws. After Buford's Massacre, Jackson tended the wounded alongside his mother and brother. At thirteen, he joined Thomas Sumter's militia as a messenger. Later in the Revolutionary War, Jackson and his brother Robert were captured after a Loyalist turned them in. At one point an officer ordered Andrew to shine his boots, to which the defiant teen's reply was, "Sir, I am a prisoner of war, and claim to be treated as such." The officer swung his sword down on Jackson's head, splitting his left hand and permanently scarring his head. When the officer turned to Robert Jackson to make the same demand, Robert also refused and received a terrible blow in response. On April 27, 1781, shortly after this incident, Robert died of smallpox.

Jackson's other brother, Hugh, had died of heatstroke nearly two years earlier, during the Battle of Stono Ferry on June 20, 1779. And Jackson's mother had contracted cholera during the war while serving as a nurse for American prisoners. Jackson was left an orphan at fourteen, with no surviving family. The guerrilla war in the Waxhaws and the deaths of his siblings and mother left him with a deep-seated hatred of the British and a brutally won understanding of unconventional warfare.[14]

Major General Andrew Jackson. Stipple engraving of the future president, here portrayed during the period of the War of 1812. MIRIAM AND IRA D. WALLACH DIVISION OF ART, NEW YORK PUBLIC LIBRARY

By the War of 1812 Jackson had risen to prominence on the Tennessee frontier and was the steely forty-five-year-old commanding general of Tennessee volunteers. After the Fort Mims massacre several poorly coordinated militia forces campaigned in Creek country. After seesaw campaigning in 1813, in March of the following year Jackson led a mixed body of four thousand regular forces, Tennessee riflemen, Cherokee, Lower Creek and Choctaw warriors, and colorful characters including David "Davy" Crockett and Sam Houston after the Red Sticks. On March 27 Jackson's force found the Natives at a fortified twist of the Tallapoosa River known as Horseshoe Bend. Jackson sent his Native allies and the mounted men under General John Coffee's command to the far side of the river to surround the position, while he advanced directly to the breastworks the Red Sticks had constructed across the bend. He began by firing his two small cannon at the works, without causing much damage. Meanwhile, Coffee and the Natives crossed the river and assaulted the village from the rear. With the enemy in confusion, Jackson ordered a bayonet charge by his regular forces. The charge was successful, and the defenders were hemmed in on all sides. They refused to surrender, and approximately eight hundred of the force of one thousand Red Stick warriors were killed. In contrast, Jackson had less than fifty men killed and 154 wounded. The surviving fighters fled south to the protection of their Seminole kin in Spanish Florida. In August 1814 the victors forced the Creek Nation to sign the Treaty of Fort Jackson, effectively giving up half of Alabama and some of southern Georgia. This victory—and his even greater win over the British regular army at New Orleans—made Jackson a national hero, propelling him to the White House fifteen years later.[15]

After his success punishing the Red Sticks, Jackson was promoted to major general in the U.S. Army and given command of the South. In December 1814 a force of British regulars, all with experience fighting the French, landed south of New Orleans. On the night of December 23, Jackson launched a surprise attack on the British force. The redcoats held their own, with both sides sparring into the New Year. Jackson fell back to a plantation called Chalmette, placing his men in line facing south behind an eight-foot-deep canal where they fortified their line. Jackson's command consisted of one of the most diverse groups of fighters in American history. The force of 4,732 men included almost one thousand regulars, Jackson's Tennessee militia, French Louisiana militia, Mississippi dragoons, Choctaw warriors, an Irish regiment, and two battalions of mostly free black men. The force was even joined by Jean and Pierre Laffite's pirate band. Jackson was also eagerly awaiting the arrival of two thousand Kentucky riflemen making their way down the Mississippi River. When they arrived on January 4, Old Hickory was rudely surprised. In the dead of winter, the men lacked basic equipment including tents and blankets. In addition, only 550 of them were armed, causing the general to later remark that it was the first time he had seen a Kentuckian "without a gun, pack of cards, and a jug of whisky."[16]

Jackson placed the hapless new arrivals on the west side of the river guarding an artillery battery. Officers placed a great deal of field artillery along the rest of his fortified lines, aimed to rake much of the open field to their south. The right of Jackson's line rested on the Mississippi. To his left he placed Coffee's Tennesseans and their Native allies in a swamp. The artilleries of both armies engaged in a preliminary duel on January 1, but General Edward Pakenham, the seasoned British commander, elected to hold off on a general assault until the rest of his force was up. Pakenham devised a complicated plan for an assault on January 8. He would send a force to the west side of the river to capture the battery that the Kentuckians were guarding, hopefully turning it on Jackson's force on the east bank. He also sent a flanking force of West Indian troops through the swamps on the American left. The main attack would come directly at the center of Jackson's fortified line behind the canal. The attacking troops were to carry bundles of sugarcane to be used as fascines to create a crossing, in addition to ladders to scale the works. The plan went awry from the beginning. The attack on the guns on the west bank was delayed by problems caused by the river crossing. The British eventually scattered the Kentuckians and took the battery, but at that point the outcome of the battle had already been decided. The West Indians attacking the Americans left found more than they had bargained for when they were met by Tennessee riflemen and Choctaw warriors in their native swamplands. The main assault on the center was initially covered by morning fog, but as the British approached the American lines, the mist cleared—permitting the well-placed American artillery to rake the enemy's exposed lines. The British forces were successful in overrunning part of the American line along the river, but their assault was unsupported: One officer had failed to have his men bring up the fascines. In the last mistake of his life, General Pakenham directed the 93rd Highlanders away from supporting the successful breach on the left to support the right side of his line where men were being mercilessly exposed to artillery fire. The courageous veteran had a horse shot out from under him and was wounded twice, but continued to direct the battle. He finally suffered a mortal wound by grapeshot, a type of shot that essentially turns a cannon into a giant, short-range shotgun. Many of his compatriots met the same fate. Some huddled in the canal only to be raked with cannon or shot down from above. A few brave attackers attempted to swim the canal and scale the walls, but were shot down or taken prisoner.[17]

The Battle of New Orleans was one of the most lopsided victories in American history. The British left around 1,500 killed and wounded on the field and saw about five hundred men captured. Meanwhile, Jackson reported fewer than one hundred casualties. However, the British did not leave the theater after the battle. After attempting to capture one of the forts guarding the Mississippi line of approach, they continued to campaign in the area, moving on to Mobile Bay and advancing until news reached them—rather belatedly—that the war had been ended with the Treaty of Ghent, signed nearly a month before on Christmas Eve.[18]

To this day historians debate the importance of the Battle of New Orleans and the many myths that arose in its wake. Some have argued that the fight was a completely needless waste of human life. Although the December 24 treaty still needed to be ratified by both countries, had both sides known of it, the battle might not have been fought. Others argue that Pakenham may well have continued the campaign; New Orleans was one of the most important ports in the United States, and denying access to it might have led the western states to leave the Union. In addition, the British and their Spanish allies had never recognized President Thomas Jefferson's Louisiana Purchase. At a minimum, some have argued, the British would have granted the area to Spain.

Word of Jackson's victory arrived in the burnt capital of Washington at the same time as the news of peace, giving the impression that America had won the war in combat. In the minds of the populace, Jackson had risen to the nearly mythic level of Washington. In reality, though, the war did not effect major changes stateside. The nation had not been successful in its attempt to take Canada, and the Treaty of Ghent returned the belligerents to *status quo ante bellum*. The battle also gave rise to the myth that the British were defeated by Old Hickory and a band of stoic backwoods riflemen. According to this well-worn story, the parade-ground advance of the Old World redcoats was no match for the Kentucky and Tennessee riflemen who picked off the attackers as they would hunting squirrels. There is some truth to this: The Tennessee men, supported by Natives, performed very well in the swamp on the east. However, the Kentucky men on the west bank of the river ran from the field, as many other militia units had done during the war. Jackson was so incensed that he wrote Secretary of War James Monroe, "The Kentucky reinforcement, in whom so much reliance had been placed, ingloriously fled." In addition, it is unlikely that those in the center of the American line were carrying rifles; they were likely armed with standard .69-caliber U.S.-issued muskets. The factor most responsible for the majority of British casualties was well-placed and -directed American artillery. One British officer watched as the Americans used a thirty-two-pound naval gun loaded with canister shot as a giant shotgun, which "served to sweep the center of the attacking force into eternity."[19]

The end of the war did not bring an end to American partisan bands in arms. Indeed, they continued to be involved in unconventional warfare well into the nineteenth century. Many Americans took up "filibustering," the practice of arming American insurgents with the express goal of overthrowing foreign states and setting themselves up as rulers. Although this violated the Neutrality Act of 1794—and the government did charge some of the raiders—filibustering continued up until the Civil War. Perhaps the most famous use of American volunteers in a foreign war was that of Southern volunteers who rushed to support the Texas Revolution. In 1821 young *empresario* Stephen Austin, following in his late father Moses Austin's footsteps, received permission from the nascent

Mexican government to bring colonists to Texas. The cotton boom and expansion of its slave-driven economy had fueled Southerners' desire for more land. Born in Virginia and raised in Missouri, Austin would be personally responsible for attracting around 1,500 families to Texas, and other settlers soon joined them. By 1831 the new settlers outnumbered the original *Tejanos* by a ratio of more than two to one; by 1836 there were perhaps 35,000 American settlers, who now outnumbered the original inhabitants by ten to one. Under the liberal Mexican Constitution of 1824, Texas—which was part of the Mexican state of Coahuila y Tejas—enjoyed great autonomy: Mexico never forced the Catholic state religion on the American settlers and it turned a blind eye to the numerous slaves kept as "contracted" workers. This began to change in 1833, after General Antonio López de Santa Anna was elected president. In time Santa Anna rejected the liberal policies of his predecessors, seized near dictatorial powers, and repudiated the Constitution of 1824. Revolts erupted in many states, including Alta California, but the general chose to make a special example of Texas.[20]

Fighting between Mexico and the American settlers commenced on October 2, 1835, at Gonzales—one of the first Anglo-American settlements west of the Colorado River—after a Texas militia company refused to turn over a cannon to Mexican troops. Initially the Texans were poorly organized, and few could agree on what their ultimate reasons for fighting were. Was it to restore the Constitution? Demand more autonomy? Or declare independence? Southern newspapers in the United States sensationalized the unfolding events as a clash between Protestant whites and Mexicans, and thousands of white, Southern filibusters subsequently flocked to Texas. As disorganized as the settlers, the new arrivals spent as much time arguing among themselves about the chain of command as they did anything else.[21]

The following spring, Santa Anna resolved to punish the Americans. He would personally lead one force into Texas while another cleared the Gulf Coast. José María Tornel, the Mexican secretary of war, had no respect for the fighting abilities of the Americans. "The superiority of the Mexican soldier over the mountaineers of Kentucky and the hunters of Missouri is well known," he asserted. "Veterans seasoned by 20 years of wars can't be intimidated by the presence of an army ignorant of the art of war, incapable of discipline, and renowned for insubordination."[22]

As news of Santa Anna's actions spread, the Texans bickered over how they should defend their territory. In the face of a two-pronged invasion they elected to split their forces, leaving around three hundred men under the command of Colonel James Fannin to defend east Texas at Goliad and a second, smaller force of around two hundred at San Antonio. They fortified an abandoned mission known popularly as the Alamo. The defenders were a colorful lot, the most well-known being Colonel David Crockett (commonly known as "Davy," he actually used the name David), a famous rifleman, Indian fighter under Jackson, and former congressman from Tennessee. Upon arrival in Congress, he was said to have boasted, "I can wade the Mississippi, leap the Ohio, ride a streak of lightning, slip without a scratch down a honey locust, whip my weight in wildcats, hug a bear too close for comfort, and eat any man opposed to Jackson." He eventually fell out with Jackson and the Democrats over the cruelties of their Indian Removal of 1830 and was voted out of office. After failing to be reelected, he told a friend he was heading "for the wilds of Texas." At the Alamo he was under the command of native South Carolinian William Travis, a lieutenant colonel in the Texian army, and frontiersman James Bowie, who is still famous for his fighting knife.[23]

On February 23, leading a 2,500-man army of transcripts, General Santa Anna laid siege to the Alamo. He could have spared many lives had he waited for his artillery to come up and for its defenders to succumb to supply shortages and bad water. (His guns alone would have made short work of the compound.) However, when he learned that the Americans were not considering surrender, "our commander became more furious," recalled one Mexican officer. "He believed as others did that the fame and honor of the army were compromised the longer the enemy lived." On March 6, four days after Texas delegates at Washington-on-Brazos signed a declaration of independence from Mexico, Santa Anna ordered a pre-dawn attack on the Alamo. Within ninety minutes, at a cost of about a third of the force, the attackers had scaled the walls and overwhelmed the defenders. Taking the field after the fight had ended, Santa Anna ordered the execution of all male prisoners. They were brutally hacked to death. Most historians agree that Santa Anna ordered Crockett's execution after surrender as well. He spared the women, children, and slaves in the compound from the bloodbath, freeing them to spread the news.[24]

Travis had originally called for reinforcements at the Alamo, but Fannin failed to do the same at Goliad. Soon his force was also surrounded by a vastly superior Mexican army. Fannin accepted terms of surrender, but once again, Santa Anna ordered the execution of the prisoners. At Goliad, 342 men were massacred while twenty-eight managed to slip away. Sensing the fall of the revolution, Santa Anna subsequently split up his forces and took off in pursuit of around nine hundred men commanded by Sam Houston, former governor of Tennessee and close friend of Andrew Jackson. Discounting any threat from Houston's army, on April 20 Santa Anna made camp in an open field near the San Jacinto River. The next afternoon, while the Mexican army was at rest—with many men napping, washing, and eating—Houston's force overran their camp, yelling "Remember the Alamo!" and "Remember Goliad!" While Mexican soldiers scattered, Houston and other officers attempted to rein in the killing; it continued for hours, however, with 650 Mexicans killed and 300 more captured—including Santa Anna himself, who was taken the next morning wearing a private's uniform. Only eleven Texans lost their lives and thirty, including Houston, were wounded.[25]

When Santa Anna was brought before Houston, who was laid out having been shot in the ankle, many called for his execution. Instead Santa Anna agreed to call for the rest of the Mexican army to leave Texas, and in mid-May signed the Treaties of Velasco recognizing the independent Republic of Texas. Predictably, the Mexican government would never ratify the treaty, and the Texans were convinced it was just a matter of time before another army attacked. News of the fighting swept across the American South, and hundreds of eager filibusters raced to fight under the Texas flag. Texas also requested annexation into the United States so the resources of the U.S. military could be used to guard its border. But Presidents Andrew Jackson and, later, Martin Van Buren both demurred. Northern abolitionists had long believed that the American invasion of Texas was simply a thinly veiled attempt by the filibusters

Houston, Santa Anna, and Cos. Published by Henry R. Robson in 1836, this imaginative lithograph portrays the surrender of Mexican commander Santa Anna and his brother-in-law General Martin Perfecto de Cos to American leader Samuel Houston following the Battle of San Jacinto in late April 1836. In reality, Santa Anna was captured the morning after the battle wearing a private's uniform, and Houston—having been shot in the ankle—was unable to stand when Santa Anna surrendered. PRINTS AND PHOTOGRAPHS DIVISION, LIBRARY OF CONGRESS

to expand the Southern slave dominion. Thus the Texas Republic would remain independent for almost ten years.[26]

The Texas Revolution is the most blatant example of American fili-busters attempting to overthrow a foreign government. But these actions continued until the Civil War. Most of them were sponsored by groups hoping to establish and expand slave-based empires in Latin America, but such fighting occurred even along the Canadian border. In 1837 the Scotsman William Mackenzie led a rebellion against British rule that included American-born insurgents. American forces led by Rensselaer Van Rensselaer began organizing New York volunteers who called them-selves "Patriots"; the force was being supplied by an American-owned vessel, the *Caroline*. On the night of December 29, 1837, a force of Canadian militia drove off thirty-three crew members and overnight guests, killed an onlooker, and captured the steamer. They then set it ablaze, cut it loose, and set it adrift over Niagara Falls. The *Caroline* affair, as it became known, inflamed simmering border antagonisms that dated back to the previous wars with Great Britain. President Martin Van Buren had no intentions of letting a New York mob instigate another war with the British. He sent one of the heroes of the War of 1812, General Winfield Scott, to Buffalo to single-handedly defuse the situation. Scott convinced Van Rensselaer and his followers to disband.[27]

But the Patriots were not through. They reorganized themselves into what they called "Hunting Lodges" and continued filibustering. In May 1838 they paid the Canadians back for the *Caroline* affair by setting the Canadian ship *Sir Robert Peel* on fire. Later, in November and December, 1,400 Hunters invaded Canada, where they were met by a mixture of Canadian militia and regulars. The Hunters were defeated, with perhaps twenty-five killed and the rest taken prisoner. Seventeen were later executed and seventy-eight were sent to the British penal colony in Tasmania. The rest were permitted to return to the United States. The Canadian government thus exhibited firm control over its sovereignty, and in time the movement lost its appeal to Americans. However, American-inspired foreign insurrections would continue.[28]

After the Mexican-American War, filibustering increased dramatically, driven by both the concept of Manifest Destiny and Southern dreams of a slave republic stretching from the Caribbean to Brazil. Many saw the fall of Spain's power in the region as an opportunity to take one of its last bastions, Cuba. In the United States, Venezuelan-born Narciso López represented other wealthy Cuban slave owners who feared that Spain would abolish slavery on the island. He sponsored several attempts to overthrow the government, the last one ending with the capture of his force including fifty Americans. López was publicly garroted while thousands of Cubans in Havana cheered. The Americans were also executed. Meanwhile, having already failed to take Baja California in 1853, American William Walker launched a filibustering expedition to Nicaragua. After taking command of rebel forces, he proclaimed himself president in 1856. He worked to reinstate slavery in the country and to drum up pro-slavery support from the United States. However, he soon alienated his supporters as well as prominent business interests including the British and Cornelius Vanderbilt. After losing the presidency in 1857, he attempted to retake Nicaragua by force in 1860. He was captured by the British navy, turned over to Honduran authorities, and executed by firing squad.[29]

The frequency of armed partisan uprisings did not decrease much following the American Revolution. In fact, the fear of uncontrolled uprisings like Shays' Rebellion spurred the Founders to meet in Philadelphia to create a much stronger federal government with the power to tax and raise its own forces. Washington found this to be an effective tactic, especially as it enabled him to put down the Whiskey Rebellion, the first major threat to the fragile new government. As commander-in-chief he was able to call on the militia of several states to quell the uprising in western Pennsylvania. Meanwhile, Natives attempting to keep control of the area west of the Appalachians used the tensions that presaged the War of 1812 to defend their homelands. Here too frontier militia practiced well-developed methods of total warfare on Native villages and non-combatants to drive their warriors to sue for peace. The Battle of Fallen Timbers, the Canadian campaigns, and Jackson's war on the Red Sticks effectively ended large-scale Native resistance east of the Mississippi River. Ironically, Native-style guerrilla warfare was championed in the public imagination: Despite being earned by keen military strategy and regular forces supported by militias, Jackson's victory at New Orleans solidified the myth of the frontier rifleman who could easily defeat a trained, seasoned soldier. The peace following the War of 1812 did not see an end to partisan-driven actions. The Texas Revolution was fought mainly by white Southern filibusters, inspiring a movement that both sought to overthrow several Latin American governments and threatened the border with Canada. This background of irregular frontier-style warfare, which had scarcely waned following the American Revolution and the War of 1812, foreshadowed much of the guerrilla strife that would ensue during the nation's darkest hour: the American Civil War.

CHAPTER SIX

"Swamp Fox Rangers"

AFTER MANY YEARS OF DISREGARDING GUERRILLA AND UNCONVEN-
tional warfare during the Civil War, historians have returned to reexam-
ining their role in the country's bloodiest conflict. For generations, Civil
War–era historians justified this oversight by pointing out, as did Revolutionary War–era historians, that the Civil War was won by conventional
forces. This is true to a point, but the scale of guerrilla warfare during
the conflict and its impact on the civilian population have long been
underestimated. As was true during the Revolution, guerrillas did little
to advance either Confederate or Union forces. However, they did sub-
stantively change the way the war was fought, often increasing the level
of violence targeted against civilians. Combat began with Northern and
Southern commanders attempting to fight a conventional war between
standing, uniformed armies. But wherever Union forces occupied Southern territory, guerrilla uprisings occurred. Unable to cope with insurgents
in occupied areas, Federal forces turned on Southern civilians who, they
believed, harbored guerrillas in reprisal. During the Civil War, the same
methodology long applied against the Natives—targeting homes and
property—would be turned toward Confederates and those who harbored
them, with one notable exception: As a general rule, non-combatants
were not killed. Nevertheless, by the end of the war (which cost more
than 600,000 lives) hundreds of towns and cities were reduced to ashes;
countless farms, barns, crops, and farm animals were destroyed; and the
Union had waged what historian Clay Mountcastle has described as a
"punitive war" against the civilian population of the South. The motive for

this wanton destruction went beyond the necessity of withholding supplies from the Confederate army or destroying any infrastructure present
in the South. Beyond the material, it was also political and psychological:
Northern commanders retaliated against civilians who harbored guerrilla
bands. Crushing support for the rebellion on the Confederate home front
became a major goal of Northern commanders. As historian Daniel E.
Sutherland notes, these policies "led to profound changes in military
policies and strategy. Those changes, in turn, produced a more brutal and
destructive war that led to Confederate defeat." As these policies were
implemented and the war became increasingly bloodier and more desperate, many Southerners who had once considered themselves Rebels
and looked to guerrillas to defend them abandoned the cause and their
newly formed government. However, when the war began, the South
embraced its historic guerrilla heritage.[1]

At the outbreak of the Civil War, Southerners were already looking
back on their young history with a perhaps exaggerated pride in the
accomplishments of their ancestors. To them, the Texas Revolution was
won by the wily Kentucky and Tennessee riflemen (and Texas Rangers)
who drove Santa Anna from Texas, the same frontier fighters who had
brought Great Britain to her knees in the Battle of New Orleans. Southerners took the greatest pride in the partisan bands who drove away the
redcoats and won the Revolution in the South. These views certainly
contained a grain of truth and were deeply held values in Southern
white culture. William Gilmore Simms, perhaps the most influential
novelist and historian of the antebellum South, focused on many aspects
of Southern life in his work. He is best known today for his unashamed
defense of the indefensible—slavery. However, he was a popular and
influential historian of the region, and his 1844 *Life of Francis Marion*
was on the bookshelf of many Southern homes. The following excerpt is
typical of the florid prose that glorified South Carolina guerrillas of the
Revolutionary War era:

> *While Sumter stands conspicuous for bold daring, fearless intrepidity
> and always resolute behavior; while Lee takes eminent rank as a
> gallant Captain of Cavalry, the eye and the wing of the southern lib-*

erating army under Greene; Marion is proverbially the great master
of strategy—the wily fox of the swamps—never to be caught, never to
be followed,—yet always at hand, with unconjectured promptness, at
the moment when he is least feared and is least to be expected.[2]

When the Civil War began, Simms became a leading advocate of guerrilla warfare. He suggested to a local commander that each Confederate company (on paper, one hundred men) allocate ten men to act as guerrillas. This reflects the Revolutionary War practice of augmenting regiments with companies of light infantry. But Simms went far beyond that, calling for such guerrillas to be disguised and painted as Native warriors and armed with "rifle, bowie knife & hatchet." As he explained, "If there be any thing which will inspire terror in the souls of citizen soldiery of the North, it will be the idea that scalps are to be taken by redmen."[3]

Southern whites looked to the Revolution as a guide to the current conflict. They saw themselves being as oppressed in their current predicament as the Patriots had been in theirs, and even adopted the symbols of the Revolution for themselves. They continued to celebrate the Fourth of July and placed the likeness of an equestrian George Washington on the official seal of their slaveholding republic. The federal government replaced England as their enemy, with Abraham Lincoln assuming the throne of King George III. Southerners even took to calling Unionists "Tories." As men enlisted, volunteer companies proudly embraced their Revolutionary War guerrilla heritage by naming themselves "Swamp Fox Rangers" or "Marion Men." Others took names that echoed even further back, calling themselves "ranger" companies. Although the conflict's ultimate outcome was clearly decided by conventional forces, it could be argued that the war itself was sparked by guerrilla raids.[4]

The Civil War was instigated by the Southern white oligarchy's determination to protect and expand its "peculiar institution" of slavery to the west in the face of abolitionists' rising power. The abolitionist cause was greatly boosted by the nascent Republican Party's opposition to the expansion of slavery. It is no surprise, then, that guerrilla actions predated the war—instigated by an uprising on the Kansas frontier, where settlers had been left to decide the question of slavery for themselves. An

The Confederate States of America: 22 February 1862—*deo vindice*. Lithograph of the seal of the Confederate States of America, by Andrew B. Graham. The Confederacy adopted much of the symbology of the American Revolution, curiously combined with Old Testament validations of slavery. As seen here, its seal portrayed a mounted George Washington under the motto *Deo Vindice*—Latin for "Under God, Our Vindicator." PRINTS AND PHOTOGRAPHS DIVISION, LIBRARY OF CONGRESS

already incendiary situation was then exacerbated by John Brown's failed guerrilla raid on Harpers Ferry in Virginia. Following the election of Republican president Abraham Lincoln along a sectional vote, both sides agreed that a force of arms would be the only way to settle the matter.

In 1854 Illinois congressman Stephen Douglas pushed through the Kansas-Nebraska Act, permitting the settlers of both territories "popular sovereignty" to decide the fate of slavery for themselves. Both pro- and anti-slavery settlers flocked to the Kansas Territory, with the full intention of settling the issue with arms if need be. Many settlers traveled from the neighboring slave state of Missouri to settle pro-slavery communities, including Atchison and Leavenworth. At the same time, Northern abolitionists sponsored by the New England Emigrant Aid Company settled abolitionists in Lawrence, Manhattan, and Topeka. Fearing a Yankee takeover, thousands of "Border Ruffians" from Missouri crossed the state line and stuffed ballot boxes with votes for pro-slavery candidates to a territorial legislature that would legalize slavery. Free-Staters, who opposed slavery, complained to Federal authorities to no avail; some took to advocating violence. According to legend, Henry Ward Beecher—one of the most prominent ministers in New England, a fervent abolitionist, and brother of Harriet Beecher Stowe—shipped Sharps breech-loading rifles out West in crates marked "Bibles." In Kansas the weapons would be dubbed "Beecher's Bibles."

In a short time pro-slavery and anti-slavery legislatures began vying for control of an increasingly heated situation. In the fall of 1855, armed insurgents began killing each other. Then on May 21, 1856, mounted Missouri Border Ruffians sacked the anti-slavery town of Lawrence, burning a hotel and the offices of an abolitionist newspaper. This action was the last straw for Ohio abolitionist John Brown. Up to this point Brown had failed in every endeavor he had ever attempted, and he had now dedicated his life to the abolition of slavery by any means necessary. He attracted a religious group of believers who held the same views. On the night of May 24 Brown led a band of abolitionists, included his sons, to the pro-slavery settlement of Pottawatomie Creek, where they dragged several men from their homes—none of whom owned slaves—and butchered them with short swords. Brown and his followers then went into hiding while fighting continued between the two factions.[5]

On October 16, 1859, Brown and his guerrilla band emerged from hiding to lead a raid to capture the weapons from a U.S. arsenal at Harpers Ferry, in present-day West Virginia. Brown had been in hiding since commencing his bloody work in Kansas, but was financially supported and armed by many wealthy Northern abolitionists. On the night of October 16 he led a force of twenty-one men, including his sons and many Bloody Kansas veterans, into Harpers Ferry. The raiders first took Colonel Lewis Washington, the president's great-grandnephew, hostage.

Two unidentified Border Ruffians with swords. Albumen print by "Blackall," a photographer in Clinton, Iowa, of "two pro-slavery activists who crossed over into Kansas Territory between 1854 and 1860." PRINTS AND PHOTOGRAPHS DIVISION, LIBRARY OF CONGRESS

They then fell on the town, successfully disabling the telegraph that could have alerted Federal forces some sixty miles away in Washington, DC. The raiders hoped to instigate a massive slave uprising in Virginia; ironically, though, the first person killed was a free black man, a railroad baggage handler who confronted them. Brown had hoped to capture thousands of weapons with ammunition, then push south through Virginia to arm the slaves. But because of his insistence on secrecy, the word had never reached the enslaved. The gunshots did alert the people of Harpers Ferry, however, who fought back and turned out under arms. As local militia companies and civilians surrounded them, on the morning of October 17 Brown and his raiders took nine hostages and retreated to a firehouse where they holed up.

In Washington, President James Buchanan organized a response, ordering Colonel Robert E. Lee, on leave from his 2nd United States Cavalry regiment, to take command of a company of Marines to put down the insurrection. The next morning Lee sent his volunteer aide, Lieutenant J. E. B. Stuart, to demand the surrender of the force. Brown declined, and the Marines stormed the building. Using a wooden ladder as a ram, the Marines broke through the barricaded doors. The officer leading the charge recognized Brown and cut him down with his dress saber. After slashing him, he attempted to run him through, but the parade-ground sword simply bent in half. In just a few minutes the Marines freed Colonel Washington, captured the surviving raiders, and ended the event.

Brown was turned over to the Commonwealth of Virginia to stand trial. He was found guilty of treason and hanged on December 2, 1859. Academics have since argued heatedly about Brown's place in history. Some today have asked whether he was America's first "domestic terrorist." After the war the general consensus among many white historians was that he was an unhinged fanatic who helped drive the nation into a needless war. African Americans including W. E. B. Du Bois disagreed, deeming him a misguided martyr who gave his life in a poorly planned effort that was a harbinger of far bloodier events to come—events that eventually led to the liberation of millions. What is certain about the raid, however, is that it ignited Southern extremists known as "Fire-Eaters." These men became erroneously convinced that the sectional northern Republican Party was composed of supporters of Brown. The failed guerrilla raid set the tone for the election of 1860 and secession. However, Brown had started his guerrilla career along the Kansas/Missouri border—where the partisan war was ignited, far from Fort Sumter.

Missouri was a border slave state that did not join the Confederacy. Lincoln knew that keeping these border states, which also included Kentucky and Maryland, in the Union was key to winning the war. But as fighting began in the spring and summer of 1861, these areas exploded with guerrilla violence. Missouri had a mixed population that, in addition to pro-slavery Southerners, also included many recent German arrivals who would steadfastly defend their new country—the United States. Long-simmering neighborhood disputes were now used as justification for fighting. Unionists established their own militia called the "Home Guard." The "Dutch," or Home Guard of St. Louis, particularly enraged native-born Southerners.[6]

By the end of June pro-Union guerrilla bands in Kansas, known as jayhawkers, took the opportunity to seek retribution on their Border Ruffian neighbors in Missouri. "They have a grudge against Missouri and the South that they will never forget it until it is wiped out with blood," one Kansan opined of the jayhawkers. As they moved through, no Southern men were safe, and neither was their property. What the jayhawkers could not steal, they destroyed, and they took considerable delight in liberating slaves. Here and elsewhere in the Civil War, many men did not volunteer to join a national army and fight grand battles. Their fights would not be at Shiloh, Gettysburg, or Vicksburg. Instead they would fight on the home front, forming largely unsanctioned home guard units to defend their neighborhoods against the other side. As had been true during prior conflicts in American history, the best way to defend one's own way of life was to attack and destroy the homes and property of one's enemies. Prominent Kansas abolitionist James Montgomery, who raised his own jayhawker raiding band, viewed the issue in very simple terms. "They have called me to lead them," he announced, "and I promised ... to keep them [the Rebels] from our doors, by giving them something to do at home." Keeping his word, his guerrillas swept into Missouri, destroying homesteads and freeing slaves in the process.[7]

James Henry Lane (1814–1866), politician and leader of the Free State Party of Kansas. Portrait of the most zealous of Kansas jayhawkers, Senator and Union General James Henry Lane, by famed Civil War-era photographer Mathew Brady. PRINTS AND PHOTOGRAPHS DIVISION, LIBRARY OF CONGRESS

Perhaps the most infamous jayhawker was political opportunist James H. Lane, who, due to his unprincipled ways, proved to be far more of a liability than an asset to the abolitionist Free State movement. Although elected to represent Kansas in the U.S. Senate, Lane returned to Kansas in August 1861 to personally take to the field, recruiting his own brigade of jayhawkers and ravaging the Missouri countryside. As one Southern onlooker reported, "We found the country for 20 miles laid waste, the inhabitants plundered, several persons killed & the people in much alarm for their safety." Missouri erupted in violence, as the threat of Border Ruffian raids reached southern Iowa. In response the Iowans launched counter-raids into Missouri, where, short on weapons, they armed themselves with "knives, hatchets and clubs."[8]

On August 10, 1861, at Wilson's Creek near Springfield, Missouri, a combined army of more than 12,000 Confederates and Missouri State Guard troops under Brigadier General Benjamin McCulloch attacked 5,400 Union troops in a bloody encounter that forced the Federal troops from the field. The commander of U.S. forces in Missouri, General Nathaniel Lyon, lost his life. But the victorious Confederates vacillated as to their next move. Falling back to the southwestern part of the state, pro-Confederate governor Claiborne Jackson and General Sterling Price argued about what they should do. Meanwhile, news of the Wilson's Creek victory—in addition to Rebel victories in Manassas, Virginia— emboldened Southern partisans, especially in the northern part of the state. Federal troops from St. Louis attempted to maintain the railroad and lines of communication, but even though more Union troops under Federal control arrived in the state, the situation failed to improve. Now even men in officially recognized regiments were being accused of serious crimes including murder, theft, and destruction of property. While observing the army one Northern correspondent noted, "The Missourians believe very generally that we came here to steal their niggers, hang the men and ravish the women." However, these reports were made during the first months of the war, during which time Northern volunteer soldiers also had little in the way of discipline.[9]

In July 1861 Union Brigadier General John Pope took command of much of Missouri. An 1842 graduate of the U.S. Military Academy at West Point, Pope had been promoted several times during the Mexican-American War. However, he had soon fallen out with his commander, Major General John C. Frémont, and established a reputation as a braggart. Pope found complete anarchy in northern Missouri. He originally thought a quick campaign would bring the guerrilla war to an end, but the situation proved to be much more challenging than anticipated. "It was impossible," Pope wrote, "for any man living in the country, away from considerable towns, to avoid taking up arms against somebody." He quickly discovered this was not a war fought between armies, but between neighbors. He wrote, a "war was precipitated on the people of Missouri by their own leaders; not war in the open field and by armies duly marshaled for battle, but war by one neighbor against another."[10]

Keeping the North Missouri Railroad safe from destruction became Pope's first priority. Having quickly grown frustrated with the lawless interior, he became the first Union commander in the war to take up the tactic of reprisals and mass punishment of civilians. On July 21 he warned the civilians of northern Missouri that he was holding them responsible for the safety of the railroad, "and it is my purpose to give them strong inducements to do so." He complained that when the line had been damaged it was impossible for Federal authorities to learn the names of the culprits, "although they were well known to everybody in the neighborhood." So in the future, he warned, "I therefore notify the inhabitants of towns, villages, and stations along the life of the road that they will be held accountable for the destruction of any bridges, culverts, or portions of the railroad track within 5 miles of each side of them." The nearest community would be held financially responsible, "and a levy of money or property sufficient to cover the whole damage done will be at once made and collected."[11]

On August 16 guerrillas fired on a train carrying Union recruits heading west from the Marion County town of Palmyra. One volunteer was reported killed and another wounded. This occurred in northeastern Missouri, an area thought to be infested with Confederate sympathizers. Pope responded by proclaiming, "it is my purpose immediately to inflict such punishment as will be remembered" on the community. The next day, he dispatched troops to the area with an ultimatum for local residents: They had six days to turn in the gunmen who had fired on the train. If they refused, a brigade of troops would enter the county and "contributions" would be "levied to the amount of $10,000 on Marion County and $5,000 on the city of Palmyra." When no men were turned over, Federal troops arrived and began confiscating property. One officer even went so far as to take a prominent civilian Southern sympathizer and order that he be tied to the top of a railroad engine as it was heading out. The populace did not take these actions lightly and complained to elected officials and military commanders about having their property stolen and homes searched. Perhaps realizing that Missouri was indeed still part of the Union—and that such actions would never be supported by a civilian court, much less the Lincoln administration—Major General Frémont ordered an end to the reparations.[12]

John C. Frémont was an interesting choice for command of the Department of the West. A former filibuster who had played a prominent role in California's Bear Flag Rebellion during the Mexican-American War, he probably had as much experience with guerrilla warfare as anyone in the army. Acting on instructions from President James K. Polk (instructions that remain unknown to historians), in May 1845 Frémont raised a heavily armed, sixty-two-man filibuster force in St. Louis and set out for California. There he led a band of volunteers that claimed the abandoned presidio at Sonoma, where they briefly raised the Bear Flag and proclaimed independence on July 4. The Bear Flag Republic was very short-lived; American warships arrived in Monterey three days later, and California was annexed into the United States. A great explorer of the West, abolitionist, and in 1856 first Republican Party candidate for president, by the beginning of the Civil War Frémont was a household name in the United States.

The guerrilla uprising in Missouri convinced General Frémont that it was time to use the hard hand of war against the pro-Southern population. Without consulting the Lincoln administration, on August 30 he issued a proclamation of questionable legality to the citizens of the state, which in time cost him his command. First Frémont proclaimed martial law throughout Missouri, arguing that it was essential to "repress the daily increasing crimes and outrages" that were being committed by "bands of murderers and marauders." Anyone found under arms, he continued, would be given a military court-martial and, if found guilty, would be put to death. Persons caught destroying telegraph lines, bridges, or rail lines would "suffer the extreme penalty of the law." Pro-Southern civilians who supported the guerrillas would have their personal property seized, including slaves. In fact, Frémont proclaimed, all slaves being held by pro-Southerners in the state would be set free. The order was intended to put down the guerrilla war being waged in the north of the state. But the caveat including emancipation was far more than the administration could support. Lincoln's goal in the first year of the war was to maintain as much of the Union together as possible, and he had gone out of his way to convince the border slaveholding states of these intentions. Frémont's proclamation was precisely the kind of provocation that might send essential states like Kentucky, Maryland, and Missouri into the hands of the waiting Confederacy.[13]

Lincoln intervened immediately. First he ordered Frémont to modify the order, removing emancipation and forbidding his forces from executing any civilians without presidential authority. He believed the Confederates would respond in kind and such actions would continue, "and so, man for man indefinitely." The president was correct: The Rebels were outraged. Confederate Brigadier General M. Jefferson Thompson promised to "hang, draw, and quarter" Union prisoners or their civilian supporters for every Southerner Frémont killed. He swore that he would "make all tories that come within my reach rue the day that a different policy was adopted by their leader. . . . I will retaliate tenfold, so help me God!" Lincoln was incensed. He sent a commission to investigate Frémont's command, and they returned with a biting report. The commission found the department in a complete shambles, operating under a conceited and incompetent commander. One member even declared that Frémont was nothing but a "nincompoop." But as much as he wanted to cashier him, Lincoln realized Frémont had powerful Republican friends and relatives; his wife, author Jessie Ann Benton Frémont, was the daughter of the late Senator Thomas Hart Benton and held considerable pull in Washington. Instead of cashiering him Lincoln transferred him east, a move that would later prove to be a disaster.[14]

Kansas and Missouri sparked the Civil War by continuing and expanding on the bloody fighting that had marked the previous decade. But contrary to what many historians have thought, this guerrilla war was not isolated to any single area. Fighting was most brutal in border regions that lacked unified civil governments. Tennessee, Kentucky, and the area that became West Virginia saw bloodshed throughout the war. Some guerrilla activities even spilled over into Ohio, Iowa, Indiana, Pennsylvania, and Illinois. In fact, on October 19, 1864, one intrepid group of Confederate raiders took over the town of St. Albans, Vermont, fifteen miles south of the Canadian border. When announcing that they were taking the town, they were greeted with laughter by some. But after the guerrillas discharged a few shots over the Yankees' heads, the latter realized the Southerners had not come in jest. The raiders then robbed the banks and attempted to set the town ablaze. The fire failed to take hold and the band was chased north to Canada, where local authorities captured them. But guerrilla fighting continued to be fiercest in border areas that were not under the firm control of either army.[15]

In Virginia during the first year of the war, many Rebels advocated launching a guerrilla campaign in Union-occupied areas. In July 1861 George Fitzhugh, a lawyer and prominent defender of slavery, called for guerrilla operations in *DeBow's Review*, the most widely read magazine in the South. At that time, most Americans believed the war would last no more than a few weeks. If it became extended and the Federals occupied the interior, Fitzhugh argued, the Confederacy's "chief reliance" should be on "irregular troops and partisan warfare." Moreover, the terrain of the South was ideally suited for guerrilla fighting. The dispersed population, ill-maintained roads, and mountainous interior would be ideal for "irregular defensive warfare." Another leading defender of slavery, sixty-seven-year-old Virginian Edmund Ruffin, believed the war had to be won using conventional forces, but that in occupied areas, "Home Guards" would be essential for keeping a lid on slave insurrections and repelling marauding Federals. Such a force would be composed of old men and boys who could not be drafted into the army. But Ruffin also advocated arming women: "I am trying to persuade all

the ladies of my acquaintance in the neighborhood to learn to shoot &
become familiar with using guns & pistols," he boasted.[16]

Early in the war the Southern states and the Confederate government accepted untold numbers of "rangers" and guerrilla companies
into their ranks. Some of these units would eventually be absorbed into
Southern armies, while others would operate for months or even years
as totally autonomous home guard units. Defining exactly which units
were composed of guerrillas and which units were composed of regularly enrolled troops who fought using guerrilla tactics has been a challenge for historians. Many famous Confederate raiders, including the
commands of Generals Nathan Bedford Forrest, John Hunt Morgan,
and Turner Ashby, were actually composed of regularly enlisted state
volunteer cavalry regiments. To one extent or another, these men joined
uniformed regiments that maintained a chain of command within
the Confederate military, wearing uniforms and recognizing rank and
authority. What set them apart, however, was their use of guerrilla
tactics. They fought as scouts and raiders, sometimes traveling miles
behind enemy lines, disrupting communications, burning bridges, and
capturing prisoners and supplies. Other units were clearly supported by
the Confederacy as classic guerrillas—that is, as self-sufficient forces
ranging far into occupied enemy lines, blending in with, and being supported by, the local population. For example, after the Union occupied
Northern Virginia, the Confederacy authorized Major John Singleton
Mosby and other rangers to operate independently. But "Mosby's
Rangers," as they were known, still maintained a chain of command,
with Mosby himself answering to General Robert E. Lee's officers. A
last group of fighters were pure guerrillas, though. They appeared in
every theater of war and in every state in the South. Some began as
militia and home guard at the call of the governor, while others were
self-constituted bands who answered to no one but themselves. This last
group cared nothing for chains of command.[17]

Many partisan units rushed to Confederate service in Virginia after
that state left the Union. Turner Ashby, a militia cavalry commander
of the "Mountain Rangers," was assigned to General Thomas Jonathan

"Stonewall" Jackson's command in Northern Virginia. In time Ashby rose to command the 7th Virginia Cavalry, a large legion of combined infantry and cavalry companies that considered itself partisan. These men may have inherited the spirit of their close former neighbor, General Daniel Morgan: Their preferred weapon was the bowie knife, not the cavalry saber. Under Stonewall Jackson, Ashby's men did their best in screening what became known as Jackson's incredible Valley Campaign of the spring of 1862. Although Jackson considered Ashby and his men undisciplined, he performed well in the first months of the war, but was killed in a skirmish near Harrisonburg, Virginia, on June 6, 1862.[18]

Most citizens of the northwestern counties of Virginia remained loyal to the Union, however, and eventually withdrew from their neighbors to form their own state. The population here had long enjoyed economic and social ties to the Midwest and Northeast, and the limited amount of arable land in the northwest had never made large-scale, slave-based agriculture tenable. Additionally, many of the hill people had long resented the planter oligarchy that dominated state politics, and when the state voted to secede, they called on their northern neighbors for assistance. They reorganized themselves, formed a pro-Union government, and in 1863 entered the Union as the state of West Virginia. However, their claims included many counties with a sizable population of Rebels, and a guerrilla war quickly broke out. Southerners rallied behind the colors of the "Moccasin Rangers," a home guard company formerly under the command of Perry Connolly (or Conley). Splitting off from a less violent faction of the band, Connolly and his sixteen-year-old girlfriend, Nancy Hart, took to settling old political scores against several counties north of Charleston.[19]

Not surprisingly, the pro-Union guerrilla unit that rose up in opposition to the Moccasin Rangers called itself the "Snake Hunters." Captain John P. Baggs recruited unit members over the summer, and while they did perform some scouting for Union troops, their primary objective was to protect their homes from the Moccasin Rangers. These Unionist guerrillas were just as comfortable in the mountains with their knives and rifles as their pro-Rebel antagonists were. In true guerrilla fashion they shunned uniforms and drill, and their profane six-foot-two captain regularly dismissed them by stating, "Put down them thar blasted old guns and d----d to you! . . . Now to your holes you ugly rats, and don't let me see you again until I want you!" The Snake Hunters may have been crude, but they proved to be very effective for the kind of fight they were engaged in.[20]

The best-known Confederate partisan leader in western Virginia was Albert G. Jenkins. His semi-autonomous Border Rangers, of the 8th Virginia Cavalry, held the same organizational state as Turner Ashby's men. Colonel Jenkins and the 8th threatened Ohio settlements across the river during the first summer of the war. Northern troops under George B. McClellan occupied the state, but found capturing the guerrillas nearly impossible.[21]

Early in the war the border areas of Kentucky and Tennessee were riven with strife, as neither the Confederacy nor the federal government was fully in charge. Kentucky remained in the Union, but thousands of its residents openly supported the Confederacy. In like fashion, although Tennessee seceded from the Union, large enclaves of Tennesseans— especially the residents of the mountainous east—refused to accept secession. In the first year of the war, a brutal form of political cleansing emerged in the eastern areas of both states. Many Tennessee Unionists fled to Kentucky, while many Blue Grass men retreated to Confederate strongholds in the Volunteer State (as Tennessee had been known since the War of 1812). Here both Union and pro-Confederate guerrilla units combed the countryside to drive out the enemy. Political enemies up to and including family members were driven from their homes, beaten, and stripped of whatever property they possessed. As was true in Kansas and Missouri, for many men here the war was not to be fought by joining a national army and marching off to a distant battlefield. The threat here was personal and local; the real fight was over their homesteads. Some local groups actually cared little about the greater political aspects of the war. Taking advantage of the lack of civil and military control, they simply plundered the countryside.[22]

Out of this chaos emerged Champ Ferguson, a guerrilla whom historian Noel C. Fisher has labeled "perhaps the most successful partisan leader in the East Tennessee war." During the Civil War Ferguson was

Champ Ferguson. Detail of CDV (from *carte-de-visites*, inexpensively-produced albumen prints popular during the Civil War). One of the most infamous guerrillas of the Civil War, Ferguson claimed to have killed more than a hundred men. He was convicted of killing fifty-three, and hanged in Nashville on October 20, 1865.

an infamous guerrilla fighter, but for unclear reasons, until recently he has been overlooked by historians of the period. Ferguson was not originally from Tennessee; he was a native of Clinton County, Kentucky, a Unionist enclave just over the state line. When the war began, one of his brothers joined the Federal army, and Champ claimed to support the Union until news of the First Battle of Manassas changed his mind. "I was a Union man in the beginning; I was a Union man, till after the battle of Bull Run," he stated. "But finding that war must decide, I allied my self with my section." Ferguson's "section" was with the slaveholders of the South. A rising farmer by the time the war erupted, he had $2,000 worth of land and several slaves, placing him as a very well-off man in his native county. Ferguson had other incentives to side with the Southerners. But after becoming a vocal supporter of the Rebels, he found his neighborhood to be a dangerous place to remain; at one point he was taken by a Unionist home guard and managed to escape to Tennessee. However, he had his problems with people in the pro-Confederate areas of the state as well. Prior to the war he had a fallout with two Tennessee brothers, Floyd and Alexander Evans, who, he claimed, had swindled him on a livestock deal. To settle matters he filed lawsuits against them and then began nighttime visits to their barn to "attach" property to take back to Kentucky. On August 12, 1858, the situation came to a head at—of all places—a Presbyterian camp meeting in Fentress County, Tennessee. During the meeting the Evans brothers and an acting constable, James Reed, accosted Ferguson with an arrest warrant. The encounter turned violent and, now being chased by a sizable crowd, Ferguson was caught and found himself in a hand-to-hand fight with the constable. He wound up killing him with a pocketknife, after which the crowd cornered him in a house and forced him to surrender. Ferguson was dodging prosecution at the time the Civil War began and was still out on bail when he joined a local guerrilla band in Tennessee and had the charges dropped. As he later recalled, "I was let out on bail, when the war broke out I was induced to join the army on the promise that all prosecution in that case would be abandoned. This is how I came to take up arms."[23]

In time Ferguson would raise his own independent company composed of men from across the area. Of seventy-three men who were riding with him in 1862 (and he rarely appeared with more than a handful), most were farmers; however, one was the Fentress County jailer, another was a slave trader, one was a teacher, and another was a student. About a third came from Ferguson's home county (Clinton County, Kentucky), and the remainder from the countryside surrounding his new home in Sparta, Tennessee. Ferguson and his followers may well have reflected a study conducted of Tennessee Union and Confederate guerrillas, which found that out of about one hundred combatants, the Rebels tended to be "farmers with substantial land holdings. Their average amount of real property was three times that of loyalists, and their personal property holdings were twice as great." Ferguson's wealth clearly placed him in this group.[24]

Facing Ferguson in Tennessee was a group of poor farmers from Fentress County, Tennessee, led by "Tinker Dave" Beaty. According to tradition there were so many members of the Beaty clan in the area that Dave received the nickname "Tinker" to differentiate him from another Dave Beaty, a drinker known as "Cooly Dave." Tinker Dave and Champ had known each other for perhaps twenty years prior to the war and had no previous animosities. The cause of their wartime feud may have been no more complex than the fact that Champ was a Confederate supporter and Beaty and his boys were Republicans. Beaty and his Independent Scouts operated much like Ferguson and his band did. Until the last months of the war, neither unit was officially mustered into the forces of the Union or the Confederacy. They did not respond to any chain of command, and neither did they receive rations, uniforms, or pay. But both did claim official sanction for their bushwhacking. "We were told," noted Tinker Dave, "we were doing more good the way we were doing [it]." Of the sixty men who rode with Tinker Dave during the war, almost all of them were his Fentress County relatives and neighbors. Most were small-scale highland farmers, but their ranks also included a saloon keeper, a cooper, a blacksmith, and at least one man who was registered on the muster rolls as a "quack doctor." Many of the men in the ranks of both forces were deserters and draft dodgers. Six or more of Beaty's men had deserted from the Confederate army. Their motives remain elusive; they may have been forced into the Rebel army by the 1862 draft, or perhaps, learning of the unrest on their own home front, deserted to defend their families from the likes of Ferguson. Much like the Snake Hunters and Moccasin Rangers of western Virginia and the jayhawks and Border Ruffians of Kansas and Missouri, Ferguson's and Tinker Dave's men remained on the home front during the war, hunting each other.[25]

The idea of joining guerrilla units rather than field armies was attractive to men on both sides for a variety of reasons. In addition to their belief in the myth of the frontier riflemen, independent service held many attractions. As time wore on, the reality of war set in. For example, potential soldiers learned that exposure to camp life and disease posed a far greater threat to one's health than enemy bullets, and with that knowledge the option of avoiding the draft by signing on to a guerrilla unit gained traction. Guerrilla units fought the war on their own terms, with many men coming and going as they pleased. When they did fight, they had the option of laying in ambush, making a raid, or, if overwhelmed, simply disappearing into the population as they saw fit. Guerrillas shunned military discipline, drill, guard duty, and routine. One Arkansan pointed out that the partisans he served with "preferred the free but more hazardous life of an independent soldier or scout, to the more irksome duties of the regularly organized forces of the Confederate Army." Other incentives included the opportunities for plunder. In fact, plunder was the main motivation for most of Champ Ferguson's independent raids. While he gained nationwide notoriety in the press for murdering unarmed civilian or military prisoners (some even sick and bedridden when he murdered them), those instances occurred when he stumbled across them on pillaging expeditions.[26]

By early 1862 Confederate authorities knew they needed to rein in the guerrillas. Partisan bands were sapping critical manpower by draining it from the armies in the field. Too many were becoming freebooters, preying on friend and foe alike. In addition, the men who comprised the Confederate high command were primarily graduates of the U.S. Military Academy at West Point and fundamentally believed, like Washington did during the Revolution, that the only way to win the war and earn foreign respect was through victory with a regular standing army. Confederate president Jefferson Davis and General Robert E. Lee were both academy graduates with experience dealing with irregulars in the Mexican-American War. Many Confederate officers had fought Natives in Texas and Seminoles in Florida, both of whom regularly used guerrilla tactics. Davis and Lee both believed unconventional warfare was the last resort of uncivilized societies and recognized the ranger-rifleman myth for what it was. Men like Francis Marion were helpful auxiliaries, but historically wars were ultimately won by standing armies.[27]

The Confederate Congress attempted to rein in and organize growing partisan bands by passing the Partisan Ranger Act on April 21, 1862. On the one hand, it encouraged the enlistment of partisan units; on the other, it attempted to limit their numbers by bringing them under Confederate control. The act authorized the president to commission and organize partisan rangers with the same pay and services as the army. However, the act was also intended to limit and control the guerrillas by bringing them under the Confederate command. The law created confusion as well. It was enacted at the same time that thousands of soldiers were seeing their one-year enlistments end, but instead of being permitted to go home, Congress passed a conscription law forcing them to remain under arms. Many units applied to be reenlisted as rangers, but the law forbade that. To make matters worse, newly conscripted civilians now believed they could join a local ranger company and avoid the draft. The problem became so acute that Congress passed an amendment to the law in July, barring draftees from service in the rangers. However, once the law was established, it was ignored by many. Most freebooting bands operated out of reach of any military or civil authority and charted their own course until the end of the war.[28]

CHAPTER SEVEN

"I ain't killed but thirty-two men since this war commenced"

Champ Ferguson

THROUGH 1861 AND 1862, CONDITIONS CONTINUED TO DETERIORATE IN Missouri. After Major General John C. Frémont was transferred east, Major General Henry Wager Halleck was given command of the newly reorganized Department of Missouri. "Old Brains," as he was known in the regular army, was a Military Academy graduate who had published numerous manuals and articles for the army and was considered one of the finest intellectuals in the service. He was also slow to act and exceedingly sensitive to criticism. When he took command of the department, the Union victory in Missouri seemed assured; most of the conventional Confederate forces in the far southwest of the state were melting away. However, guerrilla raids by both sides intensified during this period, which saw one of the most brutal guerrilla raids of the entire war.

The escalation of retaliatory actions was sparked by the "Great Jayhawking Expedition," as it came to be known, which was led by one of the most famously violent Kansas abolitionists, Charles Jennison. The jayhawks entered Missouri from Kansas City in November 1861. Jennison's force included a company of cavalry commanded by John Brown Jr., a son of the martyred guerrilla. Captain Brown's jayhawk company of the 7th Kansas Cavalry included several black men, a sight that surely horrified Missouri rebels. Their mission was to punish the Southerners, "stir up an insurrection" within the slave community, and essentially rob, pillage, and burn. The jayhawkers differentiated little between Unionists and Southerners; they even threatened areas on the Iowa border. Their indiscriminate marauding likely drove many men who were trying to avoid the war to take up arms with Confederate guerrillas. After receiving a cascade of complaints from Unionists and Iowans on the fence alike, in mid-January 1862 Major General Halleck finally ordered the jayhawkers back to Kansas.[1]

The escalating guerrilla war called for desperate measures to be taken. Halleck had clearly learned a lesson from observing Frémont's excesses and asked the administration for permission to establish martial law as "the mass of the people here are against us." On December 26, 1861, he issued General Order No. 34, instituting martial law with a focus on controlling openly hostile populations along railroad lines. He also declared that guerrillas who were captured and found to be "not commissioned or enlisted" in recognized units would be tried as criminals and executed if necessary. But as attacks on rail lines continued unabated, Halleck dispensed with all formalities and simply proclaimed, "these men are guilty of [the] highest crime in the code of war. . . . Any one caught in the act will be immediately shot."[2]

In July 1862 Lincoln promoted Old Brains Halleck to general-in-chief of all U.S. armies, a position that enabled him to move the guerrilla problem to the proverbial front burner in Washington, DC. Well versed as a legal scholar himself, he turned to Dr. Francis Lieber, one of the nation's leading experts in the field, for advice. Halleck had become familiar with the German-born legal scholar early in the war, and in August wrote to him to ask how the army should deal with insurgents. In response Lieber produced an essay titled "Guerrilla Parties Considered in Reference to the Laws and Usages of War" in which he discussed the history of guerrilla warfare in Europe and during the Napoleonic Wars. Lieber made distinctions between organized and mustered partisan units and unorganized freebooters. Bushwhackers who were captured out of uniform and found to not belong to any recognized military company, he argued, were no better than everyday killers, guilty of "homicides which every civilized nation will consider

Francis Lieber. Engraving of German-American jurist, political philosopher, and author of the Lieber Code (General Order No. 100), which codified—for the first time—the manner in which civilian populations, insurgents, and prisoners of war should be treated. MIRIAM AND IRA D. WALLACH DIVISION OF ART, NEW YORK PUBLIC LIBRARY murder." In contrast, the part-time guerrilla who occasionally left his field and plough to fight in "small bodies of country people" and then return to his farm was simply an outlaw and should be treated as such. In order to widely disseminate these fine distinctions, Halleck had fifty thousand copies of Lieber's essay circulated within the army.[3]

Halleck then called on Lieber to work with a committee of general officers to establish guidelines for how the army should deal with insurgents. The committee quickly produced a set of recommendations based almost entirely on Lieber's existing works on the topic. Commonly known as the "Lieber Code," or General Order No. 100, according to historian Clay Mountcastle, the code "eventually became one of the most noteworthy developments in American legal history." It was a watershed, the first time any nation had attempted to codify the laws of war. In the following decades many other western nations developed their own similar codes, based directly on General Order No. 100. The order protected civilians and their property, defined "combatants," and outlined the rights of prisoners of war, ultimately exerting "a profound effect on the international law of land warfare." However, given that the code was produced in direct response to the situation unfolding during the Civil War, much of the work focused specifically on codifying an anti-insurgent policy for the United States. Lieber sought to clarify as much as possible who could be defined as a legal combatant, judicially protected as a prisoner of war if captured, as opposed to who could be deemed a freebooting outlaw, liable to criminal prosecution. His guidelines are straightforward:

> *Men or squads of men, who commit hostilities, whether by fighting, or inroads for destruction or plunder, or by raids of any kind, without commission, without being part and portion of the organized hostile army, and without sharing continuously in the war, but who do so with intermitting returns to their homes and avocations, or with the occasional assumption of the semblance of peaceful pursuits, divesting themselves of the character or appearance of soldiers—such men, or squads of men, are not public enemies, and, therefore, if captured, are not entitled to the privileges of prisoners of war, but shall be treated summarily as highway robbers or pirates.*

Lieber was also a realist who understood that such distinctions were often made in the field of battle. As he had written to Halleck, "indeed, the importance of writing on this subject is much diminished by the fact that the soldier generally decides these cases for himself." Legal codes produced by academics in the safety of their offices probably exerted little influence over the actions of men in the field. "The most disciplined soldiers," Lieber continued, "will execute on the spot an armed and murderous prowler found where he could have no business as a peaceful citizen." It is unclear if the Lieber Code had much influence on Union officers during the war; it was rarely cited in wartime reports and correspondence. The code seems to have become more important later in the nineteenth century, as American expansionist efforts crossed the globe.[4]

While generals in Washington struggled to come to grips with the guerrillas, the insurgency grew with Missouri as its flash point. William C. Quantrill stands out as one of the bloodiest outlaws of the war. Before Fort Sumter he had been a wanderer from Ohio, ending up in Bleeding Kansas where at first he sided with the abolitionists. However, like Champ Ferguson—a Unionist before the war—Quantrill also changed allegiance to the slaveholders' cause. With a pre-war habit of rustling cattle and stealing slaves, Quantrill had long been a ne'er-do-well. He had originally joined the Confederate army in Missouri, but when Sterling Price's forces retreated to Arkansas, like many others he returned home. Quantrill then joined a home guard militia unit in Jackson County, on the Kansas border, whose members vowed to protect their neighbors from raiding jayhawkers. However, in a short time the band grew into a notorious "gang of robbers" and thieves. Like the pro-Southern guerrillas in Tennessee, Quantrill's followers came from thriving yeoman farms where the majority owned slaves. With the departure of the Confederate army from Missouri and in the absence of any reliable civil authority, the men banded together for mutual defense against the raiding jayhawkers. But many of them were simply freebooting cutthroats in search of adventure, plunder, and the opportunity to kill without either authority or consequences. While some of the guerrillas certainly joined the band in order to protect their homesteads, Quantrill also attracted vicious killers—including his second-in-command, George Todd, well known for being "callously brutal."[5]

The war on the Kansas/Missouri frontier became one of bloody reprisal after bloody reprisal. The greatest cycle of violence came in retaliation for a September 1, 1861, raid on Osceola, Missouri, by jayhawks under Senator James H. Lane. The town was plundered and nine of its residents were executed following a drumhead court-martial. Exacerbating the situation, in April 1863 Union general Thomas Ewing Jr.—politician, brother-in-law to William T. Sherman, and thirty-four-year-old commander of the District of the Border, which included Kansas City and neighboring Missouri counties—began arresting family members of western Missouri guerrillas. Troops scoured the countryside for their mothers, wives, and sisters, then transported and packed them into makeshift jails in Kansas City. On August 13, 1863, one of the prison buildings collapsed, resulting in the deaths of five women and injuries to several others. Among the dead were several close relatives of Quantrill's men, including Josephine Anderson, the fifteen-year-old sister of William Anderson. Their sister Jenny survived but was crippled. When news of the collapse reached Quantrill's band, they went wild. Unfounded rumors circulated that the building had been purposely undermined by the Federals so it would collapse. Quantrill's guerrillas had already been set to launch a raid on Kansas and now needed no more coaxing. Anderson in particular became a veritable terror: The death of one sister and permanent crippling of another unleashed a rabid fury in him, and he would eventually become known as "Bloody Bill" for his habit of placing the scalps of the men he had killed on his saddle and bridle. The revenge undertaken by Quantrill's men would rank as the worst atrocity of the war by far.[6]

Quantrill's men selected Lawrence, Kansas, as the target of their retribution. With two thousand inhabitants, Lawrence was both the former home of the Free State movement during the pre-war guerrilla bloodbath and the current home of ruthless jayhawker Jim Lane. On August 19, 1863, Quantrill and a force of 450 men headed into Kansas. The trip took two days. Along the way they picked up local farmers to use as guides; if they recognized them as Union men, they killed them. At dawn on August 21, 1863, the raiders galloped into Lawrence, taking the town completely by surprise. The guerrillas knew both the

The destruction of the city of Lawrence, Kansas, and the massacre of its inhabitants by the Rebel guerrillas, August 21, 1863. From September 1863, a *Harper's Weekly* illustration of one of the worst war crimes committed during the Civil War—the massacre of approximately 200 men and boys of Lawrence, Kansas by pro-slavery guerrillas under William Quantrill. PRINTS AND PHOTOGRAPHS DIVISION, LIBRARY OF CONGRESS

settlement and their enemies well. They took special delight in overrunning a recruiting depot for African American troops; here they shot seventeen enlistees, killing some while they were still in their blankets. Senator Lane heard the commotion in town and ran for the cover of a cornfield dressed in his nightshirt. The raiders narrowly missed him, but did pillage and burn his house—taking the general headquarters flag and gold sword from it. They then proceeded to break into every single home and business in Lawrence, looting everything that could be carried off. Many of the men headed directly to the saloons, their planned rampage rendered worse by drunkenness. Having already overrun the recruiting depot, Quantrill's men then turned on the remainder of the male population. Any man or boy large enough to hold a gun was murdered in cold blood. Women and younger children watched in horror as husbands, fathers, and brothers were cut down in front of them. Those who attempted to hide inside buildings soon succumbed to flames and smoke inhalation as the force torched the town, leaving 185 buildings in ashes. Ultimately, as many as two hundred men and boys were murdered in Lawrence. According to historian Richard S. Brownlee, "eighty widows and 250 orphans were left crying in the dusty streets. Hated Lawrence was almost wiped from the map."[7]

General Ewing's response to the raid nearly matched Quantrill's in its brutality. Three days prior he had issued General Order No. 10, which ordered Rebel families from western Missouri to be removed to Arkansas. "While the families are here," he explained to his father, "the men will prowl about & the country is so well adapted by nature for bushwhackers that it is next to impossible to kill the scoundrels." On August 25, after the Lawrence Massacre, Ewing issued General Order No. 11, which called for the expulsion of almost all the inhabitants of the four Missouri counties bordering Kansas. The order was enforced by Kansas jayhawkers who, leaving destruction in their wake, spread across the countryside like locusts. According to historian Albert Castel, "Order No. 11 was the most drastic and repressive military measure directed against civilians by the Union Army during the Civil War. In fact, with the exception of the hysteria-motivated herding of Japanese-Americans into concentration camps during World War II, it stands as the harshest treatment ever imposed on United States citizens under the plea of military necessity in our nation's history."[8]

Celebrated Missouri artist George Caleb Bingham was a true Unionist who had served in the army, but he was appalled by the order. Bingham met with Ewing in his Kansas City headquarters and, following a heated exchange, demanded that the general rescind it. Ewing refused. "If you persist in executing that order," Bingham replied, "I will make you infamous with pen and brush as far as I am able." He lived up to his word. After the war Bingham painted *General Order No. 11*, which fictitiously places General Ewing on horseback with loot draped across his saddle at the head of a column of Red Legs (the most notorious of all the jayhawkers) in the act of murder and pillage. The lifeless body of an unarmed man lies at the feet of Ewing's horse as a woman mourns over him. The scene focuses on an elderly gray-haired man surrendering to the jayhawkers while a woman embraces him and one of the Red Legs reaches for the revolver at his waist. In the background, other Red Legs are seen looting and setting fire to a house; columns of smoke puncture the horizon, showing the same story unfolding over and over again as far as the eye can see. A procession of refugees, packing all they can carry on carts and wagons, march off the canvas to an unknown future; several are seen turning their faces away from the carnage. In the foreground an African American father does the same as he leads his son away from the bloodshed. The painting caused a sensation, but did little to slow Ewing's rising political career. Few people noted that Ewing did permit some Unionists to remain near military outposts and within a few months allowed loyal Unionists back into the area. When another district commander took Ewing's place, all former residents of the area were allowed to return to the ashes of their farms.[9]

Predictably, General Order No. 11 may have actually backfired on Ewing. Rather than driving the guerrillas and their families out of the area, the order created a no man's land where Quantrill's men found forage, untouched smokehouses, and miles of open land to live off of. Unsurprisingly, the area descended into total anarchy. By 1864 one resident complained, "Our country is desolate, indeed almost entirely a wilderness. Our farms are all burned up, fences gone, crops destroyed, and no one escapes the ravages of one party or the other."[10]

Quantrill's men decided to spend the next winter in the warmer climate of Texas. On October 6, 1863, while riding south, Quantrill and about four hundred men inadvertently encountered a Union column escorting Major General James Blunt—a close ally of Senator Lane—near Baxter Springs, Kansas. The outcome was predictable. Quantrill's men, who were wearing Yankee uniforms, were able to bluff their way fatally close to the Federal column. The general managed to escape, but his escort did not. Of the hundred men with him, ninety were killed. Many had been members of Blunt's military band; several were incinerated with their wagon train. When Quantrill's guerrillas arrived in Texas, the Confederate commander, General Henry McCulloch, welcomed them but distanced himself from their actions, stating that "certainly we cannot, as a Christian people, sanction a savage, inhuman warfare, in which men are shot down like dogs." With no immediate goal in sight, in North Texas the guerrillas spent most of their time drinking, terrorizing the citizens, and fighting among themselves. Ultimately Bloody Bill Anderson and many other men broke away from Quantrill.[11]

Bloody Bill was driven by a single motive: "revenge and revenge alone permeated and took possession of every fiber" in his body. In the fall of 1864 he and his band, including the brothers Frank and Jesse James, tagged along with Confederate general Sterling Price in a forlorn invasion of Missouri. With around eighty men, on September 27 Anderson's gang took the tiny town of Centralia, where they stopped a train as it arrived at the depot and robbed its passengers. Finding about a dozen unarmed soldiers on board, they ordered them off, stripped them of their uniforms, and murdered them. After leaving town the guerrillas realized they were being followed by a cavalry detachment of about 115 Union troopers. Reinforced with other Rebels, about four hundred men under Anderson set an ambush for the riders. The unlucky Federals were cut down almost to the man. Many were butchered as they attempted to surrender and several were scalped as well. Their bodies were found mutilated in the most grotesque fashion. Frank James later claimed that the cavalrymen were riding under a black flag, meaning no quarter would be given. He asserted they would have killed every one of Quantrill's men had they had the chance. "What is war for," James asked, "if it isn't to kill people for a principle?" But Bloody Bill's days were numbered. As Price's army limped back to Arkansas, a Missouri militia unit caught the guerrillas in an ambush and Anderson was gunned down. His body was then put on display and photographed. With Anderson's death, the guerrilla war in Missouri began to subside.[12]

While Confederate guerrillas attract much attention on the part of historians, there were also many Union men in the South who refused to accept the dominance of the slaveholding planter elite. The Virginia mountain counties that eventually became West Virginia are notable for such actions, as is Floyd County in southwestern Virginia, a haven for deserters and draft dodgers known as "Sisson's Kingdom." In Virginia, many Confederate deserters banded together to form a secret organization called "Heroes of America"; by the end of the war these

Body of William "Bloody Bill" Anderson, several hours after his death. Bloody Bill and his men were responsible for the Centralia Massacre, one of the most infamous guerrilla actions of the Civil War. Dr. Richard B. Kice of Richmond, Missouri, took this photograph several hours after he was killed in an ambush near Albany, Missouri. According to the website of the Trans-Mississippi Photo Archive, "after his death . . . His body was placed on public exhibition in Richmond. He was decapitated, with his head placed on top of a telegraph pole, and his body was dragged through the streets before being buried in an unmarked grave." IMAGE COURTESY WILSON'S CREEK NATIONAL BATTLEFIELD men were openly defiant of Confederate authorities. In the hill country of Texas, German settlers refused to support the Confederacy, and in Jones County, Mississippi, a local insurrection was driven by an alliance between impoverished whites and escaped slaves.[13]

The area of the Leaf River where Jones and Covington Counties converge became the Free State of Jones. In the spring of 1864, pro-Unionist guerrillas led by Newton Knight toppled the Confederate government and raised the Union flag over the courthouse in Ellisville. Many of these men, including Knight himself, had begun deserting the Confederate army after its 1862 defeat in Corinth, Mississippi; others had joined the countless Rebel soldiers who deserted after the fall of Vicksburg in 1863. For most of them, the Civil War was never their war. The guerrillas who comprised Knight's company were farmers from the piney woods. Of ninety-five men in the company, almost all owned land but only eleven owned slaves or lived with family members who did. Knight, who had deserted from the 7th Battalion of Mississippi Infantry following the Corinth defeat, had become disillusioned with the Confederacy—as had many others—after the Confederate Congress passed the "Twenty Negro Law." The law exempted those who owned or supervised twenty or more slaves from service, rendering the conflict, as many Southerners saw it, a "rich man's war and a poor man's fight."[14]

The Confederacy responded to the increasing number of deserters by sending a regiment of men under the command of Major Amos McLemore to hunt them down. The regiment had rounded up more than one hundred deserters in Jones County when McLemore was assassinated, most likely by Knight himself. Deserters from the adjoining counties then formed themselves into a company, elected Knight as their captain, and promised to support the federal government by defying tax collectors. As Confederate lieutenant general Leonidas Polk reported to Jefferson Davis, by March 1864 the area was in "open rebellion," with Knight's guerrillas "proclaiming themselves 'Southern Yankees.'" Polk then sent two regiments under Colonel Robert Lowry to put down the rebellion. The Confederates captured some of Knight's men with the assistance of tracking dogs, hanging ten. But like Francis Marion, the Swamp Fox, Knight and the majority of his company were able to disappear into the marshlands. After Lowry's raid, Knight's men reemerged to defy and skirmish with the Confederates until the end of the war. After the war Knight was vilified in Mississippi for supporting Reconstruction efforts—and for committing the far more immoral "crime" of marrying a former slave.[15]

In the borderlands of Tennessee, local guerrillas supported Rebel forces whenever they passed through the area. Champ Ferguson always claimed that he operated under orders from General John Hunt Morgan, a famous Confederate raider. However, Ferguson's company was never enlisted into any regiment that Morgan commanded. In fact, until the very end of the war, Ferguson and his men do not appear on any Confederate muster rolls or returns. But Ferguson and his men did act as guides and scouts for Morgan on three of his famous raids into Kentucky. In 1862, when Morgan's men raided Burkesville, Kentucky, Ferguson heard that one of the town's prominent citizens had offered a $100 bounty for his head. Ferguson sought the man out, and according to one witness he told him "that he understood he had offered a reward for one hundred dollars for his head, and he had bought it himself, and wanted the money." At first the man denied ever offering the bounty. Seeing that the guerrilla did not buy his story, he then offered him a hundred dollars in Confederate money. That would clearly not do, so he offered Ferguson Kentucky script or banknotes. He refused. Perhaps realizing his life was truly on the line at this point, the man offered Ferguson a hundred dollars in gold. The guerrilla had held him to his word.[16]

In the summer of 1862, Morgan's brother-in-law Basil Duke met Champ Ferguson. Duke observed that Ferguson "had a reputation of never giving quarter, and no doubt deserved it (when on his own private expeditions), although when with Morgan, he attempted no interference with prisoners." (This was a blatant lie.) Duke further described Ferguson as "a man of strong sense, although totally uneducated" and warned that "while with us" he must follow "the rules of civilized warfare, and he must not attempt to kill prisoners." "Why Colonel Duke," Ferguson replied, "I've got sense. I know it ain't looked on as right to treat reg'lar solders tuk in battle that way." However, he continued, "when I catches any of them hounds I've got good cause to kill, I'm going to kill 'em."

Duke later asked him, "How many men have you killed?" The outlaw gave a spirited reply: "I ain't killed nigh as many men as they say I have; folks has lied about me powerful. I ain't killed but thirty-two men since this war commenced." Ferguson later lived up to his promise to kill "hounds I've got good cause to kill," and while on a raid with Morgan murdered men he had long sought. Ferguson was not riding with Morgan during his famous 1863 raid into Ohio, where he and his command were captured. Even though Morgan escaped, it does not appear that Ferguson and the other guerrillas were willing to have much more to do with him. His star had faded.[17]

By the summer of 1864 Federal authorities began targeting the civilian population in the central Tennessee area around Sparta, which supported Ferguson and several other gangs. During a Union raid in July, Major Thomas H. Reeves of the 4th Tennessee (U.S.) infantry brought about one hundred men into Sparta. Ferguson had just returned from a successful raid into Unionist East Tennessee, bringing back more than one hundred captured Federal horses. Reeves decided to vent his wrath upon the civilian population, whom he considered to be "aiders and abettors of the thieving band." Upon arrival in Sparta on July 15, he declared martial law and arrested all the males in town. "For two hours the cries of women and children were intense," he reported, "for they all expected the town to be burnt up and all the citizens killed." They had reason to fear: most of the town was indeed incinerated, and the entire surrounding countryside was looted. This scenario would be repeated across the borderlands of the Confederacy, wherever Confederate guerrillas operated. In time local populations no longer saw Rebel guerrillas as protectors, but rather as instigators of Union acts of reprisal. When Confederate troops passed through Sparta a few weeks later, John Coffee Williamson of the 5th Tennessee (C.S.) Cavalry was appalled, recording in his diary that "most of Sparta had been burnt by the Yanks." However, he also knew the destruction was in retaliation for harboring Ferguson: "Champ Ferguson had operated in this vicinity," he added. "All are Southern but opposed to Champ."[18]

Ferguson found central Tennessee to no longer be a safe refuge. Union patrols were putting his men to death whenever they were caught, and as one Southerner observed, "it got so hot thereabout, the Federals were swarming so in Tennessee (like bees) that [Ferguson and his men] concluded the better part of valor was to get away." Ferguson and part of his band found refuge in General John S. Williams's depleted cavalry division. "Cerro Gordo" Williams, as he was known from the Mexican-American War, was then called to far southwest Virginia to help General John C. Breckinridge defend the essential Confederate saltworks from a Union raid from Kentucky.[19]

The Federal advance on Saltville was led by General Stephen G. Burbridge, who in addition to using cavalry and mounted infantry utilized parts of two new African American units, the 5th and 6th United States Colored Cavalry from Kentucky. On October 2, the Confederate defenders had assembled a hodgepodge force of 2,800 old men and boys from the local militia, in addition to a few regular troops. However, they were well placed in fieldworks, and Burbridge poorly deployed his 4,500-man force in three uncoordinated assaults on the works. When dismounted black troops advanced in front of Ferguson's section of the line, "the cry was raised that we were fighting negros," one Southerner remembered. But the real killing started after the Union forces were driven from the field. That night the Federals built large fires to fool the Confederates into believing they were going to continue the contest in the morning. In reality Burbridge's force was utterly defeated, and the survivors slipped away under the cover of darkness. The force was entirely mounted and had brought no ambulances or wagons to carry off the wounded. They left them to the mercy of the Rebels.[20]

Many Confederates awoke to the sound of gunshots in the fog the next morning. Confederate George D. Mosgrove mounted and rode forward to see if it was the start of another attack. "Presently I heard a shot," he recalled, "then another and another until the firing swelled to the volume of a skirmish line." Riding to Ferguson's section of the line, "I came upon a squad of Tennesseans, mad and excited to the highest degree. They were shooting every wounded negro they could find. Hearing firing on other parts of the field, I knew the same awful work was going on all about me." At the head of this appalling "work" was Champ Ferguson. Wounded white prisoner Harry Shocker, from the 12th Ohio Cavalry, looked on in horror as Ferguson calmly walked the field killing black and white prisoners alike. Crawling off to hide, he watched as Ferguson approached another wounded man, Crawford Henselwood, and asked him why he had come here "to fight with the damn! niggers?" He then demanded, "Where will you have it, in the back or the face?" Henselwood sat up and begged, "For God's sake don't kill me soldier!" "I heard the report of a pistol," Shocker recalled, "and saw my partner fall over and he was dead." In the end, as many as forty-six black soldiers died at Saltville.[21]

The Confederates then moved many of the wounded from both sides to nearby Emery and Henry College, which was being used as a hospital. In the days following the fighting armed men forced their way into the college and killed two blacks who had survived the first spree. Soon after, Ferguson and one of his lieutenants, William Hildreth, visited the hospital and again threatened Harry Shocker. Ferguson asked Shocker what unit he was in, and when he replied that he was from the 12th Ohio Cavalry and had been in Kentucky, Ferguson said, "I suppose you have heard of me. My name is Champ Ferguson." He then asked Shocker if he knew the whereabouts of another wounded prisoner, Lieutenant Elza C. Smith of the 13th Kentucky Cavalry. When Shocker refused to answer, Ferguson flew into a rage: "You damn yankee, you know him well enough but you don't want to know him now." As the two guerrillas headed to the door, Ferguson snarled "I have a *be*grudge against Smith. We'll find him."[22]

Elza Smith was a relative of Ferguson's late first wife. He had joined the 13th Kentucky Cavalry in Clinton County in 1863 and had been in many close scrapes with Ferguson's men. But on this day, Ferguson's motivation was a comrade's death: Ferguson believed Smith had murdered a close friend and fellow guerrilla, Colonel Oliver P. Hamilton, after he had been taken prisoner. According to Smith, Hamilton attempted to escape while being transported and was shot while running away. It is doubtful that many soldiers, Union or Confederate, believed this story; the "no quarter" rules of the fight had been well established. At the college hospital, Ferguson found Smith in an upstairs room. The wounded man looked up from his bed and asked, "Champ, is that you?" At that point Ferguson approached the bed, slapped the stock of his musket, and asked, "Smith, do you see this?" Smith attempted to lift his head and pleaded, "Champ, for God's sake don't shoot me here!" Ferguson was unmoved: He aimed the barrel of the weapon a few inches from Smith's head and pulled the trigger. It misfired. The cap failed to ignite the charge, and he had to cock and fire it three times before it finally discharged. When it did, it took off the top of Smith's skull. Standing nearby holding a carbine and pistol, Hildreth spoke up: "Champ, be sure your work is well done." Ferguson took a look, saw that "his brains were oozing out on the pillow," and concluded, "He is damned dead." The two guerrillas then went off in search of other wounded Union officers to murder. At great risk to their own safety, the Confederate hospital staff refused to relinquish them. The next day Confederate authorities shipped the survivors by rail to Lynchburg, Virginia, far from Ferguson's reach.[23]

It was one thing to wage a no-quarter guerrilla war in the areas of Tennessee and Kentucky that, through much of the war, were considerably lacking in either civil or military control. It was quite another to calmly murder unarmed enemy prisoners on the battlefield and in a hospital. Complaints about the murders rose all the way to General Robert E. Lee. Lee's aide-de-camp, Walter H. Taylor, told Breckinridge the general was "much pained to hear of the treatment the negro prisoners are reported to have received, and agrees with you in entirely condemning it." Lee was also apprised of rumors that Texas general Felix H. Robertson might have been personally involved in the massacre. But Robertson had been out of the department with General Joseph Wheeler's cavalry in Georgia. He was wounded the next month and never returned to duty. In the meantime, in the early months of 1865 General Breckinridge had Ferguson and Hildreth held for trial in Wytheville, Virginia. While investigating Ferguson, Breckinridge attempted to discover exactly who had authorized him to raise his guerrilla band. He was told that earlier in the war General Kirby Smith had authorized Ferguson to raise a company "for service on the Kentucky border." On April 5, 1865, during the Confederacy's final hours, General John Echols freed the two "in view of the long arrest to which they have been subjected and the impracticability of procuring witnesses for the trial of their cases."[24]

The guerrilla war in Virginia peaked in severity in 1864. In the first three years of the war two regularly enlisted partisan units under the respective commands of Captain John McNeill and Colonel John S. Mosby had terrorized rail lines and Federal lines of communication between Washington and what became the new state of West Virginia. These two units were now all that remained of the Confederate Partisan Ranger Act. Confederate authorities including Robert E. Lee found the system to be a failure overall and convinced the Confederate Congress to repeal the act. Guerrilla units not only drained manpower away from regular forces, but far too many men became like Ferguson—nothing more than common brigands who preyed on friend and foe alike.[25]

In August 1864, General Ulysses S. Grant dispatched a veteran anti-guerrilla cavalry fighter, Major General Philip H. Sheridan, to the Shenandoah Valley of Virginia. Earlier that year Grant had sent expeditions into "the breadbasket of the Confederacy," as the German farms were known, but had done nothing to impede guerrilla activity in the area. The months following Sheridan's arrival proved to be devastating to the civilian population of the valley. While some historians have compared the destruction of the Shenandoah with William T. Sherman's contemporaneous March to the Sea, their goals were different. Sherman focused first on the infrastructure that the Confederacy needed to survive. Homes and crops were destroyed as well in order to demoralize the South and deny much-needed supplies, but they were not the linchpin of Sherman's campaign. In contrast, Sheridan's actions echoed those taken under General Order No. 11, which had mandated the virtual destruction of four Missouri counties and the displacement of thousands of civilians. In short, Sheridan launched a scorched-earth anti-guerrilla campaign.[26]

Grant ordered Sheridan to leave the valley "a barren waste," denying the use of its food and fodder to Lee's Army of Northern Virginia. "Our cavalry are burning all the grain, every mill, and every barn," Pennsylvania trooper Henry Keiser recorded as the destruction began in early October. "The valley is ablaze in our rear." The campaign would soon become something far worse. The spark came on October 3 with the death of Lieutenant John R. Meigs—a member of Sheridan's staff and son of Montgomery Meigs, quartermaster general of the army. Meigs was killed by guerrillas outside the Shenandoah Valley town of Dayton. Enraged by the death of a friend and staff member, Sheridan commanded the 5th New York Cavalry regiment to torch every building within a three-mile radius of the attack, including Dayton. Targeting this population proved most troublesome. Most of the residents were members of German pacifist sects, including the Dunkard Brethren and Mennonites. Many of Sheridan's officers were appalled by the orders: "When I heard the work we had to do," one recalled, "I was heartsick." Although Sheridan decided to spare Dayton itself at the last minute, the entire countryside for miles around was engulfed in flames. One soldier watched from a few miles away and observed, "The sky tonight is lit up by the burning of the little town of Dayton in retaliation for the murder of Lt. Meigs." Sheridan had now turned the focus away from barns and granaries to homes and personal property, targeting the civilian population for harboring guerrillas. While Sheridan was nominally operating under Grant's orders, the destruction of Dayton "was not an integral part of Grant's directed destruction of the valley," historian Clay Mountcastle explains. "There was no strategic or operational purpose for the burning of homes and barns around Dayton. The small town provided little, if any, substance for the Rebel army. Sheridan's intent was purely retaliatory in nature; one might even say vengeful."[27]

Following another guerrilla raid the next month, Sheridan ordered the burning of the town of Newtown and all dwellings within five miles of the attack. He had just destroyed the last regular Confederate force in the valley, an army under General Jubal Early at Cedar Creek. Tellingly, he complained to Grant that "the refugees from Early's army, cavalry and infantry, are organizing guerrilla parties and are becoming very formidable and annoying me very much." He concluded, "I know of no way to exterminate them except to burn out the whole country and let the people go North or South."[28]

Sheridan's next target was Loudoun County, Virginia, long known as "Mosby's Confederacy." John Singleton Mosby had been one of the most successful Confederate partisans of the war. Operating in Northern Virginia, raiding Union supplies and lines of communication, his men had wrought havoc on the enemy throughout much of the war. They were actually sanctioned by the Confederate army and wore uniforms on their raids (albeit covered by a rain poncho or coat). Unlike Ferguson and countless other guerrillas, Mosby and his 43rd Battalion, 1st Virginia Cavalry operated within the chain of command. In March 1863 his raiders surprised a Federal camp near the Fairfax County courthouse, capturing a sizable part of the garrison—including Brigadier General Edwin H. Stoughton, whom Mosby personally rousted from his bed—without firing a single shot. The situation escalated in 1864 when General George Armstrong Custer captured six of Mosby's men and had them summarily executed. Mosby retaliated in kind: He had a group of Custer's men who had been taken prisoner draw straws, and several of them were executed in turn. Mosby did subsequently write to Sheridan, requesting that both sides honor their prisoners, but the army's "no quarter" practice when dealing with guerrillas was already well established.[29]

Toward the end of November Sheridan wrote Halleck in Washington, "I will soon commence on Loudoun County, and let them know there is a God in Israel. Mosby has annoyed me considerably, but the people are beginning to see that he does not injure me a great deal, but causes a loss to them of all that they have spent their lives in accumulating." The next day he ordered Major General Wesley Merritt and his 1st Cavalry Division to clear Fauquier and Loudoun Counties in an attempt to uproot Mosby's Confederacy. At the beginning of December Merritt's men executed the order. Merritt saw no guerrillas, but found barns and mills easy to catch. James H. Stevenson, one of his men, added that they "laid Mosby's Confederacy in ashes; carrying off every animal of any value that could be found." He estimated the total value of the property destroyed at $2.5 million (approximately $36 million in 2016). Sheridan instructed the Federal commander at Harpers Ferry that should any civilians complain about their loss to "tell them that they have furnished too many meals to guerrillas to expect much sympathy."[30]

After Appomattox, most fighting across the country ended as news spread of Lee's capitulation. Lee advised against any continuation of a partisan war against the occupying Federal forces. Union department commanders met with their Confederate counterparts first for a ceasefire, then for men to be paroled. Organized units promptly turned them-

Group portrait of Col. John Singleton Mosby (top row, second from left, standing) and some members of his Confederate battalion. One of the few guerrillas whose men operated under a government-sanctioned chain of command, Mosby's native Loudoun County, Virginia was known as "Mosby's Confederacy" during the Civil War. PRINTS AND PHOTOGRAPHS DIVISION, LIBRARY OF CONGRESS

selves in, but many guerrillas were reluctant to do so. Even Mosby's men, who seemingly fit the definition of legitimate combatants under the Lieber Code, hesitated to surrender. Instead Mosby simply disbanded the unit and told his men to go home. In Tennessee, many of the guerrilla leaders Champ Ferguson had been riding with quietly headed for Texas, perhaps fearing reprisals from their victorious Union neighbors. They packed their belongings and may have scratched "G.T.T." ("Gone to Texas") on their doors. Ferguson might have survived the war had he taken this route; he might even have gotten away with taking a parole, swearing the oath, and returning home. However, well after news of Appomattox and the end of the war had spread, he decided to just keep on fighting. After being freed by the Confederates, he returned to his old haunts in Tennessee. At the end of April 1865, Ferguson and some of his men surprised his old nemesis, "Tinker Dave" Beaty, as he was sitting down for supper at a friend's house in Jamestown, Tennessee. They took Beaty prisoner, forced him to mount up, and rode out. Beaty managed to escape, but suffered two wounds doing so. In the following days, Ferguson and a small band continued launching raids, killing several more Unionists. On May 16, 1865—having arranged for many Confederates in the area to turn themselves in—General Lovell Rousseau announced that "Champ Ferguson and his gang of cut-throats having refused to surrender are denounced as outlaws, and the military forces of this district will deal with and treat them accordingly."[31]

Instead of fighting to the end, Ferguson agreed to turn himself in without incident when troops came to his farm. His court-martial in Nashville, Tennessee, during the summer of 1865 was closely followed across the country. During the war itself, the Union had held at least 4,271 military trials of Confederate soldiers and civilians. Ferguson was far from being the only one found guilty of breaking the laws of war and executed. However, most Confederates were simply permitted to lay down their arms and go home; even Frank James, who had ridden with Quantrill, was able to take the oath. It is notable, therefore, that so many others went free while the eyes of the nation focused on Ferguson. With the war over, his trial became a major theme of national news that summer. Ferguson posed for numerous photographs and his likeness was sold throughout Nashville. A woodcut of him standing with his guards even graced the front page of the most popular paper of the time, *Harper's Weekly*. Charged with murdering fifty-three men and convicted as a "border rebel, guerilla, robber and murderer," Ferguson was hanged on October 20, 1865. Guarding the scaffold, part of the 16th United States Colored Infantry watched as justice was served.[32]

Although the Civil War was fought and won using conventional forces, the guerrilla war was far from a sideshow. Pro-Union and Confederate partisan forces engaged each other in bloody raids of retaliation across the South. In response, with Lieber's General Order No. 100 the U.S. Army adopted the first legal code of war that defined the roles of combatants, outlaws, and civilians. As the bloody consequences of irregular warfare escalated, Confederate authorities first tried to exert control over guerrilla bands with the Partisan Ranger Act, then outlawed them almost entirely when the act failed. The ugliest aspect of the war was the targeting of civilian populations during raids and reprisals. The burning of Lawrence, Kansas, and the subsequent General Order No. 11 that depopulated several Missouri counties stand out as the worst examples. Later the deliberate targeting of homes and food supplies served to demoralize and cripple Confederates, continuing the cycle of the American way of war.

CHAPTER EIGHT

"We must act with vindictive earnestness against the Sioux"

William Tecumseh Sherman

THROUGHOUT THE NINETEENTH CENTURY THE U.S. ARMY WAS forced to deal with numerous guerrilla insurgencies in the absence of any established doctrine regarding unconventional warfare. Instead soldiers fell back on well-known practices developed in the past. To combat Native uprisings, the military focused on destroying homes, villages, and, most importantly, the American bison the Plains tribes were vitally dependent on. During the Philippine-American War, veteran commanders of the Indian Wars and the Civil War would draw on earlier lessons learned in putting down guerrilla uprisings to target Filipino civilians and their villages. They even used America's first anti-guerrilla doctrine, General Order No. 100, to define the difference between outlaws and legitimate combatants. As America emerged as an ascendant world power in the early twentieth century, its armed forces would be mobilized to put down insurgencies everywhere from the Mexican border to the Caribbean and Latin America.

In the first half of the nineteenth century, many Americans hoped to create a permanent Indian reserve west of the Mississippi River. In 1830 Andrew Jackson and his supporters sponsored the Indian Removal Act, which encouraged tribes remaining east of the Mississippi to voluntarily trade or sell their property in exchange for transportation and land in the

West (what was then called Indian Territory). In order to enforce the act, American commanders fell back on anti-insurgency tactics they had developed over two centuries of frontier warfare with the Natives—tactics that punished guerrillas while breaking civilian morale to keep on fighting. Of course there was nothing voluntary about the ethnic cleansing inherent in the Indian Removal Act. Some tribes, including the Cherokee, attempted to use both public opinion and the courts in their defense; others, such as the Seminoles of Florida, elected to stand their ground and fight. Several Seminole wars occurred during the nineteenth century, with Jackson himself instigating the first one in 1817. In response to Seminole raids along the border, Jackson invaded Florida, deposed the Spanish governor, took several towns, and destroyed several Seminole villages. In the process he captured two British subjects and, following a drumhead court-martial, had them executed. This blatant act of war against both Spain and Britain set off a firestorm of protest, but the Spanish ultimately realized they had no real control over the fate of Florida. They sold it to the United States, and by 1835 fewer than five thousand Seminoles remained in the territory, in addition to their many black allies.[1]

The Second Seminole War (1835–1842) was a long and costly effort by the army to forcibly move remaining tribe members to what is now Oklahoma. Here the Native warriors developed outstanding guerrilla tactics, avoiding stand-up battles but excelling in raids and ambushes. Eight U.S. commanders attempted to round up the fighters in Florida with little initial success. In 1841 Colonel William J. Worth took command and adopted the same hard-war policies that had been successful against Natives in the past. He targeted their crops and villages in a summer campaign that destroyed their fields and homes, guaranteeing that the tribe would starve the following winter. In August 1842, with a mere two hundred famine survivors still free, Worth ended the war. His victory was almost complete, but the conflict had been incredibly costly. Perhaps as many as forty thousand Federal troops fought in Florida at some point during the conflict, and—having lost more than 1,500 comrades, mainly from disease—they universally despised their service. The last Seminole survivors rose up for a third time during the 1850s, with most ultimately removed to Oklahoma.[2]

The idea of an independent Indian territory in the West utterly failed during the nineteenth century. The wishful thinkers who proposed one underestimated the American lust for gold and land and what was perceived as the God-given right of Manifest Destiny. The fertile lands of the Willamette Valley of Oregon were first settled by Euro-Americans in the 1840s, and more settlers soon followed south into California. With the discovery of gold in the 1840s and silver in the 1850s, by the Civil War floods of settlers were arriving in these areas, spurring confrontations with western Natives. In fact, fighting in the West was well under way by the time the Civil War began. The regular army had garrisoned forts in the West prior to the war, and after the attack on Fort Sumter soldiers were withdrawn to the East and western outposts were left to local authorities. Many settlers resented the army's presence because at times soldiers were bound to protect the rights of Natives and their property.

When western defenses were left to local authorities, they often raised militia units who led bloodthirsty strikes on Natives. In Northern California, for example, the Gold Rush brought throngs of settlers to Humboldt Bay, a culturally and linguistically diverse area that was home to several Native tribes. On the eve of the Civil War, Humboldt Bay was the site of one of the worst anti-Native atrocities in the history of the West. A few residents of Eureka, the major town established on the bay, and the surrounding area formed a guerrilla unit with a single purpose: killing Indians. A number of peaceful Wiyot people lived on an island in the bay, which they considered the spiritual center of their world, and in surrounding settlements. Moving out in secret on the night of February 26, 1860, the militia attacked a settlement on the island ("Indian Island") where many Wiyot had gathered for an annual ceremony and advanced on several other Wiyot settlements in and around Humboldt Bay as well. Avoiding gunfire, which would have alerted the populace, the attackers massacred everyone within reach—the majority of whom were women and children—using mostly hatchets, axes, and knives. Casualty estimates range widely from 80 to 250 people. This would not be the end of anti-Native actions in the area: During the Civil War, after state and Federal troops had been reassigned away from nearby Fort Humboldt, the local militia again took to the field, rounding up as many Natives as they could to either be cut down or forcibly removed to reservations away from the coast.

A better-known incident was the 1864 Sand Creek Massacre, during which Colorado militia under the command of Colonel John M. Chivington also butchered a number of women and children. Chivington and his men attacked a camp of peaceful Cheyenne and Arapaho living with Chief Black Kettle, who had raised both an American flag and a white flag over his tepee. The Colorado militia killed as many as two hundred people in an act of wanton brutality, an occurrence all too common during the Civil War period.

The extirpation of Natives only escalated following the end of the Civil War. There was no permanent Indian territory to which Natives could be driven off, and with white settlement constantly pushing the frontier westward, the only alternative Euro-Americans could find was to round up Natives and force them onto reservations—usually the least desirable land in the West, totally unsuitable for the continuation of their traditional lifestyles. Western Natives were very different from the bands east of the Mississippi with whom settlers had long been in conflict. For the most part, eastern Natives were hunter-gatherer bands that also depended on semi-permanent settlements, agriculture, and, in time, perennial orchards and domesticated animals. By targeting their food, shelter, and villages, whites in the East could force Natives to stand and fight, surrender, or flee. In contrast, the Plains tribes—long a nomadic hunter-warrior culture—had adopted the horse (imported by the Spaniards in the 1500s) and evolved into one of the world's greatest horse cultures, roaming the Great Plains in search of the American bison.

The greatly reduced postwar U.S. Army found the task of rounding up nomadic bands of Indians almost impossible. Some of the most experienced guerrilla fighters of the Civil War took on this duty. As expected, many were repulsed by Native forms of warfare that included the torture and mutilation of captives. The army found itself undermanned and under siege as it attempted to guard the Bozeman Trail, which connected the goldfields of Montana to the Oregon Trail. In December 1866 a wood-cutting party of eighty men who had ventured out of Fort Phil Kearny under Captain William Fetterman came under attack by Lakota Sioux

and their Cheyenne and Arapaho allies. The Natives left eighty-one soldiers' horribly mutilated bodies strewn across an impromptu battlefield.
Department commander William T. Sherman's reaction was predictable,
given his Civil War experience with both guerrillas and civilians: "We
must act with vindictive earnestness against the Sioux," he announced,
"even to their extermination, men, women and children."[3]

Yet not all military officers entirely denounced the Natives and
their guerrilla tactics. General Philip Sheridan, one of the most brutal
anti-guerrilla fighters of the Civil War, understood the Natives' point
of view. "We took away their country and means of support, broke up
their mode of living, their habits of life, introduced disease and decay
among them, and it was for this and against this they made war," he
wrote, poignantly adding: "Could anyone expect less?" But the army
was caught in a difficult position. Settlers on the frontier demanded
immediate, even violent, action against freewheeling bands of Indians,
while humanitarians back East called for the benevolent treatment
of oppressed people. As General Sherman bluntly summarized the
situation, "There are two classes of people, one demanding the utter
extinction of the Indians, and the other full of love for their conversion
to civilization and Christianity. Unfortunately the army stands between
them and gets the cuff from both sides."[4]

With most of the postwar army on Reconstruction duty in the
occupied South, frontier commanders faced innumerable obstacles while
attempting to rein in the Natives. The western tribes were some of the
finest light cavalry fighters in history. In the absence of permanent settlements they could pack up an entire community in no time, and even
encumbered with women, children, and herds of horses, they could out-
distance any U.S. Army command. For most of the year, catching them
proved nearly impossible. The geographical logistics of the West alone
proved to be a nightmare for the army. Unlike Natives, soldiers—and
their horses and mules—required food and fodder. They had little ability
to live off the land and were dependent on supplies that usually arrived
from hundreds of miles away. Even their weapons proved ineffective.
While Natives had nothing that could effectively combat either artillery
or the newly developed Gatling gun, towing these weapons proved to

be impossible when following fast-moving Native bands. The standard-issue sidearm after the war, the 1873 breech-loading black-powder Springfield single-shot rifle and carbine, was in fact a major step back in military technology. During the Civil War, the army had adopted the Spencer seven-shot repeating rifle and carbine. In the last year of the conflict, most of the Union's cavalry had been armed with either this weapon or the privately purchased Henry repeater. In some engagements in the West after the Civil War the Natives carried superior weapons, and some were even armed with the latest Winchester repeaters.[5]

American commanders did have some advantages, though, a few of which had existed since the colonial period. For the most part Natives fought as individual warriors, whether in combat or on a raid. A chief or group might suggest a tactic on the field, but it was always up to the individual to move and react as he saw fit. The idea of a tight chain of command and European-style order and discipline was never their way. In fact, in many instances discipline was so weak that it was possible to creep up on camps and villages at night because there were no posted sentries. When waging war, American settlers usually planned, organized, and supplied large campaigns with hundreds of troops trained to answer to a single leader. Back East the Indian village was the primary target of campaigns, which habitually forced defenders to stand and fight, capitulate, or flee. With far fewer permanent villages in the West, commanders began splitting their forces and using converging columns to flush Natives from known enclaves. Natives were particularly vulnerable during the harsh winters, when they had to put up food and find forage for their horses. Led by Native scouts, converging army columns would once again force them into battle or to surrender under threat of being stripped of food or shelter or leaving their horses to succumb to starvation or exposure.[6]

In the fall of 1868 Major General Philip Sheridan fine-tuned some of the tactics he had learned and developed during the Civil War for use against the Natives. Clearly basing his plan on attacks he had conducted on Confederate guerrilla communities back East, he planned to force the Southern Cheyenne, Arapaho, Kiowa, and Comanche on to reservations by attacking their winter camps in the Texas panhandle and present-day western Oklahoma. "Little Phil," as he was known, knew the Natives' grass-fed ponies were weak and the tribes had settled into camps pre-pared with the food and shelter they needed for winter. Native guides led three separate columns that struck these camps. On November 29, 1868, Civil War guerrilla fighter Brevet Major General (now reduced to Lieutenant Colonel) George Armstrong Custer's force struck the camp of Cheyenne chief Black Kettle, who, as previously noted, had already suffered the loss of more than two hundred innocents at Sand Creek. Since the massacre, Black Kettle had been an advocate for peace with the whites. However, he did not speak for all the warriors in his camp, some of whom continued to raid and brought the wrath of the army on themselves and their compatriots. Custer's men surprised the camp along the Washita River and cut down Black Kettle and his wife—along with around one hundred other Indians—as they attempted to cross the river.[7]

While the strategy of fighting Indians in the West was clearly derived from the anti-guerrilla campaigns of the Civil War, racial ani-mosity added a brutal new element to the final extirpative campaigns that took place on the American frontier. Sherman approved of this kind of warfare and just before the campaign told his brother, "The more we can kill this year, the less will have to be killed the next war, for the more I see of these Indians the more convinced I am that they all have to be killed or maintained as a species of paupers. Their attempts at civilization are simply ridiculous." Encouraged by the success of the campaign, Sher-man wrote his officers that he found he was "well satisfied with Custer's attack. . . . I want you all to go ahead; kill and punish the hostile, rescue the captive white women and children, capture and destroy the ponies, lances, carbines &c &c of the Cheyennes, Arapahos and Kiowas." He then encouraged them to herd the remaining Natives onto reservations.[8]

The Indian Wars that took place between 1866 and 1890 provide classic—and tragic—studies in guerrilla warfare. As had been true for nearly four centuries of conflict against European settlers, Natives used the elements of stealth, surprise, and lightning raids to lure unsuspecting pursuers into bloody ambushes. They engaged in battle on their own terms, although very few fights were large enough to be considered "bat-tles" in the European sense of the term. The most infamous Native victory in American history, against famed guerrilla fighter George Armstrong

Custer, took place at Little Bighorn in June 1876. Custer's fight was part of the Great Sioux War of 1876–1877. The conflict was sparked by the discovery of gold in the Black Hills of South Dakota, sacred to the Sioux. They refused to give up their land, leading to U.S. Army attempts to force them off of it and onto reservations. Sheridan originally hoped to duplicate one of his prior successful winter campaigns, but logistical problems forced him to delay any action until the spring of 1876. Utilizing a three-pronged approach, three columns of soldiers under the respective commands of Colonel John Gibbon, General George Crook, and Custer's 7th Cavalry under General Alfred Terry advanced on the Natives from different directions. What the army was slow to come to terms with, however, was the size of the Native force it faced. Many Indians had left the reservation to join Lakota chiefs Sitting Bull and Crazy Horse, who actively opposed the reservation system. Custer and the army were totally unaware of the fact that the Natives had banded together into a massive encampment of perhaps 8,000 Sioux and Cheyenne, including as many as 1,500 to 2,000 warriors. Upon discovering the village, Custer committed a series of deadly mistakes. First, he failed to adequately reconnoiter the Natives to ascertain their precise location and the size of their force. Second, he divided his regiment into four parts. Leaving one part behind with the wagon train, he sent Captain Frederick Benteen, commanding three companies, to the south to seek out the Natives. He then sent Major Marcus Reno, also with three companies, across the Little Bighorn to attack the village that had been spotted. Custer himself kept five companies and advanced north behind the bluffs on the east side of the river. Unbeknownst to Custer, Reno's force was overwhelmed and driven back over the river. Custer rode directly into a swarm of enraged warriors and was killed along with every single man in his 210-man force. Reno and Benteen held out on a ridge until reinforcements arrived on June 27.

The Native victory was overwhelming but short-lived. Sheridan doubled down in his efforts to track down the Natives. Following a brutal winter campaign almost all of the warring bands were confined to reservations within a year, their sacred lands falling into U.S. hands. Other tribes, including the Apache and Nez Percé, would fight on, but unforgiving winter campaigns would prove effective in bringing them

Sitting Bull. Photograph of the Hunkpapa Lakota holy man (ca. 1885), by D.F. (David Francis) Barry of Bismarck, North Dakota. PRINTS AND PHOTOGRAPHS DIVISION, LIBRARY OF CONGRESS

in. Natives suffered terrible conditions on the reservations. In 1889 a new spiritual movement, the Ghost Dance movement, began spreading from tribe to tribe in the West. It prophesied that those who practiced the Ghost Dance would be reunited with the spirits of their ancestors, who would help them drive away white settlers and bring back the buffalo and their traditional lifestyles. In 1890, after the U.S. government broke a treaty with the Lakota Sioux, cut their rations, and left them at risk of starvation, the people turned to the Ghost Dance. Threatened by the movement, Bureau of Indian Affairs (BIA) agents asked that more troops be dispatched to the area. Tensions between the Lakota and the U.S. Army escalated considerably. Sitting Bull was arrested for failing to stop the Lakota from practicing the dance and was subsequently shot to death in a scuffle between his people and U.S. Department of the Interior agents. Two weeks later, a band of Lakota led by Spotted Elk was camped on Wounded Knee Creek when a far deadlier confrontation occurred. When the army—including troops from Custer's own 7th Cavalry—attempted to confiscate the band's weapons, one young deaf warrior refused. A struggle ensued, a weapon was discharged, an army officer ordered the soldiers to open fire, and the Lakota took up the confiscated arms. Far outgunned, they were cut down mercilessly. Of the 153 Native dead, the majority were women and children. The Wounded Knee Massacre, as it would come to be known, would be the Natives' last stand.[9]

As it had in the East, in the West the U.S. Army succeeded in using long-established means of fighting Natives to emerge victorious. These means included the use of Indian scouts, converging columns to prevent escape during armed confrontations, winter campaigns, and the targeting of Natives' food, shelter, and ponies. But in the nineteenth century perhaps the most important element of Native extirpation was the purposeful near extinction of the American bison. American settlement in the Great Plains, spurred on by construction of the first transcontinental railroad, brought thousands of hunters to the West—and army commanders including Sherman and Sheridan welcomed them. Destroying the vast buffalo herds became a priority. In 1869, as reported in the *Army Navy Journal*, "General Sherman remarked, in conversation the other day, that the quickest way to compel the Indians to settle down to civilized life was to send ten regiments of soldiers to the plains, with orders to shoot buffaloes until they became too scarce to support the redskins." The *Journal* advocated that the only way to end the guerrilla war with the Natives and drive them to the reservations was by destroying the basis of their nomadic culture, the buffalo. Traditionally, buffalo hides had been cured by Native women and then used or traded. In 1871, after an industrial method was discovered to tan them and use the leather for belts to drive factory machines, hunters started a gold rush on hides. Other "sportsmen" simply shot the animals down for fun. By the end of the nineteenth century only a few hundred buffalo survived of a population once estimated to be in the millions. As historian David D. Smits has observed, "Generals Sherman and Sheridan, among other high-ranking commanders of the post–Civil War frontier army, applied to the Plains Indians the lessons that they had learned in defeating the Confederate states" by targeting the Indians' "commissary on the hoof." Sitting Bull made the most poignant observation of all: "A cold wind blew across the prairie when the last buffalo fell—a death-wind for my people."[10]

Guerrilla warfare in the United States was not restricted to the West during the post–Civil War period. The war had brought an end to the Southern fight for independence, but the fighting—in particular the guerrilla war—continued during Reconstruction. Whites no longer took up arms to defeat Federal forces. Instead they fought over who would dominate their state governments: the largely Democratic white oligarchy that had controlled state legislatures in the antebellum era or the newly created Republican governments dominated by northern transplants, known as carpetbaggers, who were aided by Southern white turncoats called scalawags. Above all, many Southerners feared their former slaves, who were now armed with the vote and, empowered by Republicans, had even elected black men to public office. As was true in the West, post–Civil War guerrilla warfare in the South would also be marked by virulent racism.

Historian Mark Grimsley correctly points out that a complex but loosely organized insurgency was responsible for much of the violence in the postwar South. "The struggle was conducted in the political and economic arenas," he notes, "but it was also waged through political violence so extensive that historians have begun to view Reconstruction as a 'second civil war.'" At the conclusion of the war, President Andrew Johnson quickly welcomed the former Confederate states back into the Union, and many former Rebel officials were reelected to office. The Radical Republicans controlling Congress objected to this development and refused to seat these delegates. In time Congress wrested control of Reconstruction back from the president by passing the First Reconstruction Act, which divided ten of the former Confederate states into five military districts commanded by Union generals. These generals were charged with ensuring that voting lists did not include former Rebels and that all states approved the Thirteenth, Fourteenth, and Fifteenth Amendments to the Constitution—which extended civil and legal protections to former slaves, including the right to vote for black men—before re-admittance to the Union.[11]

A wave of violence subsequently gripped the South. In 1866 riots erupted in both Memphis and New Orleans. The Memphis violence was directed at the flood of black immigrants who had moved to the city after the war; a black neighborhood was torched, leaving forty-six dead and seventy-five injured. The New Orleans riot was a reaction to the Louisiana Constitutional Convention, which would have guaranteed civil rights for blacks. The rioters attacked black delegates on the street, then followed them into the convention hall. By the time U.S. troops broke it up, forty-eight people were dead and more than one hundred were wounded. Across the South, former Confederates organized themselves into local insurgent groups. In Tennessee, a fraternal order of former Confederates calling itself the Ku Klux Klan quickly turned violent; its methods were soon replicated across the region, with similar groups under a host of names, including the Knights of the White Camellia, employing similar tactics. The mission of these domestic terrorist organizations was not to restore the Confederacy, but rather to wrest civic control from newly established, Republican-dominated state and local governments. The means Southern whites used to regain power ranged from complete and total social ostracism of white Republicans to economic isolation, intimidation, and, finally, violence. Blacks were targeted particularly viciously. African American veterans who organized themselves into political

Visit of the Ku-Klux. Wood engraving by Frank Bellew, from the February 24, 1872 issue of *Harper's Weekly,* a trenchant—and tragic—portrayal of the fatal threats African Americans faced within ten years of the South's defeat in the Civil War.
PRINTS AND PHOTOGRAPHS DIVISION, LIBRARY OF CONGRESS

groups, such as the Union League, would be intimidated on every imaginable level. They were commonly threatened with eviction from rented or sharecropped land. When that failed, those who did not comply were left to face hooded terrorist night riders who raped, burned, tortured, and killed them.[12]

Overthrowing mixed-race Republican governments and replacing them with white Democratic ones was the chief goal of the insurgents, who worked to "redeem" Southern states from what they considered imposed and illegitimate regimes. The Klan and other terrorist groups did not operate under any kind of centralized command; the battles they chose to fight were solely about local control of civil government, with similar scenarios repeated across the region. For example, in Fentress, Tennessee, "Tinker Dave" Beaty's son, prominent Republican Claiborne

Beaty, reorganized much of his father's company to fight the Klan in neighboring Overton County. In 1870 and 1871 President Grant attempted to stem the tide of Klan violence by supporting the Enforcement Acts, which permitted the use of martial law and the suspension of habeas corpus in areas under insurrection. Grant brought in fast-moving cavalry units and used informants to infiltrate the gangs, arresting thousands and bringing many to trial in federal courts. This action and a growing distaste on the part of many Southern whites for terror-driven activities brought a period of relative peace.[13]

However, the political violence was far from over. In 1873 a rally of black Republicans in Colfax, Louisiana, turned murderous when the group was attacked by whites. As many as one hundred black men were butchered, many after surrendering. A handful of the terrorists were brought to court under the Enforcement Acts, but all were later freed by the courts. The next year terrorists in Louisiana organized themselves into "White Leagues," paramilitary organizations that openly challenged the Republican government and its mixed-race militia. That September they fought a pitched battle in the streets of New Orleans and deposed Governor William Kellogg. Federal troops intervened and restored Kellogg to office, but the "redeemers," as they called themselves, now controlled the state. Paramilitary terrorist gangs rose up throughout the South, effectively intimidating Republicans from running for office or going to the polls on election days. In Mississippi, "White Liners" drove blacks away from office and the polls; in South Carolina the "Red Shirts" did the same dirty work. These men proudly paraded through Southern cities carrying weapons and wearing the uniforms of their respective organizations, some of which even boasted cavalry units and hauled artillery. Republican governors hesitated to call on Federal officers for help or to deploy their own mixed-race militias for fear of instigating a general race war.[14]

The presidential election of 1876 proved to be a tipping point in the South, presaging the end of the embattled Reconstruction effort. Even prior to the election the Grant administration, embroiled in economic problems and corruption, had lost interest in protecting the civil rights of blacks. The outcome of the 1876 election became mired in disputes over results from Republican-controlled South Carolina, Louisiana, and Florida. In 1877 Congress established a fifteen-man commission to settle the dispute. The commission resolved that Republican Rutherford B. Hayes had defeated Democrat Samuel J. Tilden. However, in a backroom deal redolent of the worst sort of political corruption, Republicans agreed to abstain from using federal force in the South—effectively surrendering the last three states to the "redeemers." Hayes did not "withdraw" troops from the South; they simply returned to their posts and were no longer used in enforcement actions. This unofficial hands-off federal policy set the stage for an American apartheid that dominated the South for nearly a century, with the implementation of Jim Crow laws that would remain in effect until the 1960s. The terrorist insurrection had been a resounding success.

Having in essence abandoned the South to the whims of insurrectionists, it is perhaps ironic that as the United States entered the world stage at the end of the nineteenth century, American military commanders found themselves falling back on lessons learned in anti-guerrilla warfare during the Civil War. The Spanish-American War (1898–1899) was largely fought with conventional land and naval forces. However, the subsequent occupation of the Philippines led to an unintended guerrilla insurrection that was far bloodier and costlier than the war with Spain had been. As was true during the American invasion of Cuba, a well-established independence movement already existed in the Philippines. On the island of Luzon the movement was led by Emilio Aguinaldo, whose thirteen-thousand-man army initially welcomed the Americans as liberators. But the U.S. plan was to occupy the Philippines as a territory without liberating the natives. In fact, before the war's end the Americans had begun clandestine negotiations with Spanish forces holding the capital of Manila, and the Spanish agreed to offer only token resistance when U.S. forces advanced. On August 13, 1898, as Filipino and American armies advanced on Manila, the Spanish quickly turned it over to the Americans—who then turned on their Filipino allies, barring their entrance to the city. Predictably, this insult and act of betrayal incensed the Filipino fighters. When the United States and Spain failed to recognize Philippine independence in the Treaty of Paris, which ended the war, the break was complete. Fighting began on February 4, 1899, in and around Manila.

Emilio Aguinaldo, Filipino insurrectionist. Photograph of the famed guerrilla fighter published in 1919, almost twenty years after his actions during the Philippine-American War (1899–1902). PRINTS AND PHOTOGRAPHS DIVISION, LIBRARY OF CONGRESS

At first Aguinaldo and the Filipinos attempted to fight the Americans with a conventional army. They outnumbered U.S. forces by a ratio of two to one, with forty thousand troops to the Americans' twenty thousand; however, the Americans had the organization, logistics, equipment, and training needed to win. Throughout the winter Americans under the command of General Elwell S. Otis, a hardened veteran of the Civil War and Indian Wars, drove the Filipinos across most of Luzon. In May Otis's forces finally stalled; the arrival of the rainy season, combined with fatigue and the expiration of many volunteers' enlistments, brought the advance to a halt. By the fall Otis had been reinforced and was able to reassume the offensive, scattering Aguinaldo's forces and taking Luzon and many other islands as well. American forces were then tasked with winning over the hearts and minds of the Filipinos. President William McKinley wanted the army to show them "that the mission of the United States is one of benevolent assimilation, substituting the mild sway of justice and right for arbitrary [Spanish] rule." American soldiers built roads and schools, laid telephone and telegraph lines, and established public health programs that reduced infant mortality and eliminated smallpox and the plague. These efforts failed to win over the insurgents, however. At this point Aguinaldo shifted gears and called for Filipinos to adopt guerrilla tactics against the Americans—starting what historian Brian M. Linn has called "a war of attrition, of wearing down an opponent over a long period through exhaustion, disease, and steady bloodletting." The newly minted guerrillas also looked to the American Anti-Imperialist League and the Democratic Party to defeat McKinley in the election of 1900.[15]

Now scattered into the hills and isolated islands, the Filipinos turned to what Americans would become increasingly familiar with in the twentieth century as classic guerrilla insurgency. It was not centrally controlled, with each island and village often differing from the next in terms of religion or language. The insurgents rarely fought in-place battles; instead they turned to raids, ambushes, sniping, and sabotage. They terrorized natives who collaborated with the Americans and formed "shadow governments" in occupied areas. They also enlisted Filipinos to work for the Americans in order to gather intelligence. American commanders fell back on their collective Civil War and Indian Wars experience to rein in guerrillas and, as they had during the Civil War, escalated retaliatory efforts against them. Civil War veteran General Arthur MacArthur invoked General Order No. 100—better known as the Lieber Code, instituted during the Civil War—to differentiate between outlaws and recognized, uniformed fighters. Men captured in uniforms belonging to recognized units would be treated as enemy prisoners of war. In contrast, those who simply picked up weapons and made midnight raids—only to reappear as civilian farmers the next day—would be treated as outlaws. This reflected the treatment of Confederate guerrillas during the Civil War. The code also protected civilians and their property while recognizing the military necessity to violate it if needed.[16]

McKinley's administration interpreted his reelection as a mandate in support of its actions in the Philippines. MacArthur began a campaign to hunt down guerrilla leaders, whom he targeted for "neutralization." Guerrilla captains would be locked up, deported, or put to death. In addition to lessons learned in the Civil War, Americans also adopted an important lesson from the Indian Wars: the use of indigenous troops. They recruited Filipinos who had served with the Spanish army, originally known as Macabebe Scouts, as Philippine Scouts. MacArthur and the colonial government, which was headed by William Howard Taft, also supported the Filipino Federal Party, an organization that advocated a transitional process of cooperation with the Americans that would offer peace and perhaps eventual statehood. By the beginning of 1901, many guerrillas had laid down their weapons. That March the scouts led U.S. forces in the capture of Aguinaldo himself, dealing a near-fatal blow to his movement. Aguinaldo subsequently issued a statement accepting American rule and calling for his followers to lay down their arms. But the war was far from over.[17]

On September 28, 1901, bolo-wielding guerrillas on the island of Samar surprised and overran a company of seventy-eight American soldiers at Balangiga, killing forty-eight and wounding twenty-one. General Jacob H. Smith was consequently tasked with pacifying the island. "Hell Roaring Jake," as the press had dubbed him, had been wounded in the Battle of Shiloh and subsequently spent the rest of the Civil War enlisting troops in Louisville, Kentucky. He had extensive knowledge of the Union's anti-guerrilla measures against the likes of Champ Ferguson. While Smith cleared Samar, J. Franklin Bell was assigned to put down a similar rebellion on Batangas. Raised in Kentucky during the Civil War, General Bell also had ideas on how to effectively deal with guerrillas. Together they waged a bloody campaign that went far beyond what had occurred stateside during the Civil War and Indian Wars. In addition to destroying villages, crops, and domestic animals, they rounded up civilians into concentration zones. General Smith directed his subordinates to kill any male who could carry a weapon: "I want no prisoners. I wish you to kill and burn; the more you kill and burn the better you will please me." When he was asked for clarification, he stated they should kill every boy over ten. While there is little evidence that American forces targeted children, the killing and destruction were nevertheless unparalleled. In July 1902 President Theodore Roosevelt—instated the previous year following McKinley's assassination—declared that the insurrection was over.[18]

Many Americans were utterly horrified by the brutality exhibited on Samar and Batangas. The press ran sensational stories and cartoons about it, and Congress was forced to investigate the matter. Several officers were court-martialed and received mild reprimands. Smith was court-martialed and found guilty, but Roosevelt simply forced him into early retirement. Although the war was officially declared over, Muslim Moros (from the Spanish for "Moors") began fighting on Mindanao and continued to do so on and off until 1913. The guerrilla war proved to be costly for both adversaries. More than 125,000 Americans served at one time or another in the Philippines, and approximately 4,000 died (mostly from disease). Perhaps as many as 20,000 Filipino fighters were killed, and the number of civilians who died as a result of starvation, exposure, murder, and disease is estimated to be in the hundreds of thousands.[19]

Secretary of War Elihu Root, who reviewed Smith's court-martial, attempted to justify the American occupation of the Philippines by summarizing the history of American anti-guerrilla warfare. Root pointed out that Smith's call for the murder of all the men on the island was largely ignored by his subordinates and argued that his "actual conduct of military operations in Samar, were justified by the history and conditions of the warfare with the cruel and treacherous savages who inhabited the island, and their entire disregard of the laws of war," adding that Smith was "wholly within the limitations of General Order No. 100 of 1863." The secretary further asserted that Smith's actions echoed those taken by the U.S. government in 1779, when "Washington ordered Gen. Sullivan, in the campaign against the Six Nations, to seek the total destruction and devastation of their settlements. He wrote 'But you will not by any means listen to overtures of peace before the total ruin of their settlements is effected. * * * Our future security will be in their inability to injure us, the distance to which they are driven, and the terror with which the severity of the chastisement they receive will inspire them.'" Root understood America's "first way of war" very well and used it to rationalize Smith's atrocities in the Philippines.[20]

Indeed, American soldiers in the Philippines had reacted to the guerrilla insurrection in a manner now recognizable as an established pattern in American history. Veterans of the Civil War and the Indian Wars had turned to well-worn methods to put down the rebellion: targeting civilians and their property. They then turned to General Order No. 100, codified during the Civil War, to determine who should be treated as a combatant and who could be executed as a freebooter and outlaw. Alternatively, American soldiers also succeeded when using the carrot-and-stick approach: Much of the population had indeed been won over by the establishment of infrastructure and health care services on the islands.

As the United States became a growing world power, American forces found themselves called on for anti-insurgency operations across many of Spain's other former holdings. With his Corollary to the Monroe Doctrine, Roosevelt justified American intervention in Latin America and the Caribbean, maintaining that in the Western Hemisphere, the United States should conduct military interventions before European powers did. This resulted in U.S. intercession across the Americas, much of which included anti-guerrilla fighting. For instance, in 1915 and 1916 naval and Marine Corps forces engaged in anti-insurgent fighting in Haiti and the Dominican Republic, respectively. Occupations and fighting lasted for years in those countries but did little, if anything, to improve the living conditions of their impoverished inhabitants.[21]

On the home front, in the late nineteenth century the U.S. military began to move away from dependence on militia units; most were reformed into National Guard units, which are controlled by states unless called on by the president for special campaigns. The Militia Act of 1903, also known as the "Dick Act" after Congressman Charles W. Dick of Ohio, divided the militia into two groups. The trained and organized militia of each state would belong to the National Guard. The unorganized reserve militia would consist of all the able-bodied men in each state. In order to standardize units as much as possible, the federal government would provide regular army pay and training to the National Guard; when training or deployed, they would receive the same pay as federal troops. The era of loosely formed American militia units coalescing into guerrilla bands had ended.[22]

The reorganized American National Guard militia system underwent its first test during the spring of 1916, in response to a Mexican guerrilla insurgency led by Francisco "Pancho" Villa. Civil war had erupted in Mexico following the overthrow of the dictator Porfirio Díaz, pitting the forces of the first president of the new republic, Venustiano Carranza, against those of Villa and his followers. Angered by President Woodrow Wilson's support for Carranza, Villa and his supporters began killing Americans in Mexico. In an astonishingly brash move, Villa then led a guerrilla raid across the border in March 1916, killing fifteen American civilians and soldiers at Columbus, New Mexico. In response, the administration ordered Brigadier General John J. Pershing into Mexico, leading a punitive expedition of ten thousand men with the mandate to track down Villa. The troops engaged in a few skirmishes with the guerrillas, including one during which a young Second Lieutenant George Patton surprised several Villa supporters, killing them with his Colt revolver. After the expedition began skirmishing with the Mexican army, however, Wilson mobilized the entire U.S. Army and sent it to the border, in addition to deploying 112,000 National Guardsmen. The American forces then withdrew across the border. While the expedition did not catch the guerrillas, the troops did protect the border, and the military gained invaluable experience that would be essential in mobilization efforts needed for the First World War.[23]

Pancho Villa. PRINTS AND PHOTOGRAPHS DIVISION, LIBRARY OF CONGRESS

Subsequently occupied with the immense undertaking of mobilizing and fighting in World War I, the American military focused little on anti-insurgency doctrine. For the U.S. Army, the plains and well-developed roads of the western European war theater heralded a return to a conflict between states that deployed uniformed armies. The idea of fighting non-state entities fell out of favor as a topic of discussion at military academies and war colleges. Both recent experience and the long shadow of history should have proved this unwise, but professional soldiers despised fighting insurrections. From the Seminole Wars in Florida and the other Indian Wars of the nineteenth century to the Philippines and years-long occupations in Latin America, these were reviled duties, generally considered a waste of manpower. But unbeknownst to American military strategists, an even greater worldwide conflagration would soon embroil them once again in guerrilla warfare.

CHAPTER NINE

"All I want to hear are booms
from the Burma jungle"

"Vinegar Joe" Stilwell

THE SINGULAR EXPERIENCE OF WORLD WAR I REINFORCED THE CON-
ception among army officers that any future conflicts would be fought
with large, conventional standing armies. Thus, when the United States
entered World War II the military simply lacked any kind of doctrine
to wage unconventional warfare. Prior to the war military innovators
looked to incorporate technological developments including airpower,
communications, and mobile armored fighting vehicles as the army's
doctrine focused on large units. The very idea of guerrilla warfare and
unconventional operations tended to offend commanders; many of
them considered unconventional warfare uncivil, devious, and even
illegal. However, the reality of the Second World War mandated tactical diversification. Commanders began to realize that in the face of
limited resources and with vast tracts of land under enemy occupation,
the training and supplying of local resistance fighters could be a real
force multiplier. With trial and error, the mission of guerrilla warfare
would eventually be handled by a semi-autonomous agency known as
the Office of Strategic Services (OSS).[1]

By 1941, as the Axis Powers continued to threaten American interests, the void in the regular army's unconventional warfare doctrine came
to the notice of the ever-pragmatic President Franklin D. Roosevelt.

Roosevelt was convinced to act on this weakness by a World War I hero and Medal of Honor winner, William J. Donovan. Since the war "Wild Bill," as he was known, had risen as a Wall Street corporate lawyer; he was also a personal friend of FDR. Donovan had traveled overseas and observed the formation of special operations units by the British and convinced the president that the United States needed to develop similar wartime capacities. Like so many of FDR's New Deal programs, the idea of a department that handled unconventional warfare would have several incarnations and acronyms—beginning in July 1941 when FDR named Donovan to form the Office of the Coordinator of Information (COI). In June 1942 this office would be renamed the Office of Strategic Services (OSS), and although never assigned to any branch of the military, it was staffed primarily with army personnel. It would eventually serve under the Joint Chiefs of Staff, with Donovan rising to the rank of major general by war's end. However, the OSS would find itself caught between the rival services of the army, navy, and civilian FBI in its mission of waging unconventional warfare and gathering intelligence. (The unit was disbanded after the war, but its core need remained; it was replaced by the CIA in 1947.)[2]

Motivated, energetic, and driven, Donovan envisioned the mission of the unit to include intelligence gathering, black propaganda (or psychological operations, "PSYOPS"), support and aid to resistance groups in occupied areas, and the use of specially trained commando units—based on the British model—that could take the lead in training guerrillas in intelligence gathering, subversion, and sabotage. By May 1943 Donovan had separated the duties of the unit into several branches, with guerrilla warfare falling under the Operational Group Command (OG). Prior to the United States entering the war he had observed the British Special Operations Executive (SOE) in Europe and as early as October 1941 had called for the creation of a separate "guerrilla corps, independent and separate from the Army and Navy." Many officers in the army refused to accept his ideas; in fact, internal resistance was so great that the U.S. army deputy chief of staff for intelligence (or G-2), General George V. Strong, deemed Donovan's proposals to be "essentially unsound and unproductive." Unconventional warfare missions, Strong believed, should

William Joseph Donovan. Dating to July 1929, this photograph far predates Donovan's career as the "father of American intelligence"; however, at this juncture he had already been awarded the Medal of Honor for service in France during World War I, and served as U.S. Attorney for the Western District of New York. PRINTS AND PHOTOGRAPHS DIVISION, LIBRARY OF CONGRESS be carried out by regular forces. Thus, he argued, "to squander time, men, equipment and tonnage on special guerrilla organizations and at the same time to complicate the command and supply systems of the Army by such projects would be culpable mismanagement." Despite FDR's endorsement, Donovan's ideas enjoyed little support from the service branches themselves. Later, when the OSS became an independent command under the Joint Chiefs of Staff, the president would convince the armed services to grant the OSS a meager allotment of support.[3]

When the United States entered the conflict, the Allies were focused on the war in Europe and the Mediterranean. Given these areas' broad plains and well-developed road networks, it was clear that the outcome of the war would depend on conventional forces. However, with so much land under Axis occupation, Great Britain took the lead in establishing special operations forces to support local resistance movements. Prime Minister Winston Churchill strongly supported the concept of British special operations across the globe: The British established their own commando units in Europe and North Africa and created the Chindits (a mixed force of British and Burmese troops) in the China-Burma-India Theater (CBI).[4]

In North Africa, American guerrillas in the OSS had some success organizing tribes into resistance movements, and by the time Allied forces had advanced up the Italian peninsula, OSS operatives were able to organize anti-German partisans. In the summer and fall of 1944, as Germans retreated to the Gothic Line, American OSS units dropped in and brought supplies and support to the growing Italian anti-Nazi guerrilla movement. In the winter of 1944–1945, as the weather prohibited resupply of the guerrillas, the Germans were able to drive them back into the mountains. However, by the spring of 1945 the movement once again went on the offensive, and the OSS was successful in organizing seventy-five teams to train and equip partisan guerrillas. In the final drive to take Italy, the guerrillas and their American advisors blocked key roadways and harassed German troop concentrations. In the end they were responsible for killing or wounding three thousand Axis troops and capturing as many as 81,000 others, in addition to preserving key transportation hubs including Modena, Venice, Milan, and Genoa.[5]

From the beginning American support for partisan operations in occupied France took a backseat to the well-developed operations of the British Special Operations Executive. American forces were far too concerned with the development of regular forces and plans for the cross-Channel landing known as Operation Overlord. While the army did train Ranger units for special operations during the beach landings, the semi-autonomous OSS worked with the British to support the French Resistance. The overall invasion commander, General Dwight D. Eisenhower, did recognize the value of guerrilla forces, stating in a March 22, 1944, secret memo, "We are going to need very badly the support of the Resistance groups in France." During and after the landing, the partisans would be organized and equipped to block or stop German reinforcements from reaching the beaches, break up rail lines, cut lines of communication, and generally disrupt German efforts. Americans worked in three-man teams with French and British operatives to form Jedburgh teams, named after partisans who had risen up in the Jedburgh region of Scotland in the twelfth century. The men parachuted into many areas of occupied Europe, contacting local resistance groups and providing support in the form of communications with the Allies, training, supply and support for resistance forces, and even raid leadership. American guerrillas were volunteers from across the army who could speak French, were in top physical condition, and had excellent skills in communications. Volunteers were trained in England and Scotland in commando fighting skills, including hand-to-hand fighting techniques. Graduates went on to the No. 1 Parachute Training School at RAF Ringway. In order to not alert the Germans, the teams did not jump into France until D-Day. Of course, the French Resistance—known as the Maquis—had been well organized and operational for years. What it needed most from the British and the Americans was logistical support. The Resistance had its greatest success in rural areas, forests, and mountains where members could launch raids and slip away undercover. From the D-Day landings in June through September 1944, 276 Jedburgh members jumped into occupied areas of Europe. In addition, twenty-two OSS operational groups (OGs) consisting of around 355 mostly French-speaking U.S. troops were inserted. The Jedburgh units and OGs supported and organized Resistance fighters as they provided intelligence, guided Allied forces, rescued downed airmen, and ambushed German forces. But the teams faced multiple problems. One of the largest was in the composition of the Maquis. Many were loyal to the forces of Charles de Gaulle, while others were openly Marxist bands with a different agenda for postwar Europe. Many American guerrillas complained that they simply had been inserted into Europe far too late and could have been far more productive had they been dropped in well prior to D-Day. By the time most of them arrived, Allied troops were only days away. Ultimately the efforts of the French Maquis and the British Special Forces, which had been organizing a guerrilla network since 1940, were far more crucial to supporting the Allies than the late arrival of the Americans. The improvised operations did, however, give the Americans an idea of how guerrilla operations might be conducted in the future.[6]

For commanders the best opportunity to utilize guerrilla and unconventional warfare measures is when the enemy occupies a territory that allied forces do not have the resources to occupy and hold. The China-Burma-India Theater (CBI) in World War II provides a prime example of where American guerrillas operating under the OSS's Detachment 101 became one of the best special operations missions of the war. After sending agents to the area, General Donovan met with the infamously cantankerous commander Lieutenant General Joseph "Vinegar Joe" W. Stilwell about establishing OSS operations. At first Stilwell evaded responding to the idea, but in the absence of a direct "no" Donovan assumed he had permission to do so. Americans' first concern was opening air and land communications with China's Nationalist forces under Chiang Kai-shek. To supply the Chinese, Allied forces needed to control northern Burma and maintain the Burma Road to China. With limited resources, OSS officers working behind enemy lines would fill the vacuum. The terrain of Burma was ideal for light unconventional units. Rugged mountain ranges and steep valleys choked with jungles halted regular forces that could only move with the support of modern rail lines, roads, and airfields. The limited transportation routes that existed were ideal targets for irregular guerrilla forces.[7]

Lt. Gen. Joseph W. Stilwell inspecting Chinese troops in India. The infamous "Vinegar Joe," on duty in 1942 in the China-Burma-India (CBI) Theater. PRINTS AND PHOTOGRAPHS DIVISION, LIBRARY OF CONGRESS

American guerrillas of Detachment 101 were organized and trained in the United States and Canada. Their first commander was Captain Carl W. Eifler, who submitted a brief plan to insert troops behind Japanese lines to begin sabotage operations. Knowing full well that it is far easier at times to beg for forgiveness than to ask for permission to act, Eifler found it necessary to quickly assemble the unit before Stilwell became fully aware of his intentions. The 250-pound Eifler, whose whisper was considered a loud roar, was ideally suited for the job. He actively used friends to recruit healthy intelligent volunteers who were experts in Asiatic cultures, medicine, demolitions, and communications. Among them would be First Lieutenant William R. "Ray" Peers, who would later command the unit. Peers first met Eifler at OSS headquarters in Washington, where according to a witness, upon introduction, Eifler "took a stiletto type dagger and drove it a good two to three inches into the top of his desk." Peers may have been a bit shocked and wondered what he was getting into, while Eifler "looked pleased." The volunteers went to an SOE school in Canada and an OSS camp in Maryland, where they were trained in British hand-to-hand fighting skills, demolitions, communications, and the use of Allied and enemy weapons. They also studied everything they could about Asian culture.[8]

Carl W. Eifler. Eifler, the first commander of Detachment 101 in the CBI Theater, was the first officer to propose contact and cooperation with Kachin natives in Burma (present-day Myanmar). Eifler was eventually able to overcome Vinegar Joe's reluctance to engage in unconventional warfare. U.S. ARMY

But when Detachment 101 arrived in the CBI Theater, they found that Vinegar Joe had little use for them. He considered unconventional guerrilla warfare "illegal action," little more than "shadow boxing." The navy already had a plan in place to train Chinese guerrillas, and they felt the presence of the detachment undermined them. Upon arriving at Stilwell's headquarters in July, Eifler was informed by the gruff commander, "I didn't send for you and I don't want you." But in time he relented. The theater was at the bottom of the list of American priorities, and Stilwell was in desperate need of resources in Japanese-occupied Burma. The Japanese had cut the only overland road to China, and Americans were attempting to complete a new route from the India-Burma border at Ledo. Japan controlled the key town of Myitkyina and harassed American flights to China from a nearby airstrip. Stilwell approved sending Detachment 101 in to at least take the airfield, telling Eifler, "all I want to hear are booms from the Burma jungle." As W. R. Peers recorded, Stilwell's orders were to "establish a base camp in northeast India and from there plan and conduct operations against the roads and railroad leading into Myitkyina in order to deny the Japanese the use of the Myitkyina airfield. Establish liaison with the British authorities to effect coordination with their operations."[9]

With little logistical support and insufficient intelligence to complete the mission, Eifler looked to Allied forces for support. Realizing that American servicemen could hardly go unnoticed behind the lines, he turned to the British-led Burmese army for help. They spent the remainder of 1942 in the Assam Province of northeast India, recruiting and training around fifty Burmese volunteers in jungle survival, hand-to-hand combat, weapons, demolitions, communications, and raiding and ambushing. The Americans took advantage of the knowledge that the English-speaking Burmese volunteers conveyed as well. They learned all they could about local culture, dress, and traditions. With many of their supplies destroyed by a Japanese bombing raid on their warehouse, they were nevertheless able to improvise and gather the parts necessary to build their own 500-mile-range portable radio set.[10]

In early 1943 Eifler proposed that Detachment 101 agents parachute behind enemy lines to make contact with friendly Kachin natives.

The first raids in Burma resulted in the destruction of a railroad bridge, but were mostly ineffectual. In fact, several disasters occurred wherein American and Allied guerrillas were captured and executed by the Japanese or killed by unfriendly villagers. The chief problem was that teams were deployed too soon and with too little support, training, and, most importantly, local intelligence. As Peers recalled, "Some of them were failures; but they taught us many lessons as to what could be done and, even more important, what should not be done." The key was to first insert local Kachins to reconnoiter the area and find out if it was safe to insert an entire team. By the end of the year they had established six small camps in northern Burma and were training the Kachin natives. They began conducting small-scale sabotage and ambushes and became very adept in collecting intelligence on the Japanese through what Peers called the "bamboo grapevine." They also began training Kachins as guerrillas and providing teams with the weapons and support needed to attack the Japanese. The Kachins, in turn, relayed targets to the 10th Air Force and rescued downed Allied airmen. Detachment members also recruited some Kachin volunteers for advanced training and smuggled them back to bases in India for three to five months' training in intelligence and radio communications. Some were returned to the bases while others were dropped behind enemy lines for independent operations.[11]

As the Allies advanced in Burma, detachment teams infiltrated Japanese lines in advance. Advance agents jumped between one hundred and two hundred miles behind enemy lines. Once in place they carefully measured the temperament of local villagers to find friendly natives. Once contact was made, teams including Americans went in to organize, equip, and train new guerrilla units in attacking the Japanese rear. This process was repeated and expanded throughout the campaign.[12]

Many of the Kachin people had tired of Japanese occupation and had begun retaliating against the occupiers prior to receiving American help. Once team members from Detachment 101 arrived, Kachins eagerly accepted support and became essential allies in the war. In April 1942 Second Lieutenant Vincent Curl's group in the Hukawng Valley was befriended by Kachin leader Zhing Htaw Naw. Detachment 101 provided support including supplies, gear, and technical expertise, while

Zhing Htaw Naw provided combat leadership, intelligence, and air targets and rescued downed airmen. His forces went so far as to construct an improvised airstrip that they camouflaged when not needed by placing portable huts on it. By early 1944 Curl's forces had organized almost six hundred guerrillas.[13]

The Kachins were adept guerrilla warriors. Detachment 101 teams were impressed by the discipline and attention Kachin fighters exhibited when planning and preparing an ambush. When setting up the site, they took care to place their automatic weapons where they would cover the trail. In addition, they placed *pungyi* sticks in the dense undergrowth on each side of the trail, carefully camouflaging the site. When the ambush was sprung, the terrified Japanese would dive for cover in the brush, only to be impaled on the sticks. Once the ambush was executed, however, Americans were surprised at how quickly the Kachins would break off contact with the enemy in order to avoid casualties. As Americans learned, the Kachins' traditional method of war was to inflict as many casualties on their enemies as practical while minimizing their own losses. Many Americans enjoyed living and working with the Kachins. While they found the local food inedible and could not understand the Kachin custom of collecting the ears of their slain, their respect for the culture grew. Americans took part in local ceremonies, including games and holiday celebrations. Kachins were also known for their trustworthiness and bravery. Once, when a supply payroll airdrop of 500,000 rupees split open, Kachin natives found and collected all of it save for a mere 300 rupees.[14]

By the winter of 1943–1944, Stilwell had come to see the advantage of using unconventional warfare in the theater. Now planning a campaign down the Hukawng Valley to attack the town and airfield at Myitkyina, he wanted to use the guerrillas of Detachment 101 to augment Merrill's Marauders and Chinese forces—collectively known as the Galahad force—in the attack. Commanded by Frank Merrill, the Marauders, as the press had dubbed them, were a special light infantry unit trained to operate independently behind enemy lines. The unit operated with limited air cover and without artillery or tank support, traveling on foot with pack mules. Without heavy weapons, the unit needed to use the elements of speed and surprise to be successful—a concept that became lost on the command. Stilwell authorized Detachment 101 to expand to around three thousand fighters and promised even more support if the campaign was successful. As Galahad moved out, Detachment 101 guerrillas screened the advance and flanks of the forces and provided intelligence. On May 17, as they approached one of their primary objectives—the airfield at Myitkyina—one of the tribesmen who was to act as guide was bitten by a venomous snake, but because he was the only one who knew the back trails he refused to quit. He was so weak he had to ride horseback, but still insisted on guiding the force—allowing the Marauders to completely surprise the Japanese garrison and take the airfield. Their next objective, the town of Myitkyina itself, would not fall so easily. Originally, Detachment 101 guerrillas reported that the Japanese had around three hundred men there. However, when two Chinese units assaulted the town, they mistakenly engaged in a firefight with each other and had to pull back. Two days later, when the full force attacked, they found the Japanese had greatly reinforced the town and were able to hold off the attackers. Now ordered to lay siege, the force lacked the supplies and heavy weapons necessary for heavy operations, a blunder that needlessly cost many lives. The siege lasted past June and into the monsoon season. The campaign decimated the members of Galahad, especially the poorly supplied light forces of Merrill's Marauders. They were already suffering terribly from disease and were nearing starvation, being dependent on limited airdrops. After suffering a second heart attack, Frank Merrill himself had to be evacuated. With little combat air support and lacking the artillery and armored vehicles necessary to fight as conventional infantry, the Galahad force struggled to capture the town. Some in the Galahad headquarters blamed Detachment 101 for inaccurate original intelligence reports, but captured Japanese prisoners confirmed that the town had about 275 defenders when the force first attacked. However, the Marauders were grateful for the support of the guerrillas. They guided patrols, screened forces, cut off Japanese lines of communication, and provided essential intelligence. Kachins even supplied elephants to haul supplies! All the while, the guerrilla force continued to expand. By August 1944, when Myitkyina finally fell, the force had close to ten thousand fighters and was conducting missions almost four hundred miles away. During the rest of the campaign the detachment's forces continued to grow and screen Allied activities. Teams conducted over one hundred missions utilizing 350 detachment personnel and continued to conduct mop-up operations until deactivated in July 1945.[15]

The Kachin guerrillas of Detachment 101 became a valuable force multiplier in the China-Burma-India Theater. Consisting of only 0.8 percent of the Allied forces in the theater, the guerrillas may have been responsible for as many as 29 percent of the enemy casualties in the campaign. Commanders including Stilwell eventually realized that Allied forces could successfully utilize native forces like the Kachins in many capacities. They acted as scouts, provided intelligence, and rescued around four hundred downed airmen. The jungle canopy was too dense for aerial reconnaissance, and the unit supplied the 10th Air Force with as much as 95 percent of its targets and most of its battle damage assessment as well. In short, the Kachins, supported by Detachment 101 teams, became exceptional guerrilla fighters and rendered the Japanese occupation of Burma untenable. As in Europe, the OSS expanded throughout the area. By the end of the war the OSS was attempting to organize and train anti-Japanese forces in China and Southeast Asia. In fact, OSS officers had begun to train Viet Minh guerrillas, including Ho Chi Minh and Vo Nguyen Giap. But OSS-trained guerrillas in China, Thailand, and what would become Vietnam were just getting organized as the conflict came to an end.[16]

CHAPTER TEN

"Bamboo telegraph"

JAPAN'S LIGHTNING OFFENSIVE IN 1941 WAS NOT LIMITED TO THE INFA-mous December 7 attack on Pearl Harbor. On December 8 the Ameri-can-held Philippines were invaded. The siege of Bataan and Corregidor followed on the island of Luzon; by May 1942 the Philippines had sur-rendered to Japan. But not all American and Filipino forces laid down their arms. Some had been cut off, others escaped from captivity and the Bataan Death March, and many American and Filipino civilians took up arms in resistance. In the beginning, with little organization and no outside support, the bands acted independently until the Americans returned. As many as 277 guerrilla bands formed with as many as 260,715 fighters, many under American leadership and support, to resist Japa-nese occupation. While resistance movements in Europe have received much historical attention, the efforts of Filipino and American guerrilla fighters are a largely unsung but outstanding example of cooperation and a shared sense of mission. Although some of the boldest American guerrillas did not survive the conflict, two American guerrillas who were indispensable in this effort were Colonel Russell W. Volckmann, on the island of Luzon, and Lieutenant Colonel Wendell Fertig, on Mindanao.[1]

Although Americans had made contingency plans for a Japanese invasion of the Philippines, they had completely underestimated the speed and competence of the Japanese army and navy. In an effort to organize the defense of the island of Luzon, on November 15, 1941—just prior to Pearl Harbor—Captain Volckmann, then serving as the execu-tive officer of the Philippine army's 11th Infantry Regiment, met with

General Douglas MacArthur, commander of the United States Army Forces in the Far East (USAFFE), which integrated American and Filipino forces under one command. Captain Volckmann pointed out to the general that his regiment lacked weapons, heavy fire support, transportation, and clothing. He then asked MacArthur, "Sir, how do you assess the situation? What are your plans?" Volckmann was surprised when the commander-in-chief responded,

> *Well, I'll tell you Russ, I haven't got anything really on paper, yet. I've got it all in my mind, but we really don't have to worry about things at this point. The Japanese have a second-rate navy and about a fourth-rate army, and we don't have to worry about them until around July [1942], or in the summer months, during the dry period.*[2]

MacArthur's overconfidence was reflected in many American officers, including one who boasted that he could whip the entire Japanese invasion force with a company of Boy Scouts. Volckmann was not convinced and returned to his 11th Infantry, who were tasked with defending the coast along the Lingayen Gulf on the western coast of Luzon.[3]

MacArthur's original plan called for holding off a Japanese attack for several months while the U.S. Army and naval forces launched a relief force from the United States. Of course, that plan hinged on the existence of a Pacific fleet based at Pearl Harbor. MacArthur had also planned on using American civilian plantation owners, miners, and businessmen, and even considered leaving Philippine reserve units behind enemy lines to form a nucleus of a guerrilla force. However, his overestimation of the time it would take Japan to take the islands, the near-total destruction of the U.S. Pacific fleet, and his overestimation of the ability of the American and Filipino forces to hold back the Japanese doomed the plan. In addition, the army lacked any formal type of guerrilla warfare doctrine, and the OSS, tasked with developing irregular warfare concepts in Europe and the CIB, was all but nonexistent in the Philippines. MacArthur insisted on having complete control of all elements in his theater and had no use at all for members of the OSS.[4]

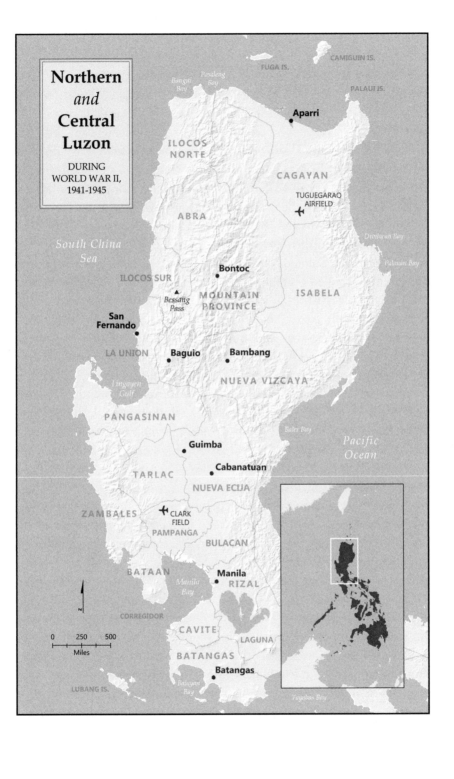

Northern *and* **Central Luzon**

DURING WORLD WAR II, 1941-1945

FUGA IS.

CAMIGUIN IS.

Bangui Bay

Pasaleng Bay

PALAUI IS.

Aparri

ILOCOS NORTE

CAGAYAN

TUGUEGARAO AIRFIELD

ABRA

Divilacan Bay

South China Sea

Palanan Bay

Bontoc

ILOCOS SUR

MOUNTAIN PROVINCE

Bessang Pass

ISABELA

San Fernando

LA UNION

Baguio

Bambang

NUEVA VIZCAYA

Lingayen Gulf

PANGASINAN

Baler Bay

Pacific Ocean

Guimba

Cabanatuan

TARLAC

NUEVA ECIJA

ZAMBALES

CLARK FIELD

PAMPANGA

BULACAN

BATAAN

Manila Bay

Manila

RIZAL

CORREGIDOR

CAVITE

LAGUNA

0   250   500
Miles

BATANGAS

Batangas

LUBANG IS.

Balayan Bay

Tayabas Bay

The swiftness and ferocity of the Japanese attack in December 1941 dispelled any notion General MacArthur may have had about defending his beachheads and establishing a well-organized insurgency. On the island of Luzon the combined American and Philippine army fell back to defend Bataan and Corregidor, leaving some units cut off. MacArthur ordered Colonel Claude A. Thorp into central Luzon to organize resistance. Several American officers and men, as well as many Filipino troops, had been cut off from the retreat. The Filipinos were lucky, as they could discard their uniforms and blend in with the inhabitants; the Americans, on the other hand, had to disappear into the jungles. The American officers included Colonel John P. Horan, Walter Cushing (an American civilian promoted to captain), Captain Ralph Praeger, and Major Everett Warner. MacArthur also attempted to establish a network of spies in Luzon and directed General William F. Sharp to establish guerrilla preparations in Mindanao and the southern islands. In April 1942, when MacArthur escaped to Australia, he had hoped to use his guerrilla base to set the stage for his eventual return. However, his replacement, General Jonathan M. Wainwright, received terms of surrender from the Japanese that called for him to order all forces in the Philippines to lay down their arms. Believing that guerrilla forces could accomplish little, Wainwright ordered all to surrender. General Sharp in Mindanao complied. The fifty-five-year-old general lacked the willpower and ability to continue, and the majority of his men surrendered.[5]

On April 11, 1942, Volckmann, now a major and intelligence officer of the Philippine army's 11th Division, learned of the surrender of his command. Knowing that Colonel John P. Horan and elements of his 43rd Regiment (Philippine Scouts) were continuing to resist, and that part of the command remained in the area of Baguia in the Mountain Province (known to be pro-American), Volckmann decided to evade capture. His commander, General William Brougher, reluctantly gave his assent. Other officers were not so supportive. "Why try?" they asked. Besides, several believed that "the Japs will treat us okay." They further argued that hiding out would be fruitless—that Americans hiding on the islands would be helpless and would be turned in by local informants in a short time. The odds were slim, but Volckmann thought it better to take

Russell W. Volckmann. A keenly successful guerrilla strategist during World War II, Volckmann—along with Fertig and Colonel Aaron Bank—was one of the founding fathers of today's Special Forces. U.S. ARMY

his chances in the jungle than with the idea that "the Japs will treat us okay." Armed with only a .45-caliber revolver, a map, and a survival knife, he and a few others headed out on a lengthy trip to the unoccupied areas of northern Luzon.[6]

In fact, many of the men behind enemy lines eventually surrendered, including Colonel Hornan and Major Warner. In October 1942 Colonel Thorp was captured and executed by the Japanese. Thorp had also received permission from MacArthur to organize guerrillas, but had failed to attract local support or the loyalty of the refugee American and Filipino fighters. According to some accounts, Thorp's sharp temper and supercilious attitude toward the Filipinos caused them to first shun his forces, then eventually turn them in to the Japanese. Captain Praeger had established radio communications with MacArthur's forces, but was also betrayed by collaborators or perhaps prisoners whom he had freed. He was captured and killed in 1943, when the Japanese were led to his camp. In October 1942 Colonels Martin Moses and Arthur K. Noble, who had assumed command of the loosely scattered forces, launched a series of attacks against Japanese positions in northern Luzon. Their actions may have been premature, and the reaction of the Japanese was swift and violent. In reprisal, the Japanese destroyed villages in the surrounding area and scattered the guerrillas. The colonels found it impossible to find food or shelter and were captured on June 1, 1943. They were eventually executed.[7]

Most Americans who escaped capture were hardly in a position to commence guerrilla operations. Perhaps as many as two hundred men had escaped prior to the surrender of Luzon, and as many as two hundred more had escaped during the Bataan Death March. Their main concern was survival. Volckmann had left with his unit's signals officer, Captain Donald Blackburn, and in time had linked up with other Americans and displaced Filipinos. They spent days traveling through the jungle avoiding Japanese patrols and convoys. Exhausted from disease, lack of food and supplies, and months of combat, escape, and evasion, in time they realized they had no choice but to turn to the natives for support. Indeed, the key to any successful operation behind enemy lines, or any guerrilla operation for that matter, is to have some level of local support. The Japanese had informants and offered bounties for American and Filipino combatants who had refused to surrender. Approaching any Filipino civilian was a life-or-death proposition. Volckmann and Blackburn were successful in realizing that local support was their only chance of surviving, much less becoming an offensive force. Fugitives wound up hiding out in jungle camps across northern Luzon, protected and supported by local tribes that fed, clothed, and nursed the scattered elements of the defeated army.[8]

The camps housed American and Filipino soldiers as well as civilians, including businessmen and plantation owners. Many people from all walks of life had retreated from Japanese-occupied areas. The men found life on the run daunting. Lack of food, low morale, and poor sanitation led to myriad diseases including beriberi, malaria, fever, and dysentery. Many died, and those who survived did so with the support of locals. It was because of Filipinos, at considerable risk to their own lives, that the guerrillas were able to survive, evade, regroup, and eventually attack the Japanese. "To these gracious natives," wrote Volckmann, "we owe our lives."[9] One of Captain Praeger's men, Captain Thomas S. Jones, clearly summarized Filipinos' invaluable assistance to the surviving soldiers:[10]

That any of the . . . guerrilla bands [were] able to survive and continue resisting during the long years between the fall of Corregidor and the invasion of Leyte [was] due almost solely to the efforts of the ordinary people of the Philippines. They—men, women, and children—made heroic sacrifices to keep the resistance movement alive. Whatever credit may go to the actual guerrillas themselves can never be so great as that which belongs to the civilians who supported them, and who bore the brunt of the enemy's anger and reprisals.[11]

The Fassoth Camp in central Luzon and the Diesher Camp on Mindanao stand out. At Fassoth, Volckmann was impressed with a large barracks that included bamboo bunks. They also had a working radio receiver that picked up San Francisco's KGEI, the only U.S. station accessible in the Pacific. Here they heard the first news of the war they had had in months. The camp included eighty enlisted Americans and eight officers. Most of the Americans in the camp were survivors of the Bataan Death March, and few were in good enough shape, mentally or physically, to resume armed resistance. In fact, the non-commissioned officers and enlisted men had commandeered all weapons and instituted their own form of discipline. Volckmann noted that Americans who were in hiding on the island fell into three groups: Some had given up everything and simply waited to die; a small percentage went to the dark side and used violence to extort what they wanted from other former prisoners and the civilian population; and finally there were the American guerrillas—those who grew strong in the hope of striking back against the enemy.[12]

Most importantly, the Filipinos began to reassess their situation. Upon arrival Japanese forces attempted to act as liberators, proclaiming Asian solidarity against western colonial powers and the advent of the Greater East Asia Co-Prosperity Sphere. They established a puppet government with a police force and instituted a series of "Neighborhood Associations" to use collaborators to keep watch over the islands. In the beginning these proclamations gained some support, but in time the Filipinos began to judge the Japanese not by their propaganda, but by their brutal treatment of family members and neighbors. As was true in all areas the Japanese occupied, subjects were treated as subhuman. In addition, the war brought economic disaster to the islands—a potent blow made even more so by widespread human rights abuses. As time wore on, MacArthur's promise to return and the approach of American forces reenergized support for the war effort. Former members of the Filipino Scouts and members of the army easily comingled with the population and began organizing and supporting Americans in hiding. Many tribal groups, including the Marxist Hukbalahaps in central Luzon, temporarily set aside their differences and allied with the Americans and other guerrillas.[13]

But the Filipino guerrilla bands themselves were never truly unified. They sprang up independently, with many starting out as local security vigilante groups that were organized to defend villages after the Japanese invasion. They acted independently and continually argued over command and jurisdiction. Some were no more than armed gangs who used force to rob, beat, and rape their neighbors and to settle old grievances. In time many groups welcomed American civilians and soldiers in hiding in hopes of receiving Allied logistical support. Early on some of the detached bands of guerrillas enjoyed some success. In a nine-month period, Walter Cushing and his private army became famous in northern Luzon for their brash raids and ambushes. This all came to an end in September 1942, when the Japanese were finally able to kill him.[14]

Lanao Maranao Battalion, Philippines, World War II. U.S. ARMY. COURTESY MACARTHUR MEMORIAL ARCHIVES, NORFOLK, VIRGINIA

The most successful early Filipino-American guerrilla organization on Luzon was Captain Ralph Praeger's Troop C, 26th Cavalry, later known as Cagayan-Apayao Forces (CAF). Most of these men had been Philippine Scouts, some of the best-trained soldiers in the army. Before the war they had all been recruited to the Philippine army as English-speaking high school graduates and were exceptionally well disciplined and trained. Praeger, their commander, had been raised on a Kansas farm and was a 1938 West Point graduate who chafed under spit-and-polish army discipline. He was a practical soldier whom one would not expect to rise as a guerrilla leader. Standing at six foot four, he towered over his men. Refusing to surrender kept his command together; by early 1942 Praeger commanded about 150 men, including many Filipino soldiers separated from other units and a handful of American civilians and soldiers. On the night of January 12, 1942, Praeger led his men in a daring night raid on the Japanese-held airfield at Tuguegarao. With homemade TNT grenades, the guerrillas of Troop C hoped to blast the handful of aircraft the Japanese had on station. With no moon and poor reconnaissance, the raiders failed to find the planes. However, they were successful in disrupting a large enemy encampment and killed perhaps as many as one hundred to two hundred Japanese. Praeger's men built on this success and later opened the first radio communications with MacArthur's command in Australia. However, they had stirred up a hornet's nest and were soon being driven by the Japanese. With his command scattered, on August 30, 1943, Praeger was captured, either by radio triangulation or the work of informers. The Japanese tortured and held him for three and a half months before he was tried and executed. He would posthumously be awarded the Distinguished Service Cross.[15]

Also on Luzon, Volckmann consolidated his command. He was forced into hiding after the first premature uprising in October 1942 and the capture of Colonels Moses and Noble. In June 1943 Volckmann assumed command of the majority of forces on the northern part of the island. His first priority was to use the "bamboo telegraph" to develop an intelligence network and open up a communications net with the scattered bands. He worked to unite rival groups and reined in lawless marauding gangs. Noting the lethal danger presented by informers and collaborators, he directed guerrillas to the Neighborhood Associations and the police. The reprisals meted by the guerrillas were brutal and lethal, leading to accusations of war crimes at the end of the conflict. Some accused the guerrillas of executing old enemies by simply labeling them as "informers" in the absence of solid evidence. But for the guerrillas, the harsh measures paid off—and after a six-month campaign, surviving collaborators withdrew to the protection of Japanese outposts. In addition, with real signs evident of MacArthur's return, Volckmann observed that "the so-called 'fence-sitters' began toppling in the right direction."[16]

Volckmann relied on American military and civilian refugees as well as Philippine army officers to organize northern Luzon into seven districts. Each district was built around a guerrilla unit based on a Philippine army regiment. He continued to learn from the previous mistakes of others. Besides learning about the dangers of collaborators, Volckmann also wanted to keep his camps away from well-developed civilian areas that were supporting his forces. The jungle camps became centers for training volunteer guerrilla forces in night operations, ambushes, and demolitions.

In the spring of 1944, upon finally making radio contact with MacArthur's forces with a jury-rigged radio, they received the command to "lie low" and support the Allied effort by sending intelligence and supporting coast watchers. Volckmann realized this would demoralize his forces, who wanted nothing less than to strike back at the Japanese invaders. However, for the most part they obeyed the directive and avoided large-scale confrontations with the enemy. At the same time, they did conduct multiple small-scale attacks that instilled confidence in the guerrillas and secured desperately needed supplies. In time these forces grew in competence and size and developed support units including artillery, hospital units, and engineers. And they formalized the "bamboo telegraph" by establishing a Pony Express–like system of stations for messengers.[17]

With communication restored under MacArthur's command came logistical and technical support. American submarines, starting with the USS *Stingray*, began supplying Volckmann's forces with much-needed medical and military supplies. With word of the October 1944 American landing on Leyte Gulf in the Philippine Islands also came news of more men, materiel, and support for Volckmann's guerrillas. With MacArthur's forces now back in the Philippines, the guerrillas on Luzon were critical to the preparations for landing. The Americans then sent the USS *Gar*, which brought thousands of pounds of weapons, equipment, and medical supplies as well as radio and explosives technicians. With this newfound American support, Volckmann was able to establish a radio net throughout northern Luzon and prepare the path for MacArthur's return.[18]

Prior to the U.S. invasion of Luzon, Volckmann informed MacArthur that the landing zone was clear and the 6th Army would face no opposition. On January 9, 1945, MacArthur's forces landed at Lingayen Gulf. Although Volckmann had informed MacArthur that the landing zone was clear, the navy played it safe and pounded the beaches with gunfire. While the United States had feigned attacking the southern part of the island, the Japanese under General Tomoyuki Yamashita— the "Tiger of Malaya"—gave up on the idea of holding the entire island and pulled back to Volckmann's area, the mountainous Cordillera Central of north-central Luzon. Volckmann's forces were essential to discovering this intelligence.[19]

Upon the U.S. landing in the Lingayen Gulf, Volckmann linked up with the Americans and traveled via PT boat to meet the commander of the 6th Army, General Walter Krueger. Krueger had met the then-captain Volckmann prior to the war while in command of the 2nd Infantry Division at Fort Sam Houston in Texas. Krueger was perplexed as to why the Japanese were not putting up a stiffer resistance; Volckmann informed him that the bulk of the Japanese had fallen back to the mountains and were digging in their heels. Volckmann later went on to meet MacArthur himself, who, instead of berating him for failing to follow the order to surrender, promoted him to the rank of full colonel.[20]

Once U.S. forces were ashore, Volckmann's guerrillas were attached to the 6th U.S. Army and joined in the fight. In addition to acting as guides and providing intelligence, they raised havoc in the Japanese rear, cutting communication lines, destroying bridges, and ambushing retreating units. Volckmann also devised a communications method that enabled his men to direct low-level bombers of the U.S. 308th Bomb Wing to targets through low cloud cover and mountains—a precursor to today's forward air controllers. As a result, Japanese front lines soon faced dire shortages. By June 1945 Volckmann's five regiments had cleared their respective districts of Japanese forces; they then joined the army to face the enemy. Now with complete logistical support, in addition to being backed with air and artillery, Volckmann's guerrillas were able to evolve from a hit-and-run unconventional force to a regular unit capable of fighting in line with conventional forces. In central Luzon, in support of the 11th Airborne Division's drive to the Ipo Dam, the guerrillas were even able to take Japanese dug-in positions. By early March MacArthur's forces had captured all the important points on the island while the Japanese retreated to the north. On June 14 three guerrilla regiments captured Bessang Pass with the support of U.S. artillery. This opened the way into northern Luzon, where the Japanese mounted their final defense. The guerrillas now held the entire Japanese command under siege and were within five miles of Yamashita's headquarters before the surrender of the Japanese on August 15. While General Yamashita had placed a price on Volckmann's head and spent a great deal of time and resources attempting to capture the American guerrilla, in the end it would be the guerrilla and the Americans who accepted his surrender. After the war Yamashita was put on trial and executed for war crimes committed on Luzon.[21]

According to Volckmann's biographer, from 1942 to 1945 the guerrilla had built up a force of more than 22,000 men who killed at least 50,000 opposing forces while suffering a loss of less than 2,000 men. MacArthur himself recognized the value of Volckmann's guerrillas as a combat multiplier, noting that his men did the equivalent of an entire army division. Volckmann also received the nation's second-highest accommodation, the Distinguished Service Cross.[22]

On Mindanao, Filipino guerrillas turned to an American officer in hiding named Wendell Fertig for training and guidance. As with many guerrilla units in the Philippines, as the indigenous population tired of the abuses meted out by their Japanese occupiers they looked to American military and civilians in hiding for support. Their choice of a leader on Mindanao may have very well created the most competent American guerrilla leader of the war. Fertig had arrived in the Philippines five years before the war as a civil engineer in mining. He was "tall [and] sandy-haired with an athletic build," in addition to "being calm, genial, deliberate and possessing a remarkable memory and a great facility for remembering names." According to contemporary observers, Fertig respected the people and "knew how to treat Filipinos." Due to the fact that he held a commission in the reserves, he was placed on active duty in June 1941. Prior to the invasion, he sent his family back to America while he assumed duties as an engineer. He first served on Luzon before being reassigned to Mindanao, organizing efforts to destroy supplies and bridges as the enemy advanced.[23]

Now promoted to lieutenant colonel, by April 1942 Fertig was supporting General William Sharp in destroying supplies on Mindanao. Refusing the order to surrender, he took refuge in an undeveloped region of Lanao Province and waited. The American forces had been brutally defeated, and it appeared that no relief was in sight. Fertig realized that if a resistance force were to materialize, it would be Filipino and it was up to the disorganized and scattered Americans to support it. In time he was contacted by the leader of a Filipino guerrilla unit, Luis Morgan,

Wendell Fertig, 1943. A civil engineer by training, Fertig—whose spectacular resourcefulness and creativity were instrumental to his own and others' survival in the theater of war—easily adapted to life in the Philippines, and was deeply respected by local *guerrilleros*. U.S. ARMY. COURTESY MACARTHUR MEMORIAL ARCHIVES, NORFOLK, VIRGINIA

and asked to assume command. Morgan had led a Catholic guerrilla unit that many felt was more intent on fighting against the Moro Muslims on the island than in resisting the Japanese. In time they turned to Fertig. Perhaps Morgan thought that Fertig would be no more than a figurehead who could add legitimacy to his command and bring in American supplies. Whatever Morgan's original intentions were, Fertig turned out to be more than capable and succeeded in uniting many of the scattered forces on the island—including the ferocious Moro, who had longstanding grievances with the Catholic majority on the island. In order to keep the peace between the factions, and over the objections of MacArthur himself, Fertig ordered that Morgan be evacuated by submarine to Australia. This effectively united most of the resistance fighters on the island and consolidated a position that in time would command as many as 33,000 members and perhaps 16,500 armed fighters. MacArthur later noted, "By perseverance and diplomacy Colonel Fertig gradually won the respect of the other guerrilla leaders, and by October 1942 he had built up a fair cohesive guerrilla organization."[24]

Fertig turned out to be the perfect man for the job. He put both his practical experience and his engineering degree from the Colorado School of Mines to use, establishing lines of communication and logistical support for much of the island. Under the occupation the islanders had become destitute. At first Fertig could offer little outside material support and used his considerable engineering skills to improvise. He was able to print and issue script for an underground currency and helped establish plants that used coconut milk to produce tuba beer in addition to alcohol that could be used in place of gasoline. By the winter of 1942–1943 he had re-emplaced many of the local leaders the Japanese had deposed in favor of establishing a shadow government on part of the island. Fertig also used his experience on the islands and a keen sense of propriety in his dealings with Filipinos, in time earning their respect. By February 1943 his men had successfully built a makeshift radio transmitter and had opened up communications with MacArthur's forces. Soon submarines arrived loaded with supplies, including matchbooks featuring MacArthur's likeness that promised his return to the island. Fertig fell into the role of a guerrilla chief, even growing a red goatee and being called "Tatay" (Father) by the Filipinos.[25]

Fertig may have gone a bit too far when he fashioned homemade stars for his shirt collar and promoted himself to the rank of "general" in command of all resistance in the Philippines. While this would aid him in consolidating his command, when he made contact with MacArthur's staff the gesture was neither appreciated nor recognized. Fertig had released the following order:

> Letter to all guerrilleros, as senior United States officer in the Islands, Lieutenant Colonel Wendell W. Fertig . . . assumes command of the Mindanao-Cisayan Force, USFIP, [United States Forces in the Philippines,] with the rank of brigadier general. All organized units resisting our common enemy are invited to serve under this command. Unified resistance is the key to success.
>
> W.W. Fertig, Brigadier General, Commanding[26]

MacArthur did not recognize the rank of general, but he did promote Fertig to colonel and awarded him the Distinguished Service Cross. He gave Fertig command of Mindanao, but retained overall command of resistance forces in the islands to himself. For his part MacArthur wanted the guerrillas on Mindanao to "lie low" and act as coast watchers, collecting information on Japanese movements. Thus information on Japanese naval and troop concentrations would become invaluable for the eventual landings on the islands. Fertig, on the other hand, wished for military aid from the United States and the ability to conduct offensive operations. He felt that this was essential in order to maintain the morale of the movement. Many Filipinos were deeply resentful of the brutal Japanese occupying forces and would reject any order to simply "lie low." A compromise was reached wherein MacArthur sent limited supplies to the island in exchange for intelligence that would be used in planning the liberation of the Philippines.[27]

By May 1943 his guerrillas had secured open control of much of Mindanao. Uniformed troops patrolled the town of Misamis (present-day Ozamiz), and Fertig had even created a small naval force that performed some incredible actions during the war and patrolled the waters of Panguil Bay. Working with Fertig's guerrillas, the town was functioning with reestablished civil government. On one occasion, when an American submarine arrived it was greeted by a band playing "Anchors Aweigh." With reestablished electricity and telephone communications the guerrillas and their government printed currency, exchanged commodities, and held regular Catholic services. The Japanese were not oblivious to these developments. Aerial photography and intercepted radio transmissions confirmed that a resistance movement had been established on Mindanao. In June the Japanese retaliated with landings on the Misamis coast, and in an attempt to cut off Misamis Occidental (the state in which Misamis was located) from the rest of the island, they advanced from Panguil to Pagadian Bay. The guerrillas had hoped to maintain order as they fell back and then strike back against isolated units, but the poorly armed and trained forces simply dissolved in the face of the Japanese. Eventually Fertig found refuge with the Moro in Lanao Province, where he had shown the Muslims a copy of *Life* magazine containing an article where the king of Saudi Arabia, Ibn Saud, had granted Islamic support for the American cause. For the next year Japanese troops poured onto the island, first to drive out the guerrillas and then to prepare for an anticipated American landing. Fertig moved from hideout to hideout, always keeping just ahead of their patrols. By August 1944 Fertig's guerrillas were without supplies, suffering terribly from malaria, and holing up in isolated Bukidnon Province. They were at the end of the line when American bombers began hitting Japanese emplacements. In response the Japanese withdrew to defend potential landing zones, leaving the guerrillas in position to reclaim much of the island's interior.[28]

When the Americans landed they were greeted by the guerrillas, who flooded out of the interior and quickly rejoined the fight. Fertig's command was incorporated into General Robert Eichelberger's 8th Army. The guerrillas secured and marked beachheads, then acted as guides and combat troops and helped the 8th Army capture or kill as many as 47,000 Japanese troops. Fertig's guerrillas had truly been a force multiplier as the Japanese committed vast resources, including over 150,000 troops who attempted to destroy the guerrilla bands. In addition the movement had denied the Japanese any material benefit of holding the island while providing naval intelligence that proved to be crucial information for the Battle of Leyte Gulf.[29]

Perhaps the finest example of guerrilla warfare in the Philippines during the war was the cooperation between the guerrillas, Army Rangers, and Alamo Scouts in a raid on the Japanese prisoner-of-war camp at Cabanatuan in central Luzon in January 1945. The camp was one of several notorious facilities used to house prisoners after the fall of the Philippines. Following the lead of guerrilla scouts, a company of the U.S. Army's 107th Rangers slipped through Japanese lines on January 29, avoiding Japanese troops and a tank along the National Highway. With Japanese forces moving through the area, the raiders remained in hiding until late on January 30. Guerrillas blocked enemy relief efforts from the northwest while Rangers captured the compound, killing around two hundred Japanese troops and freeing more than five hundred prisoners. Two died and seven were wounded during the operation, but the combined efforts of the Scouts, Rangers, and guerrillas did much to boost Allied morale and, in fulfilling MacArthur's promise to return to the islands, liberate his men. As was the case on Mindanao, these units on Luzon truly proved themselves as a force multiplier. Filipino-American guerrillas were active on other islands as well, including Leyte, Cebu, and Marinduque.[30]

The organizations developed during the war were essential to forming the postwar government of the Philippines. Presidents Manuel Roxas and Ramon Magsaysay, who had ties to the guerrillas, integrated them into the Philippine army. In fact, after the war former guerrilla fighters—including Ferdinand Marcos—would build political careers off of real (and perhaps exaggerated) accounts of their contributions to the resistance. However, the anti-Japanese forces were far from united after the war, as Moro separatists and Huc guerrillas continued their struggle for independence. But the Filipino-American guerrillas had accomplished much in resisting the Japanese. Prior to the Allied landings they had provided valuable information to MacArthur's forces and established civil-military governments in areas the enemy did not control. The Japanese had failed in their propaganda campaign of creating a "Greater East Asian Co-Prosperity Sphere," and the people of the archipelago judged them instead on how they had treated the civilians and prisoners under their control. After making contact with the Allied command, the guerrillas received the outside logistical support essential to expanding their efforts. Once the Americans had landed, several of the groups were able to assume the duties of regular line units—a rare task in guerrilla warfare. Yet guerrilla commanders were also forced to make hard decisions that fell outside the standard rules of war. Through painful lessons, they learned that the only way to deal with informants and collaborators was with brutal force. After the war the Philippine government and U.S. Army dealt with these issues with a general amnesty.[31]

The Allies clearly won World War II with large conventional forces supported by the mobilized American economy. However, the role of Americans who fought as guerrillas was no small contribution. They provided priceless intelligence, reconnoitered and captured landing beaches, rescued downed airmen, and acted as guides. The army successfully used American-supported and -trained guerrillas in the Philippines and Burma as a force multiplier to disrupt Japanese lines of supply and communication, provide intelligence, and even perform as conventional infantry. The guerrillas experienced their greatest successes when supported by local populations who provided men, supplies, medical assistance, and shelter. They became even more effective when supported with Allied weapons, materiel, and experts. They did their best work operating in rough terrain and jungle, where large infantry units are considerably slowed. Charismatic leadership was essential, but unfortunately infighting over territory greatly hampered the resistance movement in the Philippines. However, leaders had to acknowledge their limitations. As fighters they were best suited to the type of hit-and-run raids and ambushes that mankind has been practicing for millennia. Guerrilla units rarely had the logistical support, training, or firepower to withstand any kind of conventional fight, but they did fantastic work scouting ahead of and covering the flanks of Allied regular forces. Some, including Volckmann's guerrillas, were even able to move and operate as regular forces by the closing months of the war.

The army was slow to warm to the idea of any kind of unconventional warfare in World War II. Necessity forced commanders to accept guerrillas, but the lack of any prior training and established doctrine on how to conduct guerrilla warfare led to costly mistakes and delays. Looking back on the achievements of Detachment 101 and American guerrillas in World War II, W. R. Peers noted that their fervor and capabilities might have been put to even more effective use had they been properly trained and organized—a valuable lesson for the future:

Units comparable to Detachment 101 collected information behind the lines in France, Italy, the Philippines, China, and other areas. In the aggregate they represented an immense intelligence capability of a type for which, if there should be another war, there would in all probability be a strong requirement. Each of these operations, however, experienced growing pains, and there was a lag time of from one to two years before they were able to produce tangible results. It would be highly desirable, therefore, that the personnel who may be used in such operations in the future should be so oriented, trained, and organized that this critical lag could be minimized. How this is to be accomplished appears as a pressing and continuous problem for the intelligence community.[32]

CHAPTER ELEVEN

"To kill them, you'll have to kill me first"

Captain Vernon W. Gillespie Jr.

As World War II came to a close, General William Donovan, wishing to preserve the capabilities of the Office of Strategic Services, wrote a "Memorandum for the President." In it he proposed that President Franklin D. Roosevelt, his longtime supporter, establish an independent "central intelligence agency" that would answer directly to the commander-in-chief. The agency's mission would be to collect overseas intelligence for the Executive Department. Donovan pressed for maintaining his OSS operatives as the foundation for this organization. However, with Roosevelt's death Donovan's ideas were lost as well. President Harry Truman, who held a deep distrust "against cloak and dagger operations by the United States," brought the service to a close. Truman ordered the OSS shuttered as of October 1, 1945. Without Roosevelt's backing and battered by inter-service rivalries, the suspicious Federal Bureau of Investigation (FBI), and distrustful regular forces, Donovan and his force were dismissed.[1]

However, the concept failed to die. Although Donovan's direct involvement ended with the OSS, he was responsible for calling attention to the potential of using American forces in guerrilla operations behind enemy lines—and the potential of such forces to be effective auxiliaries to regular forces and force multipliers in the theater if supported by local populations. Edmond Taylor, a war correspondent and navy commander who served with Donovan on the planning board of the OSS, wrote glowingly that "the guerrilla aspects of the OSS mission probably interested him more than any other. By combining unlimited nerve, Yankee ingenuity, and self-reliance, the American tradition of frontier warfare, and the most advanced twentieth-century science or technology, Donovan believed that effectively unconventional solutions could be found to almost any strategy problem." According to special operations historian Alfred H. Paddock Jr., "Donovan must be considered the spiritual father of Army unconventional warfare."[2]

Just a few months into the emerging Cold War, Truman reconsidered his distrust of "cloak and dagger operations." In January 1946 he created the Central Intelligence Group to coordinate information. In 1947 Congress passed the National Security Act, which fundamentally restructured American military and intelligence services. Among a host of other provisions, the act established the Central Intelligence Agency (CIA). Later the National Security Council (NSC) placed paramilitary operations, including guerrilla operations, exclusively under the control of the new civilian agency. Although Donovan was out of the picture, many of his former agents flocked to the CIA.[3]

The roles of the CIA and the military in regard to guerrilla warfare inevitably clashed during the Korean War. Beginning in the winter of 1950, Americans trained North Korean dissidents. They were led, supplied, and trained by American forces, with some units fighting in conventional battles and others dispatched behind the lines in traditional guerrilla missions. Few Americans with special forces training participated in these missions. Perhaps as a result, American-organized North Korean guerrilla forces exerted little impact during the war.[4]

However, the concept of special operations was reborn with the proxy war in Korea. Brigadier General Robert McClure was named chief of the army's new Psychological Warfare Division (Office of the Chief of Psychological Warfare Division, or OCPW). Having headed Eisenhower's Psychological Warfare Division in Europe at the end of World War II, McClure was an excellent choice for the position. The army had maintained its involvement in unconventional warfare by supporting psychological warfare units, and the outbreak of the Korean War sparked the establishment of the Psychological Warfare Center at Fort

Bragg, North Carolina, and eventually the creation of the 10th Special Forces Group. The mission of the 10th focused on both psychological and unconventional warfare. At first McClure struggled to attract officers, but in time—and armed with a list of former guerrillas from the now-retired General Donovan—he assembled a cadre of talented and experienced men who would ultimately create the U.S. Army's Special Forces. Colonel Aaron Bank had served in the OSS with the French Maquis in World War II. Lieutenant Colonel Marvin Waters and Colonel Melvin Russell Blair had both served with Merrill's Marauders. Colonel Wendell Fertig and Lieutenant Colonel Russell W. Volckmann were two of the most experienced American guerrillas from the campaign in the Philippines. Volckmann had returned to the field in Korea, but had been evacuated in December 1950; McClure found him at Walter Reed Army Medical Center in Washington, DC, recuperating from what may have been the lingering effects of a World War II–era stomach ulcer. Volckmann was at first reluctant to accept an assignment with the fledgling Special Forces Group, but did so when assured that the army was serious about "behind-the-lines operations."[5]

Volckmann's service in the Korean War had not been as productive as he had hoped. He was eventually assigned to the position of executive officer of the Special Activities Group—Far East Asia Command (or SAG). The unit was composed of Marines, Army Rangers, and South Korean units with orders to operate behind enemy lines. During the first year of the war, the unit did succeed in establishing an intelligence network, but it was disbanded in April 1951. Headquarters believed that all infantry should be trained as Rangers, and furthermore that no specialized "ranger-style units" that drained men and resources from the regular forces were needed to take up such activities. However, the army and the CIA continued to train both North and South Koreans for the United Nations Partisan Infantry Korea (UNPIK, also known as the White Tigers). Here Volckmann recognized many of the same problems he had faced in World War II: The organization of guerrilla fighting was ad hoc, the leadership was indecisive and inexperienced, and the Korean partisans were mostly used on the front lines as conventional soldiers rather than behind the lines as guerrillas.[6]

Before the Korean War began, Volckmann had been tasked by the army to prepare a field manual (FM) based on his experiences. In September 1950 the army released *Operations Against Guerrilla Forces* (FM-31-20), which was similar to *The Small Wars Manual* produced by the Marine Corps in 1940. Marines had drawn on their extensive experience in Latin America and the Caribbean, dealing with insurgencies and civil affairs during occupations. In like fashion, Volckmann turned to his own experiences aiding guerrillas in the Philippines to help the army put down future insurgencies. Volckmann's *Operations* and the Marines' *Manual* became the foundation for American counterinsurgency operations. Much of the doctrine contained therein has been progressively built on in the decades since, culminating in Major General David Petraeus's 2006 *U.S. Army and Marine Corps Counterinsurgency Field Manual* (FM 3-24).[7]

In *Operations Against Guerrilla Forces*, Volckmann advised the army on the best methods it could adapt to combat the very type of insurgency he had led in the Philippines. Perhaps borrowing a page from Francis Lieber, Volckmann first defined guerrilla warfare and then provided examples from both American and world history. "American military history is replete with examples of 'guerrilla' and 'anti-guerrilla' warfare," he wrote, "from the time of the American Revolution through the Indian campaigns, the campaigns in the Philippines (1898–1901), [and] the Punitive Expedition into Mexico led by General Pershing just before World War I." He argued that the best way to prevent an insurgency is to formulate a plan that will not encourage the development of one within the occupied population to begin with. Volckmann had witnessed how the Japanese failed to treat Filipinos with any sense of dignity; in fact, they had purposely treated them as subhuman. American commanders, Volckmann pointed out, should be familiar with "the national characteristics, and the customs, beliefs, cares, hopes and desires of the people" they were dealing with. He also recognized the limits of guerrilla warfare, noting that "*operations are, by themselves, incapable of gaining a military decision*. In the attainment of a military decision, guerrilla operations are always preparatory to or in support of a regular offensive effort." Therefore, in order to defeat an insurgency, two things were essential: first, that guerrillas lose the support of the local population, and second, that they be cut off from outside providers of weapons and supplies. Once cut off and no longer receiving local support, Volckmann argued, guerrilla forces would be easy to mop up. As in the American Indian Wars, he recommended using native forces as counterinsurgents, utilizing informants, and converging columns of attack. But despite the fact that Volckmann and the Marines had developed the basic outline of insurgency and counterinsurgency doctrine for the twentieth century—based on lengthy and hard-earned experience—the army would not take their lessons seriously until the Vietnam War.[8]

In March 1951 Colonel Aaron Bank was named chief of the Special Operations Division. His World War II experience was far-ranging: First deployed as a Jedburgh in France, he organized former German prisoners as anti-Nazi guerrillas in Austria, then finished his wartime service in China with the OSS. Bank gave Volckmann much credit for "the development of position, planning, and policy papers that helped sell the establishment of Special Forces" units in the army. On the basis of Americans' experiences supporting the civilian-controlled OSS and the Filipino-American guerrilla forces of World War II, Volckmann and others advocated that the army adopt a policy of developing special operations capacity behind enemy lines. As Bank phrased it, Special Forces teams would then be created "in the OSS pattern of tiny units with the same prime mission of developing, training, and equipping the guerrilla potential deep in enemy territory." Bank clarified that these units were not to be confused with traditional Army Rangers. The Rangers had a longstanding tradition of making devastating short-range raids behind enemy lines while being lightly supported. In contrast, Special Forces units would "have no connection with ranger-type organizations" because their mission was to spend extended periods of time deep behind enemy lines, organizing local guerrilla bands. As Volckmann specified, their mission was to "organize and support, wherever possible within the enemy's sphere of influence, guerrilla or indigenous forces on a military basis that are capable of efficient and controlled exploitation in conjunction with our land, air, and sea forces."[9]

A common tendency among many historians has been to focus on the Special Forces mission to train and equip guerrillas in Southeast Asia in the 1960s while ignoring their early development following World War II. Although established during the Korean War, the prime mission of Special Forces was to "train American troops to lead indigenous soldiers in Soviet satellite states in guerrilla conflict against the Soviet Union." While the proxy war in Korea raged, most eyes were on divided Germany and the Iron Curtain the Soviets had closed around Eastern Europe and the Baltics. Conventional wisdom within the army held that there was no question "if" the Soviets would expand into Western Europe, but rather "when" the communists would attack. Knowing they would be overwhelmed by sheer numbers in the beginning of any such action, the idea of looking to allied guerrilla insurgencies gained appeal in Harry Truman's administration. Truman subsequently came to accept the CIA's "retardation" plan, which called for the CIA and the army to use the Lodge Bill of 1950—which permitted refugees from Soviet bloc nations to seek shelter in the United States—to train refugees as guerrillas. They would subsequently be deployed in OSS-style teams to infiltrate Soviet-held territories, recruit local assistance, and conduct classic guerrilla activities.[10]

The original plan called for units to be operational even before war was declared in areas of potential Soviet influence beyond Western Europe—including Eastern Europe, the Middle East, and the Far East. On September 25, 1952, the 10th Special Forces Group was transferred to Germany to implement the "retardation" plan. Half of the force remained in the United States to form the 77th Special Forces Group. But battles over funding, the inability to keep guerrilla training secret, and lack of intelligence about the size and capability of the Soviet army dimmed their prospects. One contracted study, conducted by Johns Hopkins University before the 10th Special Forces Group deployed, found that the men had few skills suitable for guerrilla operations and little ability to coordinate with native forces. The researchers found that the men might make fine Rangers—executing short raids behind enemy lines—but lacked the language skills and training essential for organizing guerrilla units behind enemy lines. In fact, many of them expressed a preference for serving in the now-disbanded Ranger units. Meanwhile, President Dwight D. Eisenhower was already turning away from Special Forces. Creating what the administration called a "New Look" military, the president insisted on relying on nuclear weapons and conventional forces in future military engagements. By 1956 the number of men in Special Forces was reduced to the point of being totally ineffective as guerrillas; instead they were trained as Rangers for raiding. By the end of the year the 77th Special Forces Group had been moved to strategic reserve status, where it would take as long as a year to remobilize. In Europe, the 10th had been stripped of its headquarters company and lost two-thirds of its manpower. Shrinking resources and service rivalries blocked effective development and deployment of Special Forces units. As had been true of guerrilla units following the Philippine-American War, many officers saw "elite" units as a drain on finances, facilities, and, most importantly, manpower. With the dawn of the 1960s, McClure, Volckmann, Bank, and most of the other founders of Special Forces retired or were reassigned.[11]

In very short time, however, the threat of communist expansion into Southeast Asia—and support from newly elected President John F. Kennedy—revived the service. In addition, in 1961 the army placed Colonel William P. Yarborough in command of the Special Warfare Center. A 1936 graduate of the U.S. Military Academy, Yarborough had extensive World War II combat experience in the airborne forces over Africa and Europe. Like "Wild Bill" Donovan and Robert McClure before him, he knew how to make the right friends. In 1961 he invited President Kennedy to visit Fort Bragg and the Special Warfare Center. In an infamous incident, during a demonstration for the president the men caught and ate a snake, earning the lasting moniker "Snake Eaters." Yarborough did far more than put on a good show for the president, though. He was also successful in attracting additional funding for Special Forces and expanding their mission. Kennedy was the president who authorized the men to wear the now-famous green beret, Yarborough's idea; during World War II he had designed the army's airborne uniform, jump wings, badge, and jump boots. These designs were incorporated into the uniforms of the 1960s. More importantly, though, he expanded the size and mission of Special Forces to include counterinsurgency operations (now known as COIN) based on Volckmann's principles. Teams now would work with foreign nations to put down insurgencies.[12]

The expanded mission of Special Forces would be tested in fire in the Vietnam War. The French left Presidents Eisenhower and Kennedy with a disastrous program of pacification for the divided country. The Soviet-backed North Vietnamese sponsored a highly successful communist insurgency in the south and in neighboring countries. Many historians believe the United States misinterpreted the nationalist, anti-colonial motives of the fighters, choosing to focus on fear of a "domino effect" of nations falling into an expanding communist sphere of influence. The North Vietnamese Army (NVA) supported South Vietnamese insurgents, whom the Americans called the Viet Cong (VC), in a sizable Maoist insurrection that controlled much of the countryside. The VC enjoyed strong support among much of the rural population and successfully controlled shadow governments, under which they effectively employed classic guerrilla tactics including the establishment of extensive intelligence networks, raids, ambushes, placement of land mines, and employment of booby traps.

Even though their star had fallen under Eisenhower's "New Look" policy, Special Forces began training the Vietnamese Army in 1957. By the mid-1960s they were supporting, training, and advising almost eighty thousand Vietnamese troops, both regular and paramilitary. Early on the United States sent military advisors to assist the South Vietnamese Self-Defense Corps (SDC), whose mission it was to pacify the interior. But the government was not viewed as either meeting the needs or reflecting the values of the countryside, and the insurgency grew.

While many Americans trained Vietnamese forces during the war, the role of the 5th Special Forces Group, which worked with the Montagnards on pacification efforts, stands as a particularly useful example of both the successes and the limitations of the program. Special Forces teams trained the Montagnards, who excelled in guerrilla tactics, for four years during the war, in addition to providing them with weapons, equipment, and other material aid. The Montagnards—whom the Americans called "Yards"—are a tribal people of the central Vietnamese highlands, hence the name derived from the French term for *mountaineers*. During the war, approximately one million Montagnards, members of some thirty different tribes, lived as subsistence farmers, speaking their own

Montagnard tribesman during training in 1962. The Montagnards (from the French for "mountaineers," now known as the Degar), indigenous people of the central highlands of Vietnam, excelled as guerrilla fighters during the Vietnam War. Fiercely independent and subjected to virulent racism from other Vietnamese, they suffered grievously because of their alliance with American forces. U.S. ARMY languages and, for the most part, practicing their own religion. Like geographically isolated peoples in many parts of the world, they had always lived independently, but exercised no political autonomy and had no protected homeland. They distrusted their countrymen in both the north and the south: the communists to the north and the South Vietnamese because of their inherent racism. While many Vietnamese considered them savages, Americans found them to be loyal and brave allies.[13]

In late 1961 the United States formed the Civilian Irregular Defense Group (CIDG, pronounced "Sidgee") among the Montagnards. Teams working with the CIA began a Village Defense Program in the highlands; the Viet Cong regularly used the area to bring in men and supplies from the Cambodian and Laotian borders. The communists were attempting to win over the Montagnards, using the discrimination they suffered at the hands of South Vietnamese officials to gain support. Some joined the VC, but as the communists began conscripting men and pressing tribes for food and labor, many others rejected them.[14]

At its peak, the CIDG would grow to include forty-two thousand irregulars. The group dispatched twelve-man American Special Operations teams that included two commissioned officers and ten enlisted men to work with the tribes. The men were cross-trained in different essential skills for working behind the lines, including as medical, weapons, intelligence, demolitions, and communications specialists, as well as operations experts. The variety of skills and cross-training permitted the teams to be divided in two if the need arose.[15]

The teams worked to integrate themselves into the villages. The medics looked after villagers, and the teams were augmented by Navy Seabees and Vietnamese forces to develop infrastructure including roads, bridges, dams, schools, and wells. Many of the men went out of their way to learn local customs and languages and to consume local foods, including wild plants, snakes, lizards, and rats—precisely the sort of thing in which the Snake Eaters excelled. Some went so far as to incorporate items of native clothing into their uniforms and participate in tribal rituals. Not surprisingly, these developments incurred the wrath of the regular brass at Military Assistance Command, Vietnam (MACV). When writing the army's history of Special Forces at war's end, Colonel Francis John Kelly, commander of Special Forces in Vietnam from June 1966 until June 1967, wrote the following:

> *The American soldier is the most generous person on earth. It follows that he runs the risk of exhibiting too much concern or extreme paternalism. Since the military and political struggles in Vietnam were being waged simultaneously, the less privileged members of local society made unwarranted assumptions from this display of generosity as to the amount and depth of American support for their cause. The genuine American concern for improving the lot for the underprivileged was given free rein in the early days of the Special Forces in Vietnam; nor was any attempt made by the group to control or limit this generosity firmly up to the time of the group's departure from the country.*[16]

In his defense Colonel Kelly was a no-nonsense D-Day veteran, a commander who despised any exhibition of Special Forces bravado that made the Green Berets stand out from conventional forces. In 1967 he told a group of recently arrived officers, "This is no game for clowns. I haven't got any time for boozers or cheaters or buglers." He defined a "bugler" as a Special Forces soldier who would go into a bar and run his mouth about how superior the Green Berets were in comparison to the regular forces in-country, a surefire way to instigate a bar fight. To ensure that the Green Berets maintained a low profile, he declared Saigon off-limits to his men. He also banned them from wearing "unauthorized items like tiger skin capes and elephant hide boots, and he told them to shave off handlebar mustaches."[17]

With or without "tiger skin capes," the teams made excellent progress with the Montagnards. Many found the highland people fascinating. Tribal chiefs were elected by their villages, animistic shamans were venerated, and the culture was largely matrilineal. Females owned all of the property, children received their mothers' names, and husbands became associated with their wives' families. Lieutenant Edward E. Bridges, a member of Detachment A-113, was impressed with the men he trained: "The Montagnards made excellent soldiers, in my opinion," he wrote, adding, "Many of them had been fighting since they were eleven or twelve years old." They excelled in small unit tactics "and seemed to know instinctively how to protect their flanks." He admired their bravery as well, recalling that "they wouldn't hesitate to run out and help a team member under fire." He also noted that they seemed to have very clear-cut values. Like the American guerrillas of this Civil War, "If you were one of the good guys, then you got their total support. If you were one of the bad guys, they might even work against you." The Montagnards disdained the Vietnamese, and the feeling was mutual—a problem that would become increasingly challenging for military strategists. Arming the tribes made Vietnamese authorities uneasy; they distrusted all minorities, and the idea of an armed and organized Montagnard force was frightening to them.[18]

In 1964 events at a CIDG camp at Nam Dong would focus worldwide attention on the Green Berets and their Montagnard allies. The camp was strategically located at the junction of two valleys in Thua Thien Province, about fifteen miles from the border with Laos, in an area that served as a natural corridor for attacks on Da Nang and Phu Bai. The camp also protected several villages that were home to about five thousand Montagnards. By July the camp had become a major VC target as conditions deteriorated. Nam Dong was commanded by Captain Roger H. Donlon, with his twelve-man Detachment A-726; it included sixty highly efficient Nung Montagnards, as well as 311 local recruits from local tribes. But the loyalties of the local villagers and recruits were in question, and Donlon had planned on scuttling the position. Many of the villages had been found to be hostile to the United States, and with high grass growing right up to the barbed-wire perimeter, the camp was not well maintained. But before Donlon and his men could relocate, the camp was attacked.[19]

The VC attacked the post at 2:30 a.m. on July 6, 1964. A reinforced, battalion-sized VC force first overran a twenty-man forward outpost, then slinked through the high grass and cut its way through the perimeter fence without being detected. Next they hit the camp with well-aimed mortar fire; then the attackers swarmed the compound. The surprise was complete. Fortunately the post had an inner line of defense, which the team and allied Montagnard forces were able to hold. During the five-hour firefight that followed, Captain Donlon seemed to be everywhere at once. He directed the defense while moving, tossing grenades and firing though a veritable hailstorm of mortar rounds and bullets. While directing the fight, he was wounded four separate times. After being hit in the stomach, he stuffed a handkerchief in the wound to stanch the flow of blood and kept going. When he spotted three insurgents attempting to blow the gate to the inner compound, he shot them down. He rallied American and Montagnard fighters, brought up ammunition through a hail of bullets, and extracted several wounded men while under fire. The battle continued into the next morning, as the VC drove off helicopters transporting a Marine relief force. Around 9:00 a.m., after the defenders were resupplied by an airdrop, the VC retreated. The attackers left fifty-four of their dead on the field, and Donlon became the first American to be awarded the Medal of Honor in Vietnam. The citation concluded, "His dynamic leadership, fortitude, and valiant efforts inspired not only the American personnel but the friendly Vietnamese defenders as well and resulted in the successful defense of the camp."[20]

Although 225 Americans had been killed in Vietnam up to that point, when announcing Donlon's award the administration of Lyndon Baines Johnson hesitated to acknowledge the deliberate escalation of the war. The White House statement simply read, "This is the first Medal of Honor awarded to an individual who distinguished himself while serving with a friendly force engaged in an armed conflict in which the United States *is not a belligerent party*" (italics added). *Time Magazine* was not fooled: In a December 11, 1964, article aptly titled "One Who Was Belligerent," the news weekly sharply criticized the administration's assertion. The article did clarify, however, that "the mild idiocy of that statement should take nothing away from Donlon" and his heroic actions.[21]

The story of the base at Nam Dong and the people stationed there has enjoyed a rich afterlife in fiction and popular culture. Robin Moore featured it in his 1965 novel *The Green Berets*. Legendary pro–Vietnam War actor John Wayne traveled to Vietnam to adapt the story of the battle into a feature film. When Wayne arrived in Southeast Asia to conduct research, he pressured Colonel Kelly to let him join the men during a mission. Kelly's daughter Moira recalled that he kept pushing him until finally, "my father said: 'I'm not going to tell you how to make movies. Don't you tell me how to run a war.'" When the film was released in 1968, the predominantly anti-war press panned it as a piece of clichéd pro-war propaganda. Although it was successful at the box office, many veterans were also unimpressed. Now stationed at Fort Bragg, Moira Kelly remembered that when her father took the family to see the movie in 1968 she noted that Wayne's fictional character, Colonel Mike Kirby, had picked up many of her father's mannerisms for the movie. As she recalled, when her father was asked what he thought of the picture, he replied that "for an action movie, he thought it was fine," but "as a depiction of what troops had to put up with," he "felt it wasn't accurate. . . . When they got to the scene where John Wayne was in a Saigon nightclub wearing a tuxedo, my father almost fell over with laughter. He said, 'All I had were two sets of fatigues.'" Kelly did not even mention the fact that he had made Saigon off-limits to the Green Berets.[22]

In training and supporting the Montagnards, the Special Forces learned a painful lesson that would be forgotten and relearned in Afghanistan and Iraq scarcely forty years later: namely that tribal groups have their own agendas that are frequently at odds with the American mission on the ground, whatever that mission may be. On the surface they may present themselves as firm allies, but in reality they often seek American military support in order to achieve their own objectives. As more men were assigned to CIDG, the group was transferred back to the army in 1963, where it fell under the Military Assistance Command, Vietnam (MACV).[23]

In 1964 the American mission was challenged by a Montagnard group called the FULRO (*Front Uni de Lutte de Races Opprimées*), an organization whose initials, translated from the French, stand for "United Front for the Liberation of Oppressed Races." In September the simmering resentment the Montagnards held toward the Vietnamese government exploded into violence in the Ban Me Thuot central highlands. Five camps rebelled during the night of September 19 and 20, killing eighty Vietnamese soldiers but sparing the Americans. Twenty Americans were taken hostage. The American advisors were later freed, and many of them—at significant risk to their own lives—took the lead in convincing the Montagnards to stand down and return to their bases. *National Geographic* writer Howard Sochurek was a firsthand witness to these events, and in the January 1965 issue of the magazine credited the teams for "pulling the firing pin from the revolt of 3,000 mountain soldiers." Sochurek was present when Captain Vernon W. Gillespie Jr. learned of the uprising in the surrounding camps. Gillespie brought in the Vietnamese commander and his Montagnard leaders and announced that he was taking command of the camp. He then told the Montagnards "not to move against the Vietnamese here. They are under my protection. To kill them, you'll have to kill me first." Gillespie subsequently oversaw negotiations between the Montagnard and Vietnamese commanders, who eventually held a friendship ceremony led by a shaman. Sochurek photographed Captain Gillespie, dressed in a loincloth, negotiating peace between a Vietnamese officer and a Montagnard chief during the two-hour ceremony. By September 28 American negotiators had established a truce in return for a joint Vietnamese and Montagnard peace conference to be held in Pleiku from October 15 to 17. Alas, the conference granted little more than lip service to the Montagnards' demands for autonomy, which included (among other things) command and control of their own armed forces, recognized land ownership, representation in the national assembly and local governments, and positions as officers and non-commissioned officers in the army.[24]

Criticism of the operation now turned toward the Special Forces. MACV blamed the teams for not instilling loyalty to the Vietnamese government in the Montagnard forces; it was painfully clear that the tribesmen were loyal to the Special Forces instead. The camp commanders were relieved of their duties, and Captain Gillespie was admonished for being photographed wearing Montagnard clothing and "telling a general officer that the general didn't know enough about Montagnards to interfere in that part of the country." The Vietnamese were extremely upset about the situation as well, and accused the Americans of arming and provoking the Montagnards without their consent. MACV realized the Special Forces had created a threat to the sovereignty of the government of South Vietnam, and the camps involved in the uprising were shut down within a year.[25]

The mission of Special Forces now changed. The teams and best-trained Montagnard forces were ordered away from their indigenous interior camps to the borderlands of Laos and Cambodia on a mission to intercept supplies and personnel entering the country via the Ho Chi Minh Trail. No longer supported by a friendly native population nor motivated to defend their homeland, the Montagnards lost their incentive. American and Montagnard forces struggled to redefine their purpose, as much of the American occupation was redirected toward the building and maintenance of fortified camps.[26]

Conditions for the Montagnards deteriorated through the end of the war and beyond. The CIDG program of supporting the tribes for local defense was completely dismantled by the army in December 1970. After the United States left Vietnam in 1973, many Montagnard fighters found that their villages and land had been confiscated and more than 150,000 became refugees. Former Special Forces master sergeant Ed Sprague returned to Vietnam with the United States Agency for International Development (USAID) to help the Montagnards. In 1975, during the fall of South Vietnam, he personally led two thousand of them to the beach at Nha Trang, hoping for an American evacuation. It never came. The war and its bloody aftermath led to the deaths of more than two hundred thousand tribesmen and tribeswomen and the loss of 85 percent of their villages. The communist victors had little use for the highland American collaborators, and their wartime leaders either escaped the country or were imprisoned. Since the 1980s the United States has permitted approximately three thousand Montagnard fighters and their families to immigrate into the United States. Many have settled near Fort Bragg, North Carolina, home of the Special Forces. The legacy of the program remains mixed. The outcome for the Montagnards became a nightmare.[27]

While Americans fought limited wars in Vietnam and Korea, their commanders focused on the possibility of fighting a major conventional—and nuclear—war against the Soviet Union. At the conclusion of U.S. involvement in Vietnam, the combat abilities of U.S. conventional and Special Forces were heavily strained. The advent of an All-Volunteer Force and the election of Ronald Reagan as president added resources to all branches.

The air, land, and sea battle doctrine developed to oppose the Soviets in the Cold War proved highly effective against conventional enemy combatants. When fighting conventional forces, Americans proved to be peerless in confrontations in Granada in 1983, Panama in 1989, and Iraq in 1991, as well as the initial invasions of Afghanistan in 2001 and Iraq in 2003. Special Operations units also played key roles in supporting allied anti-Taliban tribes in Afghanistan. But following the conflagration of 9/11, the problems in American policy were exposed when it became painfully clear that the United States lacked any judicious plans for the post-invasion occupations of Afghanistan and Iraq.

Political decisions made by the George W. Bush administration would have profound consequences for the region. Pre-existing tensions between the Shia majority and the historically dominant Sunni minority were exacerbated when the administration insisted on disbanding Saddam Hussein's army and the Ba'ath Party. While the administration celebrated the end of major combat operations in Iraq with President Bush's landing on the USS *Abraham Lincoln*, disgruntled former soldiers who distrusted their new Shiite political leaders began taking up arms. (It should be noted, however, that the infamous banner reading "Mission Accomplished" was placed there by the crew of the vessel to honor the ship's achievements during the war, not the president's purported victory.) Believing Americans would be welcomed as liberators, in 2003 Secretary of Defense Donald Rumsfeld boldly proclaimed that there was no "guerrilla war" in Iraq except for a few "pockets of dead enders."[28]

Rumsfeld would be proven disastrously wrong. By the end of 2006 the situation in Iraq was out of control. Al-Qaeda in Iraq (AQI) controlled an area larger than New England. The poorly trained Iraqi troops, often insurgents themselves, came and went as they saw fit. Tribal militias, both Shiite and Sunni, murdered and wounded thousands of civilians. On the home front the support for the war Bush once enjoyed had evaporated, and he contemplated a major change of course. Rather than bow to congressional and public pressure to pull out of Iraq, he proposed a "surge" of manpower in the country and a totally new kind of occupation. In order to accomplish this, he relieved Secretary of Defense Rumsfeld and many senior commanders and sent General David Petraeus to lead the effort.[29]

Petraeus fundamentally changed the way the United States addressed the insurgency. In addition to enjoying a reputation as an extremely hardworking and competent commander, Petraeus had established himself as a notable scholar as well. While on a teaching tour with West Point's Social Studies Department, he had completed his Princeton PhD dissertation on the lasting effects of the Vietnam War on the U.S. Army. Unlike most officers, who focused on conventional warfare, Petraeus argued that the lessons of Vietnam included that "American involvement in low-intensity conflict is unavoidable" and insisted that "the military should be prepared for it."[30]

Before leading the surge, Petraeus had already gained valuable experience in the region: In 2003, during his first tour in Iraq at the head of the 101st Airborne Division, he had worked hard to "win over the hearts and minds" of the people of Mosul. He rebuilt the war-ravaged city's infrastructure, repairing roads, bridges, and communication lines. He established an elected government and police force. Back in the United States, much of this firsthand experience was distilled into the aforementioned *U.S. Army and Marine Corps Counterinsurgency Field Manual* (FM 3-24), drawn from his own hard-earned wisdom and that of his peers in Iraq and Afghanistan. But Petraeus went beyond the often insular world of the armed forces: For his manuscript, he broke with many military traditions by seeking the advice of academics, reporters, and non-government aid workers with experience in the field. The result was unique. Building on Lieber's 1863 General Order No. 100, Volckmann's *Operations Against Guerrilla Forces* (FM-31-20), and the Marine Corps' *The Small Wars Manual*, Petraeus incorporated the lessons of successful American counterinsurgency operations from across the globe into his work.[31]

The new COIN doctrine broke significantly from the history of unforgiving retaliation against civilians who harbored guerrillas. Instead Petraeus argued that the "primary objective in any COIN operation is to foster development of effective governance . . . by the balanced application of both military and nonmilitary means." Rather than heavy-handed methods, the doctrine calls for measured use of military force. "An operation that kills five insurgents is counterproductive," he points out, "if collateral damage leads to the recruitment of fifty more insurgents." Historically, the conventional forces of western nations have executed guerrillas captured under arms not belonging to any recognized command and brutalized civilians who supported them. Now the U.S. manual called for soldiers to "treat non-combatants and detainees humanely." The doctrine called for the Armed Forces to leave their heavily fortified garrisons and interact with the population, responding to their needs and requests.[32]

The manual, first published in 2006 and revised in 2014, has been downloaded millions of times. It stands as the definitive governmental counterinsurgency publication and has the distinction of being the first military field manual to be reviewed by the *New York Times*. However, it does have its detractors. Many believe the manual lost focus by ignoring the motivations of the insurgents; it is impossible, they argue, to win over the "hearts and minds" of people motivated by medieval values of race and religion. The COIN doctrine, they argue, has turned fighters into social workers, people who have developed so much empathy for their enemies that they would never be able to defeat them.[33]

Petraeus took command of the surge in Baghdad in February 2007. Now with 170,000 coalition troops in a nation of 25 million people, he faced as many as fifty-six different insurgent groups. Using the manual as a guide, he ordered forces out of heavily fortified Forward Operating Bases (FOBs) and dispersed them into smaller stations and outposts in urban areas. Some commanders rightly worried this would leave their men more exposed to the enemy; however, as the manual pointed out, "sometimes the more you protect your force, the less secure you will be." Troops were now to leave their bases and bombproof vehicles and take up foot patrols. Petraeus encouraged his men to "secure and serve the population," "live among the people," "hold areas that have been secured," and finally, "pursue the enemy relentlessly."[34]

The surge brought the insurgency to a head. In fact, some of the bloodiest fighting of the war ensued, with more than one hundred American troops dying each month from April through June 2007. But that was the peak; the numbers began to drastically fall that summer, with only sixteen Americans dying in December 2008. Civilian casualties were dramatically reduced as well, dropping from 23,000 in 2007 to 1,600 in 2011. Much of this was due to the changed nature of the American presence in Iraqi communities. Soldiers now acted on solid tips from trusted informants before breaking down doors in the middle of the night and indiscriminately hauling off captives. In 2007 alone, Americans captured 27,000 Iraqis without triggering the backlash such operations generated at the beginning of the conflict. Much of this success was also attributable to Sunni tribes switching sides in the "Sunni Awakening" that followed. Beginning in 2006, tribal leaders around Ramadi had had their fill of the repressive measures of al-Qaeda in Iraq (where they could be punished for something as simple as smoking in public) and switched allegiances to the American forces. In all, approximately 100,000 Sunni fighters joined coalition forces to drive them out.[35]

In July 2010 President Barack Obama ordered Petraeus to Afghanistan to lead a similar surge. After a year of mixed results, Petraeus returned to the United States to head the CIA. The Taliban in Afghanistan has led an unbreakable (to date) insurgency in that country, strengthened by the provision of safe havens and other support from neighboring Pakistan. In December 2011 the Obama administration declared that the war was officially over and pulled American forces out of Iraq. This left the nation under a Shia-dominated government heavily influenced by Iran and unrecognized by the minority Sunnis and Kurds in the north. After American forces left Iraq, AQI forces reemerged from hiding and the bloodbath has continued. Some of the most violent history of the region is now being written, especially given the sectarian fighting that has erupted in the total absence of a strong central government. Historians, soldiers, and political pundits rightfully argue about whether or not the Bush administration's 2003 invasion was justified or whether it was a wise idea for the Obama administration to declare "victory" in 2011 and leave the field to insurgents. Although the new COIN concept has made significant gains in the region, it would be a stretch to call America's anti-insurgency operations in Iraq and Afghanistan successful.[36]

CONCLUSION

YOUNG GEORGE WASHINGTON'S 1754 RAID ON THE FRENCH MILITARY camp in Pennsylvania was an early salvo in what would become an established legacy of unconventional war in the United States. Americans have engaged in guerrilla warfare from the arrival of the first Europeans to the ongoing conflicts in Iraq and Afghanistan. After learning Native methods of stealth and surprise in staging raids and ambushes, Euro-Americans quickly turned the tables on Natives—targeting non-combatants and their villages and crops and, during the nineteenth century, nearly eliminating the American bison. This form of ranging warfare became endemic during the Seven Years' War and was carried over into the American Revolution, the War of 1812, and the Texas Revolution. While these conflicts were ultimately settled with conventional forces, their guerrilla elements played an important part in both warfare and politics. Guerrilla uprisings, most notably Shays' Rebellion in western Massachusetts, so worried the Founders that they were spurred to call a convention in Philadelphia to strengthen the weak central government and draft the Constitution. The American Civil War was partially instigated by guerrilla fighting and included widespread guerrilla and anti-insurgency campaigns. In reprisal, Northern commanders adopted scorched-earth policies in areas where the civilian population harbored guerrillas. The Union subsequently issued General Order No. 100, or the Lieber Code, the world's first military code of war. The code was applied by American forces during the occupation of the Philippines after the Spanish-American War. However, having abandoned the idea of establishing a firm doctrine or training regimen in unconventional warfare, by World War II the military was forced to experiment—for the umpteenth time in American history—in mobilizing, training, and supporting local guerrillas in occupied areas. The difficult lessons learned in both Europe and the Pacific germinated the CIA and Special Operations. In the last fifty years American-trained forces in Vietnam, Afghanistan, and Iraq have produced widely mixed results, with policymakers reinventing the wheel during each conflict.

Since 9/11 the United States has been involved in fighting the non-conventional, non-state forces of al-Qaeda, the Mujahedeen, and now ISIL (Islamic State of Iraq and the Levant). In the past Americans have "won" such fights by using slash-and-burn tactics—targeting civilians, their homes, and their livelihoods. On moral grounds, these methods are no longer acceptable in the modern western world; there is a profound need for new ways to counter non-state-supported radical Islamists. Thinking they can be defeated by "carpet bombing," as one presidential candidate recently stated, is grossly naïve—the equivalent of attempting to nail Jell-O to the wall. The very idea of force alone defeating ideology is misguided. Ideology must be confronted not only on military grounds, but also on moral and intellectual grounds. Radical extremists enjoy very little support in the Muslim world as a whole; if Americans expended as much energy debasing their medieval values as they do physically fighting them, perhaps the tide would turn against them. For the United States, the paramount military challenge of the early twenty-first century will be synthesizing and distilling the lessons learned over four hundred years of unconventional warfare, and applying those lessons to the most savage, tenacious, and geographically widespread insurgency it has ever faced.

Notes

Prologue
1. Fred Anderson, *Crucible of War: The Seven Years' War and the Fate of Empire in British North America, 1754–1766* (New York: Knopf, 2000), 5–7.
2. Anderson, *Crucible of War*, 5–7.
3. Max Boot, *Invisible Armies: An Epic History of Guerrilla Warfare from Ancient Times to the Present* (New York: Liveright Publishing Corporation, 2013), xxii.

Chapter 1: "Now we have just cause to destroy them by all means possible"
1. Matthew S. Muehlbauer and David J. Ulbrich, *Ways of War: American Military History from the Colonial Era to the Twenty-First Century* (New York: Routledge, 2014), 8–9.
2. Allan R. Millett and Peter Maslowski, *For the Common Defense: A Military History of the United States of America* (New York: The Free Press, 1994), 10–11; Muehlbauer and Ulbrich, *Ways of War*, 9–11.
3. John K. Mahon, "Anglo-American Methods of Indian Warfare, 1676–1794," in *In Defense of the Republic: Readings in American Military History*, eds. David Curtis Skaggs and Robert S. Browning III (Belmont, CA: Wadsworth, Inc., 1991), 3; Millett and Maslowski, *For the Common Defense*, 10–11; Muehlbauer and Ulbrich, *Ways of War*, 9–11; John Underhill, *Newes from America; Or, A New and Experimentall Discoverie of New England; Containing, A Trve Relation of Their War-like Proceedings These Two Yeares Last Past, with a Figure of the Indian Fort, or Palizado* (1638), ed. Paul Royster (Lincoln, NE: Digital Commons, University of Nebraska–Lincoln, 2007), under "Electronic Texts in American Studies," http://digitalcommons.unl.edu/cgi/viewcontent.cgi?article=1037&context=etas (accessed March 20, 2016).
4. Millett and Maslowski, *For the Common Defense*, 11; Muehlbauer and Ulbrich, *Ways of War*, 9–11; Mahon, "Anglo-American Methods of Indian Warfare," 9.
5. Millett and Maslowski, *For the Common Defense*, 10–11; Muehlbauer and Ulbrich, *Ways of War*, 9–11; Mahon, "Anglo-American Methods of Indian Warfare," 5.
6. Millett and Maslowski, *For the Common Defense*, 17.
7. Millett and Maslowski, *For the Common Defense*, 17–18.
8. Millett and Maslowski, *For the Common Defense*, 2–5.
9. Millett and Maslowski, *For the Common Defense*, 2–5.
10. Millett and Maslowski, *For the Common Defense*, 6–7; Mahon, "Anglo-American Methods of Indian Warfare," 9.

11. Millett and Maslowski, *For the Common Defense*, 6–7; Mahon, "Anglo-American Methods of Indian Warfare," 9–11.

12. Millett and Maslowski, *For the Common Defense*, 7; North Carolina Historic Sites, "Alamance Battleground," Office of Archives and History, North Carolina Department of Cultural Resources, http://www.nchistoricsites.org/alamance/main.htm (accessed March 17, 2016).

13. Millett and Maslowski, *For the Common Defense*, 6–8.

14. Mahon, "Anglo-American Methods of Indian Warfare," 12.

15. John Grenier, *The First Way of War: American War Making on the Frontier, 1607–1814* (New York: Cambridge University Press, 2005), 22.

16. James Mooney, "The Powhatan Confederacy, Past and Present," *American Anthropologist* 9, no. 1 (January–March 1907), 138; Grenier, *The First Way of War*, 24; Millett and Maslowski, *For the Common Defense*, 13, 14.

17. Muehlbauer and Ulbrich, *Ways of War*, 24.

18. Muehlbauer and Ulbrich, *Ways of War*, 25.

19. Muehlbauer and Ulbrich, *Ways of War*, 25.

20. Underhill, *Newes from America*; Grenier, *The First Way of War*, 27; Millett and Maslowski, *For the Common Defense*, 14, 15.

21. Grenier, *The First Way of War*, 30, 32.

22. Grenier, *The First Way of War*, 33; Millett and Maslowski, *For the Common Defense*, 16, 17.

23. Grenier, *The First Way of War*, 33; Millett and Maslowski, *For the Common Defense*, 16, 17.

24. Grenier, *The First Way of War*, 38, 39.

25. Grenier, *The First Way of War*, 35.

26. Grenier, *The First Way of War*, 41–45.

27. Grenier, *The First Way of War*, 45–46; Millett and Maslowski, *For the Common Defense*, 18.

28. Grenier, *The First Way of War*, 47.

29. Grenier, *The First Way of War*, 47–49, 49.

30. As quoted in Grenier, *The First Way of War*, 51.

31. Grenier, *The First Way of War*, 50–52.

32. Grenier, *The First Way of War*, 51–52.

33. Millett and Maslowski, *For the Common Defense*, 19.

34. Grenier, *The First Way of War*, 87–88.

35. Grenier, *The First Way of War*, 88–89.

36. As quoted in Grenier, *The First Way of War*, 89.

37. Grenier, *The First Way of War*, 89–91.

38. Grenier, *The First Way of War*, 92–102.

39. Grenier, *The First Way of War*, 92–102.

Chapter 2: "No army can subsist in this country without rangers"

1. Millett and Maslowski, *For the Common Defense*, 25.

2. Millett and Maslowski, *For the Common Defense*, 29.

3. Muehlbauer and Ulbrich, *Ways of War*, 57.

4. Benjamin Franklin, *The Autobiography of Benjamin Franklin*, ed. Louis P. Masur (Boston: Bedford/St. Martin's, 2003), 144.

5. Franklin, *Autobiography*, 144.

6. Muehlbauer and Ulbrich, *Ways of War*, 60; Franklin, *Autobiography*, 144. Many have disagreed with Franklin's assessment of Braddock. In his published report, Washington blamed the outcome of the event on the panic of the undisciplined regular troops. However, it is important to note that Washington was attempting to secure a commission in the regular British army and would not have advanced his cause by questioning his commander. Historian Peter Russell argues that Braddock had developed a solid plan of advance that included the use of flanking parties to avoid surprise, in addition to the use of militia and Native scouts. According to Russell, Braddock's plan failed when his officers became complacent after crossing the river and literally let their guard down. Peter Russell, "Redcoats in the Wilderness: British Officers and Irregular Warfare in Europe and America, 1740 to 1760," *The William and Mary Quarterly* 3rd Ser., 35, no. 4 (October 1978): 629–52; Sylvia Neely, "Mason Locke Weems's 'Life of George Washington' and the Myth of Braddock's Defeat," *The Virginia Magazine of History and Biography* 107, no. 1 (1999): 45–72.

7. Millett and Maslowski, *For the Common Defense*, 40.

8. Millett and Maslowski, *For the Common Defense*, 39–41.

9. Anderson, *Crucible of War*, 162; Grenier, *The First Way of War*, 125.

10. Grenier, *The First Way of War*, 125.

11. Anderson, *Crucible of War*, 160–61; two Gnadenhüttens were destroyed by war, this one (in Pennsylvania) in 1755 and a second one (in Ohio) in 1782.

12. War for Empire, "John Armstrong," http://www.warforempire.org/visit/biography. aspx (accessed May 15, 2016); Grenier, *The First Way of War*, 125–26.

13. Grenier, *The First Way of War*, 124.

14. Grenier, *The First Way of War*, 124.

15. Robert Rogers, *The Journals of Major Robert Rogers* (Albany, NY: Joel Munsell's Sons, 1883), 24.

16. Grenier, *The First Way of War*, 62.

17. Grenier, *The First Way of War*, 61.

18. John F. Ross, *War on the Run: The Epic Story of Robert Rogers and the Conquest of America's First Frontier* (New York: Bantam Books, 2009), 83.

19. Ross, *War on the Run*, 108–9.

20. Rogers, *Journals of Major Robert Rogers*, 46.

21. Rogers, *Journals of Major Robert Rogers*, 46.

22. Rogers, *Journals of Major Robert Rogers*, 49.

23. Rogers, *Journals of Major Robert Rogers*, 55.

24. Rogers, *Journals of Major Robert Rogers*, 58.

25. Rogers, *Journals of Major Robert Rogers*, 64–65.

26. Rogers, *Journals of Major Robert Rogers*, 65.

27. Rogers, *Journals of Major Robert Rogers*, 68.

28. Rogers, *Journals of Major Robert Rogers*, 70.

29. Ross, *War on the Run*, 462.
30. Rogers, *Journals of Major Robert Rogers*, 68.
31. Ross, *War on the Run*, 130.
32. Rogers, *Journals of Major Robert Rogers*, 69.
33. Rogers, *Journals of Major Robert Rogers*, 69.
34. Rogers, *Journals of Major Robert Rogers*, 71.
35. Grenier, *The First Way of War*, 128.
36. Grenier, *The First Way of War*, 128.
37. Grenier, *The First Way of War*, 129.
38. Grenier, *The First Way of War*, 129.
39. Grenier, *The First Way of War*, 130.
40. Grenier, *The First Way of War*, 130.
41. Grenier, *The First Way of War*, 131.
42. Grenier, *The First Way of War*, 131.
43. Grenier, *The First Way of War*, 131.
44. Rogers, *Journals of Major Robert Rogers*, 80.
45. Ross, *War on the Run*, 150.
46. Ross, *War on the Run*, 150–51; Grenier, *The First Way of War*, 132.
47. Grenier, *The First Way of War*, 133.
48. Grenier, *The First Way of War*, 134–39.
49. Rogers, *Journals of Major Robert Rogers*, 80.
50. Rogers, *Journals of Major Robert Rogers*, 82.
51. Rogers, *Journals of Major Robert Rogers*, 82–85.
52. Rogers, *Journals of Major Robert Rogers*, 82–85.
53. Rogers, *Journals of Major Robert Rogers*, 91.
54. Rogers, *Journals of Major Robert Rogers*, 93.
55. Rogers, *Journals of Major Robert Rogers*, 92–97.
56. Rogers, *Journals of Major Robert Rogers*, 98.
57. Rogers, *Journals of Major Robert Rogers*, 100.
58. Rogers, *Journals of Major Robert Rogers*, 140.
59. Grenier, *The First Way of War*, 62.
60. Rogers, *Journals of Major Robert Rogers*, 141–47.
61. Rogers, *Journals of Major Robert Rogers*, 141–47.
62. Rogers, *Journals of Major Robert Rogers*, 141–47.
63. Rogers, *Journals of Major Robert Rogers*, 148–49.
64. Grenier, *The First Way of War*, 116–17.

Chapter 3: "An unfair way of carrying on a war"

1. John S. Pancake, *This Destructive War: The British Campaign in the Carolinas, 1780–1782* (Tuscaloosa: University of Alabama Press, 1985), 52.
2. Don Higginbotham, *The War of American Independence: Military Attitudes, Policies, and Practice, 1763–1789* (Boston: Northwestern University Press, 1983), 87.
3. National Park Service, "Cowpens: Daniel Morgan," https://www.nps.gov/cowp/learn/historyculture/daniel-morgan.htm (accessed June 1, 2016).

4. Higginbotham, *War of American Independence*, 102.

5. Higginbotham, *War of American Independence*, 102.

6. Higginbotham, *War of American Independence*, 102–3.

7. Higginbotham, *War of American Independence*, 108.

8. Higginbotham, *War of American Independence*, 109–10.

9. Higginbotham, *War of American Independence*, 113–14.

10. Higginbotham, *War of American Independence*, 113–14.

11. Higginbotham, *War of American Independence*, 176–77.

12. Higginbotham, *War of American Independence*, 188, 190, 191.

13. Higginbotham, *War of American Independence*, 91–192.

14. Higginbotham, *War of American Independence*, 194.

15. Higginbotham, *War of American Independence*, 195.

16. Stephen Williams, "Letters Change View of Benedict Arnold, Gen. Gates," *The Daily Gazette*, March 26, 2016, http://www.dailygazette.com/news/2016/mar/26/letters-change-view-benedict-arnold-gen-gates/ (accessed June 1, 2016).

17. Higginbotham, *War of American Independence*, 196.

18. Higginbotham, *War of American Independence*, 320.

19. Grenier, *The First Way of War*, 151–53; Harry M. Ward, *The American Revolution: Nationhood Achieved, 1763–1788* (New York: Bedford/St. Martin's Press, 1995), 166–67.

20. Grenier, *The First Way of War*, 151–53; Ward, *The American Revolution*, 166–67.

21. Grenier, *The First Way of War*, 151–53.

22. Higginbotham, *War of American Independence*, 322–32; Indiana Historical Bureau, "Letter of Instruction from Governor Patrick Henry of Virginia to George Rogers Clark," http://www.in.gov/history/2962.htm (accessed June 2, 2016); *The Indiana Historian*, December 1997, 3.

23. Lowell H. Harrison, *George Rogers Clark and the War in the West* (Lexington: University Press of Kentucky, 1976), 20–27.

24. Higginbotham, *War of American Independence*, 323.

25. Higginbotham, *War of American Independence*, 324; *The Indiana Historian*, December 1997, 11.

26. Harrison, *George Rogers Clark*, 14–15, 44; *The Indiana Historian*, 14.

27. Harrison, *George Rogers Clark*, 14–15, 44; *The Indiana Historian*, 14.

28. Harrison, *George Rogers Clark*, 58–59; Ward, *American Revolution*, 176.

29. Joshua Shepherd, "George Rogers Clark at Vincennes: 'You May Expect No Mercy,'" *Journal of the American Revolution*, February 17, 2015, https://allthingsliberty.com/2015/02/you-may-expect-no-mercy-george-rogers-clark-at-vincennes/ (accessed June 2, 2016).

30. Ward, *American Revolution*, 169.

31. Ward, *American Revolution*, 170–71; Higginbotham, *War of American Independence*, 325–27.

32. Ward, *American Revolution*, 171; John W. Hall, "Washington's Irregulars," in *A Companion to George Washington*, ed. Edward G. Lengle (Malden, MA: Wiley-Blackwell, 2012), 336–37.

33. Ward, *American Revolution*, 171–72; Higginbotham, *War of American Independence*, 328–29.

34. Higginbotham, *War of American Independence*, 322; Grenier, *The First Way of War*, 147, 161.

Chapter 4: "Tarleton's Quarter"

1. Higginbotham, *War of American Independence*, 353; Millett and Maslowski, *For the Common Defense*, 72.

2. Ward, *American Revolution*, 129–31.

3. Ward, *American Revolution*, 135; Higginbotham, *War of American Independence*, 360–61.

4. Higginbotham, *War of American Independence*, 362.

5. Wayne Lynch, "John McClure Rallies the South," *Journal of the American Revolution*, December 4, 2014, https://allthingsliberty.com/2014/12/mcclure-rallies-the-south/ (accessed June 5, 2016).

6. Higginbotham, *War of American Independence*, 361.

7. Walter Edgar, *Partisans & Redcoats: The Southern Conflict That Turned the Tide of the American Revolution* (New York: Perennial, 2003), 68–69.

8. James Piecuch, "Massacre or Myth? Banastre Tarleton at the Waxhaws, May 29, 1780," *Southern Campaigns of the American Revolution* 1, no. 2 (October 2004), http://southerncampaign.org/newsletter/v1n2.pdf (accessed June 5, 2016).

9. Wayne E. Lee, *Crowds and Soldiers in Revolutionary North Carolina: The Culture of Violence in Riot and War* (Gainesville: University Press of Florida, 2001), 195.

10. Lee, *Crowds and Soldiers*, 198.

11. Edgar, *Partisans & Redcoats*, 73–74.

12. Edgar, *Partisans & Redcoats*, 75–76; Lynch, "John McClure Rallies the South."

13. Edgar, *Partisans & Redcoats*, 78; Lynch, "John McClure Rallies the South."

14. Edgar, *Partisans & Redcoats*, 79–83; Lynch, "John McClure Rallies the South."

15. Edgar, *Partisans & Redcoats*, 83; Lynch, "John McClure Rallies the South."

16. Edgar, *Partisans & Redcoats*, 89.

17. Ward, *American Revolution*, 135–36.

18. Pancake, *This Destructive War*, 107; Edgar, *Partisans & Redcoats*, 112–13.

19. Pancake, *This Destructive War*, 116; Edgar, *Partisans & Redcoats*, 115.

20. Pancake, *This Destructive War*, 69.

21. Pancake, *This Destructive War*, 116–18; Edgar, *Partisans & Redcoats*, 116–17.

22. Pancake, *This Destructive War*, 117.

23. Pancake, *This Destructive War*, 118, 120.

24. Pancake, *This Destructive War*, 118–20; Edgar, *Partisans & Redcoats*, 118–19.

25. Pancake, *This Destructive War*, 120; Edgar, *Partisans & Redcoats*, 119–20.

26. Higginbotham, *War of American Independence*, 364–65.

27. Don Higginbotham, *Daniel Morgan: Revolutionary Rifleman* (Chapel Hill: University of North Carolina Press, 1961), 121; Higginbotham, *War of American Independence*, 365–66.

28. Higginbotham, *War of American Independence*, 366.

29. Ward, *American Revolution*, 142.
30. Pancake, *This Destructive War*, 135.
31. Pancake, *This Destructive War*, 135; Higginbotham, *Daniel Morgan*, 134.
32. Pancake, *This Destructive War*, 136.
33. Pancake, *This Destructive War*, 137–38; National Park Service, "The Battle of Cowpens," https://www.nps.gov/cowp/learn/historyculture/the-battle-of-cowpens.htm (accessed June 1, 2016).
34. Higginbotham, *War of American Independence*, 370.
35. Higginbotham, *War of American Independence*, 371–74.

Chapter 5: "The Kentucky reinforcement, in whom so much reliance had been placed, ingloriously fled"
1. Robert A. Gross, "A Yankee Rebellion? The Regulators, New England, and the New Nation," *The New England Quarterly* 82, no. 1 (2009): 112–35, http://www.jstor.org/stable/20474709 (accessed June 12, 2016).
2. Ron Chernow, *Washington: A Life* (New York: Penguin Press, 2010), 517; Gross, "A Yankee Rebellion?"
3. Whit Ridgway, "George Washington and the Constitution," in *A Companion to George Washington*, ed. Edward G. Lengel (West Sussex, UK: Wiley-Blackwell), 421.
4. Millett and Maslowski, *For the Common Defense*, 94–95.
5. Chernow, *Washington*, 720.
6. Chernow, *Washington*, 720–26.
7. Millett and Maslowski, *For the Common Defense*, 96; Muehlbauer and Ulrich, *Ways of War*, 116.
8. Grenier, *The First Way of War*, 210–3.
9. Grenier, *The First Way of War*, 207.
10. Grenier, *The First Way of War*, 208–9.
11. Grenier, *The First Way of War*, 209–10.
12. Grenier, *The First Way of War*, 213.
13. Muehlbauer and Ulrich, *Ways of War*, 137.
14. Edgar, *Partisans & Redcoats*, 133.
15. Muehlbauer and Ulrich, *Ways of War*, 137–38.
16. Daniel Walker Howe, *What Hath God Wrought: The Transformation of America, 1815–1848* (Oxford: Oxford University Press, Inc., 2007), 10–11.
17. Howe, *What Hath God Wrought*, 12–13.
18. Howe, *What Hath God Wrought*, 12–13.
19. Howe, *What Hath God Wrought*, 16–17.
20. Howe, *What Hath God Wrought*, 660–61.
21. Howe, *What Hath God Wrought*, 660–61.
22. Stephen L. Hardin, *Texian Iliad: A Military History of the Texas Revolution* (Austin, TX: University of Texas Press, 1994), 98.
23. Sean Wilentz, *The Rise of American Democracy: Jefferson to Lincoln* (New York: W. W. Norton and Company, 2005), 432–33.

24. Howe, *What Hath God Wrought*, 164–65; Wilentz, *Rise of American Democracy*, 433–35.

25. Wilentz, *Rise of American Democracy*, 434; Howe, *What Hath God Wrought*, 664–67.

26. Wilentz, *Rise of American Democracy*, 434; Howe, *What Hath God Wrought*, 664–67.

27. Howe, *What Hath God Wrought*, 518–19; United States, *Treaties and Other International Acts of the United States of America*, ed. Hunter Miller, vol. 4 (Washington, DC: Government Printing Office, 1934), http://avalon.law.yale.edu/19th_century/br-1842d. asp (accessed June 21, 2016).

28. Howe, *What Hath God Wrought*, 518–19.

29. Wilentz, *Rise of American Democracy*, 669, 697.

Chapter 6: "Swamp Fox Rangers"

1. Clay Mountcastle, *Punitive War: Confederate Guerrillas and Union Reprisals* (Lawrence: University Press of Kansas, 2009); Daniel E. Sutherland, *A Savage Conflict: The Decisive Role of Guerrillas in the American Civil War* (Chapel Hill: University of North Carolina Press, 2009), x; Thomas D. Mays, "American Civil War Insurgency and Counter Insurgency," in *Encyclopedia of Insurgency and Counterinsurgency: A New Era of Modern Warfare*, ed. Spencer C. Tucker (Santa Barbara, CA: ABC-Clio, 2013), 28–31.

2. William Gilmore Simms, *The Life of Francis Marion* (Project Gutenberg).

3. Sutherland, *A Savage Conflict*, 28–29.

4. Sutherland, *A Savage Conflict*, 26.

5. Wilentz, *Rise of American Democracy*, 92–93.

6. Sutherland, *A Savage Conflict*, 14–15.

7. Sutherland, *A Savage Conflict*, 15–16.

8. Sutherland, *A Savage Conflict*, 11–17.

9. Sutherland, *A Savage Conflict*, 18–19.

10. Mountcastle, *Punitive War*, 24.

11. Mountcastle, *Punitive War*, 25; Sutherland, *A Savage Conflict*, 20–21.

12. Mountcastle, *Punitive War*, 27–29; Sutherland, *A Savage Conflict*, 20–21.

13. Sutherland, *A Savage Conflict*, 22–25; Mountcastle, *Punitive War*, 28–31.

14. Sutherland, *A Savage Conflict*, 22–25; Mountcastle, *Punitive War*, 28–31.

15. Mays, "Insurgency," 28–31.

16. Sutherland, *A Savage Conflict*, 27.

17. Sutherland, *A Savage Conflict*, 78; Mays, "Insurgency," 28.

18. Paul Christopher Anderson, "Turner Ashby (1828–1862)," in *Encyclopedia Virginia*, http://www.EncyclopediaVirginia.org/Ashby_Turner_1828-1862 (accessed June 22, 2016).

19. Sutherland, *A Savage Conflict*, 31–32.

20. Sutherland, *A Savage Conflict*, 32.

21. Sutherland, *A Savage Conflict*, 32.

22. Noel C. Fisher, *War at Every Door: Partisan Politics & Guerrilla Violence in East Tennessee, 1860–1869* (Chapel Hill: University of North Carolina Press), 62–63.

23. Fisher, *War at Every Door*, 64; Thomas D. Mays, *Cumberland Blood: Champ Ferguson's Civil War* (Carbondale: Southern Illinois University Press), 14, 32–33, 36.

24. Mays, *Cumberland Blood*, 14, 32–33, 36, 82; Fisher, *War at Every Door*, 64.
25. Mays, *Cumberland Blood*, 53, 55.
26. Mays, *Cumberland Blood*, 65; Sutherland, *A Savage Conflict*, 51.
27. Sutherland, *A Savage Conflict*, 100.
28. Sutherland, *A Savage Conflict*, 101.

Chapter 7: "I ain't killed but thirty-two men since this war commenced"
1. Sutherland, *A Savage Conflict*, 58–61.
2. Mountcastle, *Punitive War*, 34–35; Sutherland, *A Savage Conflict*, 59–61.
3. Mountcastle, *Punitive War*, 42–43; Sutherland, *A Savage Conflict*, 126–27.
4. Captain James G. Garner, "General Order 100 Revisited," *Military Law Review* 27 (January 1965): 5; Mountcastle, *Punitive War*, 42–43; Sutherland, *A Savage Conflict*, 128–29; Mays, "Insurgency," 29.
5. Sutherland, *A Savage Conflict*, 64–65.
6. Richard S. Brownlee, *Gray Ghosts of the Confederacy: Guerrilla Warfare in the West, 1861–1865* (Baton Rouge: Louisiana State University Press, 1984), 114–21.
7. Brownlee, *Gray Ghosts of the Confederacy*, 121–25.
8. Albert Castel, "Order No. 11 and the Civil War on the Border," *Civil War St. Louis*, 1963, http://www.civilwarstlouis.com/articles/order-11-by-albert-castel/ (accessed June 25, 2016).
9. Castel, "Order No. 11."
10. Sutherland, *A Savage Conflict*, 197.
11. Sutherland, *A Savage Conflict*, 199.
12. Sutherland, *A Savage Conflict*, 203; Brownlee, *Gray Ghosts of the Confederacy*, 228–29.
13. Rand Dotson, "'The Grave and Scandalous Evil Infected to Your People': The Erosion of Confederate Loyalty in Floyd County, Virginia," *The Virginia Magazine of History and Biography* 108, no. 4 (2000): 410.
14. Victoria E. Bynum, "Telling and Retelling the Legend of the 'Free State of Jones,'" in *Guerrillas, Unionists, and Violence on the Confederate Home Front*, ed. Daniel E. Sutherland (Fayetteville: University of Arkansas Press, 1999), 17–29. Richard Grant, "The True Story of the Free State of Jones," *Smithsonian Magazine*, March 2016, http://www.smithsonianmag.com/history/true-story-free-state-jones-180958111/?no-ist (accessed June 24, 2016).
15. Bynum, "Free State of Jones,'" 28–29; Grant, "The True Story of the Free State of Jones."
16. Mays, *Cumberland Blood*, 71.
17. Mays, *Cumberland Blood*, 76–77, 92–93, 97.
18. Mays, *Cumberland Blood*, 108–9; Sutherland, *A Savage Conflict*, 154, 234.
19. Mays, *Cumberland Blood*, 110–12.
20. Mays, *Cumberland Blood*, 112–15.
21. Mays, *Cumberland Blood*, 115–18; Sutherland, *A Savage Conflict*, 230; Brian Dallas McKnight, *Contested Borderland: The Civil War in Appalachian Kentucky and Virginia* (Lexington: University Press of Kentucky, 2006), 213–14.

22. Mays, *Cumberland Blood*, 119–21.
23. Mays, *Cumberland Blood*, 119–21.
24. Mays, *Cumberland Blood*, 122–25.
25. Sutherland, *A Savage Conflict*, 238.
26. Mountcastle, *Punitive War*, 128.
27. Mountcastle, *Punitive War*, 129–30.
28. Mountcastle, *Punitive War*, 129–30.
29. Mountcastle, *Punitive War*, 136.
30. Mountcastle, *Punitive War*, 131–34.
31. Mays, *Cumberland Blood*, 136–41.
32. Mays, *Cumberland Blood*, 1, 130–45.

Chapter 8: *"We must act with vindictive earnestness against the Sioux"*

1. Millett and Maslowski, *For the Common Defense*, 143–44.
2. Millett and Maslowski, *For the Common Defense*, 143–44.
3. Russell F. Weigley, *The American Way of War: A History of United States Military Strategy and Policy* (Bloomington, IN: Indiana University Press, 1973), 158.
4. Millett and Maslowski, *For the Common Defense*, 253, 255.
5. Millett and Maslowski, *For the Common Defense*, 255–56.
6. Millett and Maslowski, *For the Common Defense*, 254.
7. Weigley, *American Way of War*, 159.
8. Weigley, *American Way of War*, 160.
9. National Park Service, "Little Bighorn Battlefield: Battle of the Little Bighorn," https://www.nps.gov/libi/learn/historyculture/battle-of-the-little-bighorn.htm (accessed June 17, 2016); Alice Beck Kehoe, *The Ghost Dance: Ethnohistory & Revitalization*, 2nd ed. (Long Grove, IL: Waveland Press, 2006), 20–24.
10. David D. Smits, "The Frontier Army and the Destruction of the Buffalo: 1865–1883," *The Western Historical Quarterly* (Autumn 1994): 312–38.
11. Mark Grimsley, "Wars for the American South: The First and Second Reconstructions Considered as Insurgencies," *Civil War History* (March 2012): 6–36.
12. Muehlbauer and Ulbrich, *Ways of War*, 254.
13. Mays, *Cumberland Blood*, 150.
14. Muehlbauer and Ulbrich, *Ways of War*, 255–59.
15. Brian McAllister Linn, *The Philippine War, 1899–1902* (Lawrence: University Press of Kansas, 2000), 187; Millett and Maslowski, *For the Common Defense*, 307–8.
16. Muehlbauer and Ulbrich, *Ways of War*, 279; Millett and Maslowski, *For the Common Defense*, 310.
17. Millett and Maslowski, *For the Common Defense*, 311.
18. Muehlbauer and Ulbrich, *Ways of War*, 284; *New York Times*, July 17, 1902.
19. Muehlbauer and Ulbrich, *Ways of War*, 280.
20. *New York Times*, July 17, 1902.
21. Millett and Maslowski, *For the Common Defense*, 336.
22. Muehlbauer and Ulbrich, *Ways of War*, 284.
23. Millett and Maslowski, *For the Common Defense*, 337.

Chapter 9: "All I want to hear are booms from the Burma jungle"

1. David Hogan Jr., *U.S. Army Special Operations in World War II* (Washington, DC: Government Printing Office, 1992), 6, 7.

2. Hogan, *U.S. Army Special Operations in World War II*, 7, 8; Alfred H. Paddock Jr., *U.S. Army Special Warfare: Its Origins*, rev. ed. (Lawrence: University Press of Kansas, 2002), 25.

3. Paddock, *U.S. Army Special Warfare*, 26–27; Hogan, *U.S. Army Special Operations in World War II*, 7, 8.

4. Hogan, *U.S. Army Special Operations in World War II*, 137–39.

5. Hogan, *U.S. Army Special Operations in World War II*, 31–33.

6. Hogan, *U.S. Army Special Operations in World War II*, 47–58.

7. Hogan, *U.S. Army Special Operations in World War II*, 98–100.

8. Hogan, *U.S. Army Special Operations in World War II*, 98–100.

9. Hogan, *U.S. Army Special Operations in World War II*, 100–101; W. R. Peers, "Intelligence Operations of OSS Detachment 101," CIA Historical Review Program, September 22, 1993, https://www.cia.gov/library/center-for-the-study-of-intelligence/kent-csi/vol4no3/html/v04i3a11p_0001.htm (accessed June 27, 2015).

10. Peers, "Intelligence"; Hogan, *U.S. Army Special Operations in World War II*, 102.

11. Peers, "Intelligence"; Hogan, *U.S. Army Special Operations in World War II*, 105–8.

12. Hogan, *U.S. Army Special Operations in World War II*, 106.

13. Hogan, *U.S. Army Special Operations in World War II*, 108.

14. Hogan, *U.S. Army Special Operations in World War II*, 108–10.

15. Hogan, *U.S. Army Special Operations in World War II*, 117; Peers, "Intelligence."

16. Hogan, *U.S. Army Special Operations in World War II*, 110, 120, 127–28; Peers, "Intelligence."

Chapter 10: "Bamboo telegraph"

1. Larry S. Schmidt, Major, USMC, "American Involvement in the Filipino Resistance Movement on Mindanao During the Japanese Occupation, 1942–1945" (master's thesis, U.S. Army Command and General Staff College, 1982), 1–2.

2. Mike Guardia, *American Guerrilla: The Forgotten Heroics of Russell W. Volckmann* (Havertown, PA: Casemate Publishers, 2010), 23.

3. Guardia, *American Guerrilla*, 24; Hogan, *U.S. Army Special Operations in World War II*, 63–65.

4. Hogan, *U.S. Army Special Operations in World War II*, 63–65.

5. Hogan, *U.S. Army Special Operations in World War II*, 65–67; Bernard Norling, *The Intrepid Guerrillas of North Luzon* (Lexington: University Press of Kentucky, 1999), Kindle file, 223.

6. Guardia, *American Guerrilla*, 38, 39, 42.

7. Hogan, *U.S. Army Special Operations in World War II*, 68, 79; Guardia, *American Guerrilla*, 97, 180–81; Herminia S. Dizon, "The Complete Data Covering the Activities of the Late Col. Claude A. Thorp," Battling Bastards of Bataan, http://www.battlingbastardsbataan.com/dizon.htm (accessed June 27, 2015).

8. Chris Schaefer, "Bataan Diary," Riverview Publishing, http://www.bataandiary.com/index.htm (accessed June 29, 2015); Hogan, *U.S. Army Special Operations in World War II*, 67.

9. Guardia, *American Guerrilla*, 57.

10. Guardia, *American Guerrilla*, 51.

11. Norling, *Intrepid Guerrillas of North Luzon*, 136.

12. Jim R. Bowman, "International Broadcast Station KGEI: 1939–1994," Bay Area Radio Museum, http://bayarearadio.org/schneider/kgei/kgei.shtml (accessed June 21, 2016); Hogan, *U.S. Army Special Operations in World War II*, 67; Guardia, *American Guerrilla*, 57.

13. Hogan, *U.S. Army Special Operations in World War II*, 70.

14. Norling, *Intrepid Guerrillas of North Luzon*, 388.

15. Norling, *Intrepid Guerrillas of North Luzon*, 549, 648, 899, 1009–55, 3691–972.

16. Guardia, *American Guerrilla*, 153–57; Hogan, *U.S. Army Special Operations in World War II*, 75.

17. Hogan, *U.S. Army Special Operations in World War II*, 76, 79; Guardia, *American Guerrilla*, 117.

18. Guardia, *American Guerrilla*, 117–26.

19. Guardia, *American Guerrilla*, 124.

20. Guardia, *American Guerrilla*, 126–27.

21. Guardia, *American Guerrilla*, 127, 134, 144–46.

22. Guardia, *American Guerrilla*, 146; Hogan, *U.S. Army Special Operations in World War II*, 90.

23. Schmidt, "American Involvement," 84.

24. Morgantown Public Library, "Defenders of the Philippines: Wendell Fertig," http://philippine-defenders.lib.wv.us/html/fertig_wendell_bio.html (accessed June 29, 2015); Hogan, *U.S. Army Special Operations in World War II*, 70, 71; Schmidt, "American Involvement," 85–99; Major Michael E. Davis, "A Letter to All Guerrilleros: Unifying the Mindanao Resistance Movement and Unconventional Warfare," SAMS Monograph (Fort Leavenworth, KS: Command and General Staff College), 35.

25. John Keats, *They Fought Alone: A True Story of a Modern American Hero* (New York: J. B. Lippincott and Company, 1963), 295, 382, 393, 445; Davis, "A Letter to All Guerrilleros," 24; Hogan, *U.S. Army Special Operations in World War II*, 71.

26. Keats, *They Fought Alone*, 97–98, 122.

27. Davis, "A Letter to All Guerrilleros," 30–32.

28. Hogan, *U.S. Army Special Operations in World War II*, 74; Schmidt, "American Involvement," 125–35.

29. Davis, "A Letter to All Guerrilleros," 35.

30. Hogan, *U.S. Army Special Operations in World War II*, 85–90.

31. Major Peter Thomas Sinclair II, "Men of Destiny: The American and Filipino Guerrillas During the Japanese Occupation of the Philippines," SAMS Monograph (Fort Leavenworth, KS: School of Advanced Military Studies, 2011), 54–57.

32. Peers, "Intelligence."

Chapter 11: "To kill them, you'll have to kill me first"
1. Paddock, *U.S. Army Special Warfare*, 31.
2. Paddock, *U.S. Army Special Warfare*, 35–36.
3. Paddock, *U.S. Army Special Warfare*, 39–40.
4. Paddock, *U.S. Army Special Warfare*, 105.
5. Paddock, *U.S. Army Special Warfare*, 119, 137; Guardia, *American Guerrilla*, 168.
6. Guardia, *American Guerrilla*, 165–67.
7. Guardia, *American Guerrilla*, 163; *U.S. Army and Marine Corps Counterinsurgency Field Manual* (FM 3-24).
8. *Operations Against Guerrilla Forces* (FM-31-20); Guardia, *American Guerrilla*, 160–61.
9. Paddock, *U.S. Army Special Warfare*, 120, 123.
10. Jason Bryant Gibson, "Super-Rangers: The Early Years of Army Special Forces 1944–1953" (master's thesis, University of North Carolina, 2008), 1, 5, 24, 32–35.
11. Gibson, "Super-Rangers," 1, 5, 24, 32–35; Paddock, *U.S. Army Special Warfare*, 156.
12. Paddock, *U.S. Army Special Warfare*, 156.
13. Rebecca Onion, "The Snake-Eaters and the Yards," *Slate*, November 27, 2013, http://www.slate.com/articles/news_and_politics/american_military_history/2013/11/the_green_berets_and_the_montagnards_how_an_indigenous_tribe_won_the_admiration.html (accessed June 27, 2016).
14. Shelby L. Stanton, *Green Berets at War: U.S. Army Special Forces in Southeast Asia 1956–1975* (Novato, CA: Presidio Press, 1985), 38.
15. Stanton, *Green Berets at War*, 38.
16. Francis John Kelly, *Vietnam Studies, U.S. Army Special Forces, 1961–1971* (Washington, DC: Department of the Army, 1973), 171–72.
17. Richard Goldstein, "F.J. Kelly, Green Beret Leader In Vietnam War, Is Dead at 78," *New York Times*, January 4, 1998.
18. Kelly, *Vietnam Studies*, preface, 172; Stanton, *Green Berets at War*, 40; James R. Wilson, *Landing Zones: Southern Veterans Remember Vietnam* (Durham, NC: Duke University Press, 1991), 5.
19. Stanton, *Green Berets at War*, 76; "One Who Was Belligerent," *Time Magazine*, December 11, 1964.
20. Stanton, *Green Berets at War*, 76; *Time*, December 11, 1964.
21. *Time*, December 11, 1964.
22. *New York Times*, January 4, 1998.
23. Kelly, *Vietnam Studies*, preface, 172.
24. Kelly, *Vietnam Studies*, 67; Onion, "The Snake-Eaters and the Yards."
25. Onion, "The Snake-Eaters and the Yards"; Howard Sochurek, "American Special Forces in Action in Vietnam," *National Geographic*, January 1965, 38–65.
26. Kelly, *Vietnam Studies*, preface, 172; Stanton, *Green Berets at War*, 82.
27. Onion, "The Snake-Eaters and the Yards."
28. Boot, *Invisible Armies*, 538.
29. Boot, *Invisible Armies*, 532–34.
30. Boot, *Invisible Armies*, 537.

NOTES

31. Boot, *Invisible Armies*, 540–41; Samantha Power, "Our War on Terror," *New York Times*, July 29, 2007.
32. Boot, *Invisible Armies*, 540–41; Power.
33. Boot, *Invisible Armies*, 541.
34. Boot, *Invisible Armies*, 542.
35. Boot, *Invisible Armies*, 543.
36. Boot, *Invisible Armies*, 543.

INDEX

About the Author

Thomas D. Mays is a professor of history at Humboldt State University in Arcata, California. He came to HSU in 2003 after spending five years teaching history at Quincy University in Illinois. He was raised in the Midwest and his family's traditional home in Virginia. He is retired from the military after serving twenty-six years on active duty and in the reserves. He holds a PhD from TCU in Fort Worth, Texas; an MA from Virginia Tech in Blacksburg, Virginia; and a BA from Roanoke College in Salem, Virginia. Currently, he teaches early American history (colonial era through the Civil War) and American military history. His interests include the American Revolutionary and Civil War eras. He has three books and several articles in print.